Other People's Stories

Other People's Stories

Entitlement Claims and the Critique of Empathy

AMY SHUMAN

University of Illinois Press

Urbana and Chicago

Library of Congress Cataloging-in-Publication Data
Shuman, Amy, 1951–
Other people's stories : entitlement claims and the critique
of empathy /
Amy Shuman.
p.   cm.
Includes bibliographical references and index.
ISBN 0-252-02963-1 (cloth : alk. paper)
1. Discourse analysis, Narrative. I. Title.
P302.7.S48   2005
401′.41—dc22
2004014398

CONTENTS

ACKNOWLEDGMENTS

A book on other people's stories depends on the generosity of others on every page. I have borrowed, cited, inherited, and just listened. Within the text, I acknowledge those who shared their stories, but many others led me to those stories, and many told me stories, especially small-world stories, that I have not able to include.

Chapter 1 is based on research I did in a Philadelphia school from 1978 to 1981. Robert Allekotte, Pamela Adderly, and Charlotte Plant were my guides as I returned to be a junior high school student. Shelley Posen, Rivanna Miller, and Simon Lichman asked me the questions I would not have thought of myself. This chapter was published in *Responsibility and Evidence in Oral Discourse*, edited by Judith Irvine and Jane Hill, and published by Cambridge University Press, which has generously permitted this republication.

Chapter 2 is based on ongoing fieldwork I began in 1982 in Pietrasanta, Italy, where I rely on a large community of artists and artisans who collaborate with me on a project of reflection about their collective memories. I thank Fred Brownstein, Pietro Conti, Carmine DiBiase, Stella Ehrich, John Fisher, Anat Golandski, Luana and Enrico Lari, Keara McMartin, Sandy Oppenheimer, Massimo Pasquini, Shelly Robzen, Cynthia Sah, and Craig Schaffer. I am grateful for many conversations with Sem Ghelardini, who was the artistic and intellectual center and counterpoint of the community during his lifetime. Fellowships from the Guggenheim Foundation, the Wenner-Gren Foundation, and the National Endowment for the Humanities, as well as numerous grants from the Ohio State University, have supported this research.

The stories I discuss in chapter 3 are based on two entirely different communities. I was a student in the Orthodox Jewish community where Rebbitzen Heller teaches. I am grateful to Jenny Dilman, my longtime friend who still lives there, for sending me the story. My discussion of the second story in the chapter is inspired by Barbara Kirshenblatt-Gimblett's foundational work on the telling of parables in context and on our many conversations. Diane Schaffer collected the story as a part of her own research, and she shared it with me. A grant from the Ohio State University provided funds for transcription and translation.

I am grateful to friends who gladly sent their junk mail for chapter 5 and to Laurel Richardson who inspired me to write chapter 6 and who also provided thoughtful comments on the introduction. I have had the good fortune to be part of a reading group (p.m.s.—post-modern studies) that provided weekly intellectual inquiry and inspiration. I thank Nancy Campbell, Suzanne Damarin, Mary Margaret Fonow, Nan Johnson, Marilyn Johnston, Patti Lather, Linda Meadows, Laurel Richardson, and Pat Stuhr, all of whose ideas became intertwined with my own. Patti Lather's work on empathy inspired my own thinking on the topic. Chapter 2 is the result of an extensive dialogue with Nan Johnson. Kathy Dickey, Galey Modan, Fred Sack, Stuart Lishan, Lynda Behan, and Simon Lichman addressed the rest. Carol Bohmer, Galit Hasan-Rokem, Bonnie Burstein, Maxie Bentzen, Ann Hamilton, and Ned Lebow were the readers whose ideas first filled the margins and then made their way into the text, leaving few visible traces of many conversations and stories. I am grateful to my fellow folklorists/ethnographers at the Ohio State University for providing me a rich and vital intellectual environment. I have been blessed by having too many students to be able to list here—but who are my guides and ideal readers. I was inspired by Lore Segal, though the similarity of my book title to hers is more a matter of appreciation. Katharine Young and Ana Clara read every word and were always willing to help me to untangle the ideas. Barbara Lloyd, Dian Clare, Kyle Evans, Tim Hewitt, Pilar Venegas Hewitt, Sally Meckling, Noreen Mulcahy, and Susan Ritchie provided support of all kinds; whatever it was that they started out to do, they ended up doing more. I thank Amy Horowitz for her ear and her heart, and for helping to bring this project to completion.

John Foley and Joan Catapano made publication possible, and Angela Burton found my mistakes. The Ohio University College of Humanities provided financial assistance toward publication. I am grateful to John Roberts, Debra Moddelmog, and Valerie Lee for making this possible. The cover image, *Peace Doves*, is a paper collage created by Sandy Oppenheimer, whose work can be found at <http://www.fisheroppenheimer.com>.

I am especially grateful to my family: Amy H, Evan, Colin, Ariel, Pam, Kathleen, Paul, Rose-Helene, Judy, Lenny, Maxie, and my mother, and to my father, whom I miss everyday, and to whom this book is dedicated.

INTRODUCTION: SUBVERSIVE STORIES AND THE CRITIQUE OF EMPATHY

In every era the attempt must be made to wrest tradition away from a conformism that is about to overpower it.
—Walter Benjamin, *Illuminations*

Storytelling promises to make meaning out of raw experiences; to transcend suffering; to offer warnings, advice, and other guidance; to provide a means for traveling beyond the personal; and to provide inspiration, entertainment, and new frames of reference to both tellers and listeners.[1] I understand all of these possibilities as the promises, rather than the functions, of storytelling. They tell us not so much about what storytelling does as about the claims that can be made for it. As the stories I examine here demonstrate, the farther stories and storytelling travel from the experiences they recount, the more they promise. And stories almost always travel. The representation of experience in stories is often inadequate, failing the promise to represent and understand experience, but this failed promise, or in positive terms, the almost fulfilled promise, nonetheless provides a compelling process for making meaning of everyday life experience.[2]

Sometimes, of course, storytelling fulfills its promise. Storytelling receives credit for making meaning or condemnation for appropriating meaning, praise for representing the unimaginable, or criticism for misrepresentation. The question is, what pushes storytelling to its limits? When does storytelling as making meaning become storytelling as misrepresentation and misappropriation? One answer may be in the connection between misrepresentation and misappropriation as separate but connected ethical complaints. These two fault lines, the land mines of criticism in storytelling in everyday life, both crack open when stories travel.

The center of my study of stories that travel is what I call "small-world stories." These stories of coincidental meetings are familiar both in literature, from the epic to the novel, and in personal narratives told in everyday life. In literature as in everyday life, small-world stories can be a trope, moving the plot from behind, or the substance of an inquiry about destiny, foreclosing the plot from in front. In either case, small-world stories are about travels, and they are stories that travel, reports told by and to people not necessarily present in the experience the stories recount. They provide one example of how story-telling works and, specifically, how telling our stories beyond their original context or telling other people's stories pushes the limits of storytelling.

Small-world stories are about coincidences, but not all coincidence stories claim the world as small. My friend and colleague Ned Lebow's story is the kind of small-world story that is about fate and destiny. He has published a ver-sion of his personal story (1999), but he told me a slightly different version, which I will tell here. To tell someone else's story is either to provide news or to make an example of it; here, I tell the story as a profound example of a story about making meaning out of raw experience and as an example of a story that has traveled, and continues to travel, with this telling. I heard Ned Lebow's story the first time I met him, in a conversation that was itself about mutual connections, a small-world conversation that led to his small-world story. I told Lebow that my aunt had been a Jewish child in hiding in France throughout World War II. In 1942, the Nazis rounded up Jewish immigrants in Paris and deported them to death camps. Lebow told me that he, too, had been born in Paris and that his mother, also a Jewish immigrant, had been deported in 1942. But he learned this story retrospectively. All he knew growing up was that he had been adopted as a baby from a particular New York Jewish adoption agency. The story he has been able to put together is that his mother and he, then an infant, were rounded up and sent with the other Jewish immigrants to a stadium on the outskirts of Paris. As they were being taken to the trains to be sent to the death camps, a woman threw her baby to one of the policemen as she was being led away. The policeman defied orders and arranged for sev-eral children to be saved. The children were handed over to a group of French-born Jewish women who arranged their complicated and difficult, but ulti-mately safe, passage to a New York adoption agency. Lebow's American parents adopted him as an infant from that very same agency, in 1942. The scarcity of infants at the agency at that time suggests the likelihood that he was one of the newly arrived French Jewish children. As an adult, not many years ago, he met Paulette Fink, one of the French Jewish women who had arranged to smug-gle the children out of France, and she told him the story. Lebow believes that he was very likely the baby thrown from the death camp train by his mother to the kind French policeman.

There are many stories here: the story of the baby thrown off the deporta-tion train into the arms of a policeman who arranged his safe harbor; the story of the French woman who survived the war to be able to tell the story of smuggling children out of France; the story of Lebow as an adult meeting the French woman and hearing what might be his own story; Lebow's adoption story; and the more general story of the deportation of foreign-born Jews in Paris. The story is Lebow's but not only Lebow's. It is a personal story, but like all Holocaust stories, its magnitude is greater than the personal. He sees the story as revealing the best of human nature in the face of the worst of human nature, the Holocaust, during which people risked their lives to save a group of children. The story is his, but at the same time, it is a story that cannot belong to him, in part because Ned Lebow depends on the stories of Paulette Fink, the adoption agency, the French policeman, and his parents, and in part because it cannot depend on his mother's story. In other words, his story intersects with other people's stories and at the same time points to missing stories. This juxtaposition between the intersections and the absences, among history, memory, and trauma, pushes the limits of storytelling.

When stories travel beyond their original tellers and contexts, they often bear a trace or track a connection to that origin. Lebow traces his story through a multidimensional vortex rather than a linear chronology. The planes of places and times (the New York adoption agency, Paris, the deportation camp in 1942, the journey taken by refugee children from Paris to New York) and people (his mother, Paulette Fink, the policeman, his parents) coincide to produce the story, and yet they remain pieces, fragments linked by fragile traces and marked by traumatic absences.

Storytelling is pushed to its limits both by the use of a particular story beyond the context of the experience it represents and by the use of a personal story to represent a collective experience. In each of the following chapters, I examine instances of stories pushed to these two limits. I understand the first as the problem of entitlement and the second as the problem of the allegorical.[3] Entitlement and allegory can be described formally, at the interactional and sociolinguistic levels of conversational analysis. It is the intersection of the two limits that produces what I see as the greatest complexity and the greatest source of both the promise of storytelling and its condemnation. We ask, who has the right to tell a story, who is entitled to it? And we ask, is this representation a sufficient, adequate, accurate, or appropriate rendering of experience? Ethical questions of ownership overlap with cultural conventions for representing experience. This model of entitlement begins with the rights accorded firsthand experience: individuals have firsthand knowledge that grants them a privileged position as knowers and a legitimate stake in the interpretation of their own experiences. Competing with this premise is the historiographical view that privileges the distant knower who has perspective and, by virtue of less or different stakes in the interpretation, the possibility of objectivity. Further complicating the disputed virtues of subjectivity or objectivity and the rights they accrue, however, is the use of stories to represent not just individual, but collective, experience. The more a story represents a generalized, shared, or even human experience, the higher the stakes in asserting or challenging illegitimacy. What raises the stakes is the claim that the truth that the story represents is not only factual, representing events that actually happened, but also true in the larger sense of conveying a true understanding of human experience. The process in which the personal or the particular story acquires that larger meaning is quite complex. It is in the process of transvaluing the personal to the more than personal (human, shared, universal) that stories often make or break their promises. In this book, I describe empathy as one process of transvaluation compromised by both allegory and entitlement. Empathy is the act of understanding others across time, space, or any difference in experience.[4] Although empathy holds out a great, perhaps the greatest, promise of storytelling, it is at the same time a destabilizing element in storytelling.[5] Empathy relies on, but also destabilizes, the association among persons and their experiences. It destabilizes entitlement by creating the possibility that people can legitimately retell each other's stories. It destabilizes meaning from the personal to the allegorical. When a personal story is used allegorically, as representative, typical, or stereotypical of a situation, entitlement claims are one way to challenge the allegory. The use of entitlement claims to challenge sentimentalizing allegories sometimes undermines empathy and the possibility of understanding across differences in experience. Often, entitlement claims are alibis for a failure of empathy. My goal in this book is to understand the promises of narrative, especially as those promises are produced by uses of allegory and entitlement, and to provide a critique of empathy at the site of the failed promises.

I want, on the one hand, to observe what happens when stories stray beyond the personal and are therefore subject to challenges of entitlement (that's my story, not yours) and, on the other, to investigate the allegorical as a place where people recognize themselves in each other's stories. How do stories change when people empathize with others' experiences? What do stories that purport to be more than personal look like, and where do they potentially trivialize or otherwise distort experiences? What happens when the empathizer understands something quite different from the person who suffered the experience? And what insights can be gained by trying to describe all of this using the sociolinguistic tools of conversational analysis? On the face of it, the idea that we recognize stories as belonging to someone other than the teller is an obvious observation. At the same time, the concept of people telling other people's stories provides a lens for viewing the pervasive use of the personal story to represent both the core of all human experience and the vast difference between people's experiences. My goal is neither to privilege the personal nor to suggest a caution against telling other people's stories. Quite the contrary, I begin with the premise that we do tell each other's stories and that this is the great promise that storytelling offers. I suggest that conversational storytelling has developed culturally specific critiques of empathy and that empathy and its critiques are part of the ethics of narrative.

Storytelling is an aspect of the ordinary. In face-to-face communication in everyday life, people tell each other stories about experiences, whose ownership they negotiate. Storytelling has been touted as a healing art or as a means for transforming oppressive conditions by creating an opportunity for suppressed voices to be heard (or for creating opportunities to listen to those voices). Very often, inspiration, redemption, emancipation, even subversion, require the appropriation of others' stories. The process of appropriation depends on stories traveling beyond their owners, beyond the personal, and beyond the claim to experience. This is not in itself troubling, nor do I dispute the redemptive or emancipatory possibilities of storytelling. In listening to or even retelling other people's stories, narrators become witnesses to others' experiences, and storytelling provides some hope for understanding across differences. But I propose a caution. The appropriation of stories can create voyeurs rather than witnesses and can foreclose meaning rather than open lines of inquiry and understanding. Appropriation can use one person's tragedy to serve as another's inspiration and preserve, rather than subvert, oppressive situations. Storytelling offers as one of its greatest promises the possibility of empathy, of understanding others. Empathy is one way that understanding can travel back toward the experience to recover the distance stories create when they are far from experience. Empathy offers the possibility of understanding across space and time, but it rarely changes the circumstances of those who suffer. If it provides inspiration, it is more often for those in the privileged position of empathizer rather than empathized. Storytelling needs a critique of empathy to remain a process of negotiating, rather than defending, meaning. The critique of empathy, and the recognition of the inevitably failed promises of storytelling, avoids an unchallenged shift in the ownership of experience and interpretation to whoever happens to be telling the story and instead insists on obligations between tellers, listeners, and the stories they borrow.

This book charts a course between the local and the global, the private and the public, the personal and the political, the everyday and the extraordinary. Each of these coupled terms and its histories is useful for exploring what Gayatri Spivak has termed "the experience of the impossible," an aporia that discloses itself in the unresolved and yet formalized relationship between the two terms (1999: 426). The seemingly fixed association between the paired terms in a binary relationship creates a reification. With many other scholars, I am working this reification, using it as a place from which to think and reconceptualize.[6] I situate my discussions within other discussions of these categories, though where others have focused on contested public narratives, I draw attention to the role of personal narratives in the public sphere.[7] My work addresses how personal narratives are appropriated in political processes, toward political action. Chapter 5, for example, considers the use of personal stories in fund-raising appeals.

Storytelling is pervasive in ordinary conversations. This pervasiveness, along with storytelling's appearance in public, highly formal, or less ordinary discourses grant it the status of being simultaneously a localizing and a universalizing means for representing experience. In this book, I focus on the most ordinary and localizing of storytelling processes. Storytelling is about particular people and their unique experiences. When stories travel beyond their owners, however, by way of storytelling, in ordinary conversation, and in works of fiction, the messages they convey are larger than an individual incident or an individual life. In everyday life, the circumstances in which stories travel beyond their owners and beyond the content of shared experiences can be a source of great concern and a site for negotiation of the ownership of meaning. When stories stay with their owners, people who share experiences can attempt to produce shared interpretations. Access to meaning is controlled by access to stories. But stories very rarely stay with their owners. In fact, what might be the most compelling feature of storytelling is the possibility that its power to transfer and transform will change the meaning of experience.

This book is an effort to trace the routes stories travel in order to understand better how personal stories acquire more-than-personal meaning. If there is a trend today toward the personal, or toward increasing use of the personal to claim access to diverse realities, it is an insistence on the personal at a moment of dispersion, diaspora, and reterritorialization. Put another way, personal stories and their assumed groundedness in local experience have acquired higher status, or at least greater interest, precisely at a time when their tellers are traveling out of their locales, away from their origins.

Although stories frequently travel with their tellers, just as often the stories travel independently. Stories that travel have always accrued value as they travel, and both fiction and history are, by definition, genres in which stories travel separately from their owners. Customarily, such stories are severed from a particular teller, and their successful independence relies in part on the story's ability to stand alone and to represent more than an individual experience.

The personal, conversational stories I analyze in the following chapters still bear traces of their owners and sometimes include specific attribution to a teller or experience. The trace is a construction, a frame used to make claims of ownership. Sometimes the trace story recounts a link lost, erased, obscured, or reconfigured. In fiction and history, when stories gain this independence from their tellers, they are evaluated by different criteria, whether aesthetic, as in the case of fiction, or by measures of verifiability, in the case of history. In contrast, storytelling in everyday life is connected to the relations between tellers and listeners, whether told by the person who endured or enjoyed the experience or by new tellers in new contexts. Storytelling in everyday life is measured by sincerity. In fact, this is so true as to be the grounds on which storytelling in everyday life is disparaged. To describe a work of art as "merely" confessional is to argue that in substituting the sincere for the aesthetic, the work fails to transcend the personal and become art.[8]

Whether in published collections intended to be inspirational, in junk mail intended to persuade the recipient to be sympathetic and charitable, or in conversations that either make the ordinary extraordinary or make the extraordinary seem less singular and isolating, stories that travel far from their owners often insist that the particular experiences of a particular person might be applicable to other particular persons in their different, but equally particular, situations. This might be unremarkable were it not for the complaints made by people whose stories are borrowed, appropriated, and transformed. If global communication makes possible new ways for stories to travel from their owners and still retain traces of ownership, it also makes possible greater awareness of violations and misappropriation and new avenues for mobilizing a defense against them.

I divide my discussion of the travels of stories beyond their owners and contexts into three areas of inquiry. First, I consider the problem of ownership itself: what it means to lay claim to an experience and its representations, and on what grounds misappropriations are perceived and challenged. The specific cases I examine, from breaches of confidentiality to colonization, are part of a larger discussion of the ownership of storytelling as the management of cultural and personal territory, which I discuss as the problem of entitlement.

Second, I consider the problem of the untellable story and its possible solution: the emergence of new categories of tellability. This, like the problem of entitlement, is an ethical inquiry concerned with how norms and values are represented and negotiated in conversational storytelling. I am particularly interested in how storytelling can be a vehicle for recategorizing experience. Some stories are tellable but only if the teller is willing to live with existing categories for interpreting the experience. Narratives impose categories on experience, but people sometimes report that their experiences don't fit the imposed category because the category unfairly judges them or insists on motivations or deserved consequences. Both storyability (what gets told) and tellability (who can tell it to whom) are constrained by how experience is categorized. But sometimes, when stories travel, they acquire new meanings and create new categorical possibilities that then travel back and make available new categories to the persons whose experiences were described.

Third, in a discussion of empathy, I turn to the question of how an individual life story acquires a more-than-personal meaning. Building on the concepts of entitlement and tellability, I look specifically at how stories taken out of context are used to create sympathy for the individual whose suffering is represented in the stories. A sympathetic response to another's situation (defined as a willingness to share an interpretation of or feel compassion for another's plight) or empathy (defined as an attempt to experience the suffering of others) always creates a relationship between a storyteller and listeners. However, this relationship, and the obligations undertaken, differs markedly depending on how far, if at all, a story travels from its owner. I suggest that empathy requires a critique, or that empathy be practiced critically. The central complaint made by people whose stories are appropriated for other contexts is the colonization of personal tragedies to mobilize others in different situations who have not suffered these tragedies. Empathy puts in place the possibility that, through the luxury of storytelling, others can indirectly experience that person's suffering for their personal or collective enlightenment without enduring those tragedies, or if they have endured tragedies, they are offered transcendence through compassion toward others.[9] Generally, collective compassion, transcendent inspiration, and empathy are virtuous qualities, and inescapable even if not virtuous. At the same time, when these virtues are invoked without attention to the responsibilities between listeners and tellers, and especially, when people experience a violation in the misappropriation of their stories, the colonization of the mind, the imagination, and the experience creates misunderstanding and mistrust exactly at the rhetorical moment when empathy promises the opposite. I call this dimension of my discussion of storytelling the critique of empathy.

All three of these areas of inquiry—entitlement, tellability, and the critique of empathy—are part of the larger question of the relationships between tellers and listeners.[10] Some of the storytelling I explore is highly contextualized; it draws on the shared understandings of tellers and listeners and shifts reference back and forth between what Katharine Young calls the storyrealm (the situation of telling) and the taleworld (the events in the story).[11] One way to distinguish among the points on the continuum between the variety of storytelling situations I discuss in this book would be to say that at one end the taleworld and the storyrealm overlap to such an extent that they are barely distinguishable, and at the other end they are so distinct as to have hardly any recognizable points of similarity, hardly any mutual references between the characters and situations in the story and those listening to or telling the story.[12] However, both kinds of story are highly localized; that is, the tellers and listeners invoke a local situation. Further, even though the taleworld and storyrealm may be very distinct, in all of these storytelling situations, the relationships between tellers and listeners are paramount. The question is whether, in what ways, and to what extent the tellers and listeners acknowledge any sense of obligation to the characters in the story.

Entitlement

Throughout the book, I refer both to the larger claims made for storytelling and to the specific, localized claims made for the rights to tell a particular story or to interpret a story in a particular way. I see these two sorts of claims as linked: both are ultimately based in relationships between tellers and listeners.

The larger claims made for storytelling range from the cognitive to the social. For some (Atkinson, 1995: xii; Schank, 1990: xi), storytelling has the status of "natural" communication, a fundamental and universal way of documenting and describing experience (Coles, 1989). Sometimes, especially in the popular literature, storytelling is asserted to be a representation of either the human soul or the human brain. Just as the prehensile thumb and tool making have been used to distinguish humans from other species, so also storytelling is invoked to delineate humanity. According to this claim, humans are the only beings who can report their experiences, and storytelling is the vehicle and repository for accumulating, sorting, and making meaning out of experience. The social claims range from the observation that storytelling is a way of creating shared understanding or creating meaning out of chaos (Arendt, 1968: 104; Myerhoff, 1978: 222–23), to narrative "as a mode of thinking fully as legitimate of that of abstract logic" (Jameson, 1979: xi) to claims for storytelling as therapeutic, transformative, or subversive (Booker, 1991). From Freud's use of "the talking cure" to contemporary uses of storytelling in self-help groups, storytelling has served a therapeutic purpose, and sometimes this purpose is essentialized; that is, the practice is conflated with the process, and narrative, rather than particular strategies for its use, is claimed to be a curative, healing practice.

Claims for storytelling as subversive often pit the narratives told in everyday life (the repressed voice of the oppressed people) against the dominant narratives of histories. In these claims, the life histories of ordinary (and especially oppressed) people are considered to be counternarratives that might undercut the discourses of those in power.[13] Proponents of this theory demonstrate how constructedness of dominant discourses is concealed by claims of objectivity. Localized personal-experience narratives are no more real, no less constructed than universalizing dominant narratives (Frisch, 1990; Tonkin, 1992; Personal Narratives Group, 1989; Portelli, 1991). However, if both the localized and the universalized narratives make essentialist claims, they do so in different ways and for different motives. Each requires a different sort of critique. The universalizing narrative, which hides its constructedness and defends its truth as universal, scientific, or verifiable, requires a critique of methodologies designed to provide objectivity. Localized narratives, insofar as they insist on the unmediated reality of firsthand experience, require a critique of the essentialism of claims for experience as real or natural.[14] The promotion of personal narrative as "real" is particularly common in popular uses of local narratives that have been removed from their local contexts and that are then used to persuade or inspire distant listeners. Those uses of personal narratives make an unapologetic claim to the reality of personal experience and often an equally unapologetic display of pathos in their invocation of others' experiences as pitiable to evoke sentimentality. Is the use of others' stories for emancipatory purposes any different? Are the latter less suspect of essentialism because they promote emancipation rather than sentiment (and because they disavow essentialism)? The answer to these questions might be, yes, there is a difference, but if so, the difference is at least in part between the apologetic and the unapologetic use of others' stories. In short, the difference may be a difference in how the obligations of tellers and listeners to stories are displayed through claims, apologies, promises, and disavowals.

The claims that scholars, journalists, or popularizers make for storytelling tell us a great deal about their understandings of the obligations stories enjoin upon tellers and listeners. The assertion that storytelling is fundamental to human experience is, at the very least, a statement about the desire to be able to describe human experiences. Also, as is true for other claims for what is "natural," "fundamental," or "universal," such statements tell us that storytelling is claimed as both familiar and as exotic, and that, for all its familiarity, the pervasiveness of storytelling puzzles us. We cannot explain, either in cognitive or in social terms, the pervasiveness of storytelling, across cultural and temporal situations, nor can we explain the existence of particular forms of storytelling in particular places or periods. Consequently, we ascribe storytelling to the realm of the fundamental and natural. This claim, or promise, of narrative, to transform the inexplicable into the meaningful, describes one of narrative's most powerful failed promises. Narrative describes an aporia between the inexplicable and the meaningful, a place from which to think about the representation of experience. This dynamic is perhaps best understood when narratives describe experiences that cannot be made meaningful. Theodor Adorno's famous insistence that there can be no poetry after Auschwitz and Spivak's similar turn to poetry in her discussion of "the experience of the impossible" turn our attention to the significance of narrative in this moment of its failed promise to make meaning (Zuidervaart, 1991; Spivak, 1999).[15]

In contrast to such grandiose claims are the ways many scholars disparage storytelling in everyday life as trivial and not worthy of examination.[16] (Of course, the more grandiose the claims made in popular commentary, the more they are disparaged by scholars.) Storytelling in everyday life is additionally excluded from scholarly research on the grounds that everyday-life stories are not predictable. Scientific fields, concerned with the validation of findings, and the humanities, which base the suitability of subjects of study on the question of whether they are worthy of reexamination and retextualizing, both require a subject to be predictably repeatable. According to most scholarly conventions, only the repeatable lends itself to study. Although stories told in everyday life are in some sense repeatable, and certainly storytelling situations and stories are patterned, storytelling in everyday life is also radically unrepeatable. To study only those stories or storytelling situations that appear repeatable would be to make the mistake of reinforcing the unchallenged rule that only the repeatable is worthy of study, a rule that confuses observable pattern with the unrecognized pattern that is unrepeatable. Stories that are told only once or that change when retold in different contexts also deserve our attention. As stories travel from one teller or context to another, not only do they lose some of their recognizable patterns, but their tellers and listeners also notice some patterns and overlook others. A teller's recognition of a similarity can prompt claims of misappropriation. Repeatability itself, whether as a measure of how stories change, as social rules for who has the right to use others' words, or as the reexperience of an event through telling about it, is one of the issues of this book as is the issue of how repeatability governs the use of narrative and the validity of a narrative account of an experience.

Rather than promote storytelling in everyday life as a corrective to dominant discourses, my goal is to trouble the divide between situated lives, personal stories, and contextualized productions of meaning, on one hand, and the stories that are told as grand historical narratives with global or historical contexts, on the other. In recent years, the grand historical narrative has been critiqued as inaccurate, hegemonic, or not representative, and the study of personal experience has been proposed as an alternative. My exploration concerns, among other issues, the ways in which the presentation of situated experience provides resistance to dominant narratives.[17] In contrast to the claims for interest in situated knowledge for its own sake and its ability to reveal truths not revealed or concealed by the grand narratives, I suggest that what is interesting and significant about situated knowledge and situated stories is the ongoing relationship between the personal and the universal, the local narrative and the grand narrative, and the localized claim and the universalized claim.

I am not claiming to restore some otherwise denied primacy or contaminated situation for storytelling in everyday life. Although I am interested in the ways that these stories are promoted or disparaged, I am not suggesting that either position is correct or flawed. Instead, I am arguing that the general claims made for storytelling are a way of negotiating relationships between tellers and listeners, a way of demarcating a territory in which particular obligations are undertaken. Most specifically, in my study of stories and their travels, I observe how the claims made for storytelling shape and are shaped by efforts to support or subvert dominant narratives and dominant ideologies and discourses.

Although the claims made for narrative generally are tied to other disciplinary discourses or political agendas, the claims made for entitlement within storytelling events are more about protecting relationships between people than about protecting territories of discourse. For the most part, the issue of who can tell and hear which stories is a question of social relationships based on questions of ethics and accountability. In disputes about entitlement in conversational narrative, people negotiate the gaps between representation and interpretation and the challenge of finding meaning when meaning is impossible.[18] I propose that better understanding of how entitlement works in highly situated conversational narrative can be useful for understanding the larger claims/promises made for narrative as a means for making meaning out of the chaos of experience and for maintaining or transforming meaning as stories travel.

Tellability

Storytelling is a highly contested site for determining norms and values. From negotiations of who can tell what, through comparisons of different versions of a story, to questions of how an experience is interpreted and what significance is attributed to it, we can observe the ways in which relationships in a story intersect with relationships between the storytellers and the listeners. Storytellers and listeners manage ethical positions within stories in both form and content; this management affects the storytelling situation and the points of intersection between story and situation, especially through the use of framing (Goffman, 1974). Storytelling imposes order on events by establishing a chronology that then becomes a way of framing and understanding experience so that not only do already-identified patterns to some extent precede and inform our narratives, but narratives also identify and impose pattern on experience.[19] The chronological sequence literally orders the experience and figuratively suggests an association between the ordered, sequential narrative and unbounded, unpredictable, chaotic (seemingly not patterned) experience. Storytelling involves a desire or a willingness either to recognize pattern in experience or to impose pattern on experience. However, different sorts of patterns are formed by the negotiation of which specific experiences get made into stories, how events are framed and carved out of the flow of experience by stories, and how stories attain the status of representations of accepted social scenarios or norms. Storytelling in everyday life can be a way to make meaning out of seemingly senseless events. However, it is a mistake to define storytelling as creating meaning out of chaos when just as often storytelling creates further chaos or fails to make sense out of events. Instead, we can observe the ways in which storytelling acknowledges and invents patterns as part of a dynamic relationship between chaos and pattern.

The order that storytelling imposes on events is never neutral, although storytellers often claim that they are just telling what happened and so disavow their own intervention in framing the event. One of my goals in this book is to unpack the association between storytelling as order (that is, a sequential order of events) and stories as a way of establishing and preserving a dominant order. The order, or structure, of narrative form helps to make stories we tell recognizable. Just as folktales have a familiar structure, so do the stories we tell in everyday lives. In European folktales, for instance, if the heroine has some kind of domestic problem, then a magical being comes along to help her. Typically, the magical being also provides a warning of some sort, the heroine fails to heed the warning, and some sort of difficulty follows as a consequence of this failure. In the end, the heroine and her hero prevail, and the story ends with a royal marriage. Personal-experience narratives sometimes aspire to a similarly recognizable sequence of events. In part, talking about our experiences is a way of searching for a sequence that makes sense.

Storytelling in everyday life can be a central means for constructing world views. Narrative paradigms[20] that fit expectations of the way things are supposed to be frame socially accepted scenarios. Socially contested scenarios describe situations that defy an expected order of experience and contradict or interrupt predicted chronologies and expected sequences of events. To make sense of unexpected events, things that don't fit into available paradigms, tellers may either take exception to the available stories or attempt to create new scenarios. These two moves operate at different levels of analysis. The first, in which tellers challenge available narratives as not accurately portraying their experiences, focuses on what counts as the event.[21] In the second move, tellers and their listeners, focusing on how an event is interpreted, reconceptualize their experiences into new paradigms. Asserting the validity of one story, or one version of a story, can be a way of undercutting or devaluing the status of another.

Even when not explicitly stated as a personal opinion or a moral lesson, stories contain evaluative commentary intended to persuade the listener to accept a particular interpretation of what happened. In Hilde Nelson's terms, narrative plays a role in moral life (1997: viii). Each of the following examples describes the reshaping of a narrative category to conform to moral positions.[22] The concepts of typified narratives, paradigm shifts, substituted versions, and shared narrative are tools for exploring the possibility of counternarratives, or potentially subversive, stories.[23] Underlying the controversies over the acceptability of one version or one paradigm over another are controversies about the larger messages these stories convey.

The first example, the story of Pearl Bryant, belongs to the genre of murdered-girl ballads, typically telling the story of a young woman killed by her lover. Ann Cohen has collected ballads and newspaper articles that offer versions of what happened to Pearl, a young woman found decapitated in a field outside Cincinnati (Cohen, 1973). Describing the woman as a prostitute, newspaper accounts implied that a woman of ill repute had taken too many risks and had come to a bad end. Later, the body was identified as Pearl Bryant, and the now explicit story was that she was a girl from the country (notice the switch from woman to girl), not the city, who had left home with her boyfriend, a dentist from Cincinnati, because she was pregnant with his baby, that he botched an abortion, resulting in Pearl's death, and that he cut off her head to disguise her identity and finally dumped her in a field. The dentist protested innocence, but he was convicted and hanged for the crime. The ballad version of the event, which clearly identifies Pearl as a victim and the dentist/lover as a villain, conveys a warning to young girls not to trust young men or they would face the fate of poor Pearl. Pearl Bryant's narrative was constructed by and for different media, the newspaper and the ballad broadside, each of which provides its own constraints. The newspaper story, claiming to report an incident of interest to the readers, offered the categories of prostitute or spurned pregnant lover as facts, and the newspaper does not take responsibility for the ways that those categories shape different stories and suggest interest in different "facts." The "facts" excluded or presented are, to a certain extent, determined by the category.

The identification of contested scenarios has been one of the strategies of the feminist movement. Revising sequences that don't make sense and devising scenarios that do are both ways the feminist movement has addressed the unexpected, or hitherto invisible, aspects of women's experiences. Retelling our stories is a way of reconceptualizing the categories of our lives. How one narrates an experience can make all the difference in determining whether an event is accepted as normal or criticized as immoral or in characterizing people as victims or as willing participants. In a report on how violence is translated into the "language of love" or how murder can be described as a "crime of passion," the *Utne Reader* gives the following examples: "A man guns down his former wife and her new boyfriend; reporters call it a 'love triangle.' A man shoots and kills several coworkers, among them a woman who refused to date him; the press reports a 'tragedy of spurned love.' A man kidnaps his estranged wife, rapes her, accuses her of an imaginary affair, and chokes her to death (all in front of the children); a reporter writes that he 'made love to his wife,' then strangled her when he was 'overcome with jealous passion'" (Jones, 1995: 36). All of these are contested narratives; both versions of the events claim a different category for understanding what happened. The first version of all these stories categorizes the events as crimes against women; the version attributed to reporters—and of course they are not the only ones who use these categories—categorizes the events as crimes of passion. Violence-against-women stories portray a different course of events from crimes-of-passion stories. Which category prevails depends on which events are included and which excluded, from whose perspective the events are told, and how they are described. In either case, the categories of violence against women and crimes of passion are constructions that invoke particular narrative paradigms.

Sometimes, by telling our own stories we are able to reframe experiences into new or different categories. A good example of this is the category of date rape. Only in the last decade or so has this category been accepted; before that, sexual assault had to involve a stranger, and the assumption was that a woman who had unwanted sex with someone familiar to her (and unentitled to sex with her) was at fault for getting herself into the situation in the first place. The emergent category that critiques "blaming the victim" is a result of a reevaluation of categories in which women can tell their own stories, and this contradicts the categories invoked in stories told about them. Several years ago, at a conference on Foxfire projects organized by folklorists at Ohio State University, some high school students from Zanesville, Ohio, spoke about their attempts to write about teenage pregnancy and sexuality at their school. Using Foxfire-like methods of interviewing students at the school, they proposed to write their own pamphlets to replace the ones distributed in their health classes. The project went well

until the students decided to include a section on date rape. The principal objected to the open declaration of the category, presumably on the grounds that
the category was either irrelevant to the school experience or the topic was not
appropriate for a school publication, and the pamphlets were never distributed.
To name date rape as a problem made the rape narratives a contested paradigm. Date-rape stories place the blame on the person who imposes unwanted
sex rather than on the person who protests. A date-rape story contradicts, for
example, a story that depicts a woman as a tease or a story about how a woman
should know ahead of time what she "has bargained for." All of these stories are
told differently. In a paper on date-rape stories written for one of my folklore
courses, a student wrote about an incident in which she ended up, after an evening of drinking with friends at bars near campus, all alone with a young man
whom she hardly knew at his apartment in the middle of the night. She didn't
trust him and knew the situation was dangerous, but she thought she could han-
dle it. She felt that her alternative, to leave in the middle of the night and go
out onto the street by herself and find her way home, was more dangerous. He
raped her. For a long time, she blamed herself for getting herself into such a
situation, until she did the research for her term paper and interviewed other
women and learned that they had been in similar situations and called those situations "date rape." For her, calling the situation "date rape" was transformative. By telling the story as a date rape, she shifted the blame from herself to
the man, and a story about her poor choices and bad judgment became a story
about his criminal behavior.

In both of these examples, in which narrative is used to label and relabel
experiences, the acceptable paradigm depends on characterization. Pearl
Bryant is either prostitute or naive small-town innocent; date rape reconfigures
the characters in stories in relation to each other. These characters are not categorized by a literary typology, though in coinciding with their fate (rather than
changing and coming to know themselves better through the story) they are
closer to the epic hero, and in their immersion in everyday life and events, they
are closer to the novel hero. Genre plays an important role here in determining the relationship between narrative and counternarrative. The story of Pearl
Bryant provides a counternarrative only in the existence of a variety of versions
of a single event. In stories about date rape, the character insists on a particular version of her story, and by invoking the alternative story, she creates tension between narrative and counternarrative.

Stories rarely if ever belong to a single category of experience; more often,
storytelling demonstrates an awareness of multiple possible categories, some
compatible, some contested, some provocative or marked, and others assumed
and naturalized. My point is that the tellability of stories is in part tied to the

categories attributed to experience. Another way to understand this is to suggest a connection between Harvey Sacks's concept of "category-bound activities" and his discussion of tellability. A category-bound activity identifies individuals' actions as typical of the group of which they are members (Sacks, 1992: vol. 1, p. 180). People "monitor events by reference to 'tellability'" (Sacks, 1992: vol. 1, p. 779). Although Sacks does not pursue a connection between the two concepts, together they provide a useful understanding of the contested terrain of the categories that shape narratives. Narrative is one method for creating the connection between actions and categories.

The examples above are stories about violence against women; some are public stories, printed in newspapers or magazines or, in the case of Pearl Bryant, made into ballads. Others are the private stories told by people who knew the victims or the stories the survivors themselves tell. However, although some of the private stories report rejection of the newspaper or other publicly promoted versions of stories, the categories are not invented in the public world and imposed on the private world. Resistance may take the form of resisting public versions of stories, but this, too, is a narrative strategy. One strategy of resistance to the absence of women's perspectives and stories has been efforts to collect and publish women's stories in their own voices. But telling their own stories does not necessarily mean that those women escape the categories and labels imposed on them by dominant narratives. Resistance to dominant narratives is not a simple matter of offering the alternative of personal example. The optimism of countless books promoting personal stories as a way of providing voices for people who have not been heard is challenged by the willing appropriation of those stories in television talk shows or other media presentations that trade on the commodification of personal disclosures in public arenas. When stories travel beyond the tellers who suffered the experience, they can acquire new contexts of meaning. And if the story returns to the teller who claims to own the experience, the new interpretations of the experience can travel with it.

The Critique of Empathy

Redemptive, subversive, or other liberatory claims made for narrative are based on the possibility of counternarratives. As a genre, narrative both promises to convey meaning and to provide more than one way to tell a story. I will not rehearse the well-known debates about the usefulness of narrative in historical and ethnographic research. Narrative is by now generally recognized as a rhetorical and descriptive genre shaped by both the formal and social constraints of available narratives and by tellability and the interpretive perspectives of tellers and listeners. One difference between my concern and the concern of those debating the crisis of representation in anthropology and history is that those debates focus on the validity of stories as evidence. The entitlement claim, in which narratives are contested on the grounds of ownership and rights, sets up a different chain of responsibility than the claim to evidence. In the entitlement claims, narrators proclaim their interestedness. In ethnographic and historical narratives, interestedness (often confessed) is mostly regarded as a contamination of the record.[24] As long as stories stay with the people who have suffered the experience, the contest between narrative and counternarrative can be a question of entitlement.[25] In other words, the rights to entitlement and interpretation are linked; people who suffer an experience are presumed to understand it best. When stories travel far from their owners, the distant tellers and listeners can still presume to understand; empathy provides one means for understanding across disparate experiences. But empathy is a weak claim to entitlement; in fact, empathy is almost always open to critique as serving the interests of the empathizer rather than the empathized. In this section, I explore the connection between contested narratives about suffering and the critique of empathy that underlies some of those contests.

My research questions begin with stories about personal suffering that travel beyond their owners. Stories that travel beyond their owners are subject to a different sort of critique than those that remain situated. I begin by asking how ownership is claimed and what territory is included in that claim. To what extent is the ethos of personal experience unimpeachable? If the only challenge to the ethos of personal experience is credibility, how is credibility established in the narrative exchange, and how does this change as the story travels away from the persons who claim to have suffered by the experience? Is the testimony of personal suffering challenged? Here, the particular claim is important, whether "this happened to me" or "I suffered by this."[26] How does the ethos of the teller, once credibility is established, help to establish ownership of the experience and the narrative? If critique is located in the empathetic reaction, is the challenge directed to entitlement? Do tellers claim empathy as justification to claim ownership of the narrative?

I am neither launching a critique of stories that travel beyond their owners nor proclaiming that certain kinds of counternarrative are subversive. Instead, I am taking as a given the fact that stories do travel beyond their owners and that tellers do claim counternarratives as emancipatory. One focus of my research is the particular claim of empathy by tellers who do not claim to have suffered an experience themselves. Empathy is always open to challenges, but at the same time, stories must travel beyond their owners to do some kinds of cultural work. Counternarrative depends on the possibility of critique of the master narrative, and thus, to some extent, on empathy with the counternarrative. It is in this sense that subversive stories and the critique of empathy are implicitly linked. Empathy is one of the failed promises of narrative, but in that failure, it provides the possibility of critique and counternarrative, providing whatever redemptive, emancipatory, or liberatory possibilities narrative holds.

In response to Hayden White's charge that the Palestinians needed better narratives, Edward Said wrote:

> The narratives have been there. They're of a different sort. I don't think there's a kind of "grand narrative": it's essentially not a Western narrative. The model of wandering and exile is available. I. F. Stone always says the Palestinians have become "the Jews of the Middle East." But that's a borrowed narrative. . . . After all, this is a narrative that always has to compete with a very powerful, already existent narrative of resurgent nationalism of the retributive kind, of the sort that one associates with Zionism. So on a lot of fronts there are formal problems. Then there's the tactical problem of where's this narrative to be formed? Because the Palestinians are locked into the Arab (so-called) narrative, and that's usually tied into oil, and the Arabian Nights, and a whole set of other myths, on the one hand. And on the other, in the West it's virtually impossible for the narrative to be located hospitably in any set of allied or counternarratives. (1990: 138)

Said seems to be arguing that the Palestinians cannot have a grand narrative and that they are trapped in local narratives that never transcend themselves. The failure to transcend the local can involve a failure of empathy, a failure of the story to travel beyond the personal experience. We can begin to understand how storytelling is used in negotiations of power by asking what makes one story tellable and another story not tellable in particular historical and social contexts.

What makes one category of narrative more available than another? Stories do not exist in isolation, and it is impossible to prevent a story from being appropriated, reinterpreted, and recategorized. A related consideration rendering stories untellable in particular situations is that some categories are unrecognizable to some listeners. Date rape is one unrecognizable category for listeners who maintain that rape occurs between strangers. The date-rape stories involve a shift in perspective from the stories of the tease or the girl who invites advances and later protests. The untellability involves a lack of recognition of the category, a "this kind of thing doesn't happen" response. Sometimes, untellable categories of storytelling are about recognized categories that are specifically excluded from conversation as topics to be avoided. The tellability of these trauma narratives is compromised by the unacceptability of the events. These are stories about things that shouldn't happen, rather than about things that didn't happen.

Children dying or child abuse are good examples of the problem of narratives about things that should not happen. In the case of child abuse, some people respond by thinking that not only do these acts transgress the natural order, but also even talking about them violates what should be. It is the reification of the unthinkable as the unspeakable. Talking about children dying isn't this sort of violation, but all stories about things that shouldn't happen share a problem about how to talk about tragedies without romanticizing or somehow distancing the events from one's own experiences. The difficulty is that often we don't know how to make any sense out of tragedies—things that should not have happened—and in an effort to make sense out of what is senseless, or to make something seem all right when it feels all wrong, stories are constructed to find some thread of meaning or redemption. However, the availability of narratives is not just a matter of selecting a topic or negotiating an awkward conversational moment. Though questions of topic or situation are important for determining an accurate and appropriate match between the story and the experience, the availability of narratives also depends on larger discourse issues such as who else is using that narrative and for what persuasive purposes. On one hand, the availability of narrative is a matter of finding some way to take account of the unaccountable, and on the other, claiming a narrative as a way of understanding events is a political choice that enjoins particular obligations upon tellers and listeners. Trauma narratives foreground the possibilities of subversive stories (or counternarratives) and the necessity of a critique of empathy. Empathy is one kind of obligation, sometimes creating a possibility for understanding across differences, sometimes involving sentimentality, sometimes romanticizing tragedy as inspiration, but in any case deeply compromising the relationship between tellers and listeners.

Storytelling in everyday life is both a liberating practice that creates new narrative paradigms and a conservative practice that constrains experience into available narratives and acceptable scenarios.[27] The categories of the liberatory and the conservative are slippery here, however, because they do not map onto personal freedoms or constraints. The familiar and acceptable, insofar as it acknowledges a shared experience, can be a source of political coalition, and breaking out of expected or familiar categories is not in itself a form of liberation. Storytelling in everyday life is a good place to think about the social constraint, conservation, and subversion of meaning and to question the binary oppositions between public and private, conservative and liberatory, or subversive and status quo, that shape social thought. Storytelling about personal experience in everyday life has subversive potential, but personal narrative is not of itself an antidote to the dominant narrative; just as often as it voices resistance, personal narrative appears as the vehicle for dominant ideologies. Voices speaking from the margins reinscribe the center and reinscribe their marginality precisely by calling attention to their marginality in an attempt to undermine the center.

Sharon Boyer, an African American mother of a child who was murdered and a participant in Memorial to Our Lost Children, a project to create a memorial to murdered children, is particularly concerned about ways that people distance themselves from such tragedies by telling the stories as if the events could not happen to their children, as if children who get murdered are poor or black or neglected or drug users.[28] The group Parents of Murdered Children contradicts this stereotype; murdered children do not represent any race or class. And as Boyer said at a meeting of the group in 1994, it does not make any difference if one's child was an honor student or a drug user. She says, "The mother whose murdered child was a drug user has lost her child not once, but twice, first to drugs and then to murder." So why do we tell their story differently? Why is it different to tell a story about a drug user who was murdered? The easy answer is that the drug user who is murdered is like the tease who is raped; in such stories, the victim is, at least in part, to blame. Stories construct categories of victims, innocent saints, and evildoers. A story asking for sympathy for a drug user can be as untellable as a story asking for blame for a charming, intelligent, and handsome young man who rapes his date. One of Boyer's main efforts as a member of Parents of Murdered Children is to tell the story as she sees it. She resists the stories in newspapers as sensational. Further, she argues that because the particular facts are not at issue, the question is not from whose perspective the story is told. Nor is the issue blame and innocence. The issue is murder: an undeserved, tragic, senseless death. She cuts to the heart of the problem of untellability by refusing to permit any effort to make sense of the senseless. Constructing binary categories of blame and innocence does just that. At the same time, the formulation of the binary opposition between blame and innocence provided the parents of murdered children group with a productive site to conceptualize their shared counternarratives.

Storytelling can resist the constraints of appropriate situations as well as the constraints that label and categorize experiences. One of my students, Peggy Gerds, who had been a nurse in the Leukemia Wing at Children's Hospital in Columbus, Ohio, collected stories from the parents of her former patients. She asked parents whose children had died to tell her their stories. (And here, "their" is deliberately ambiguous, referring both to the parents' stories and the children's stories.) The parents welcomed the opportunity to talk about their children with Gerds. They were angry about what I am calling the untellability of tragic stories. Other people's discomfort with death, or cancer, or children dying competed with what was most important to them, which was that their children be remembered. For example, one parent told about meeting an acquaintance in the supermarket who introduced her to another person by saying, "She has two children." The parent corrected her, "No, I have three children, but one of them died of leukemia." The parents wanted and needed to remember the child and to have the child remembered by others. A story about a child dying of leukemia is sometimes untellable, and it is particularly untellable in a casual conversation such as this supermarket encounter. Mentioning the child might have created the opportunity for the story to have been told, and since the story belonged to the mother, the acquaintance was in the impossible situation of either misrepresenting the correct number of children or inappropriately introducing the story as a topic for conversation. One way to understand a society's presumed unmentionable topics is to explore the relationship between tellability and entitlement. I consider this issue extensively in my conclusion, on disability narratives.

In all of the cases I've mentioned so far, the storytellers insisted on telling their stories, even as they recognized that these stories might not be heard, understood, or considered socially appropriate. Telling untellable stories accomplishes several things for the tellers. As I mentioned, sometimes telling the story is a way of reconstructing the category of the event by taking exception to the available stories. In other cases, this recategorization of an event is a way of working against the way the story is understood by creating a new scenario. The issue for these tellers is not just telling the story but telling it in a particular way or in a particular situation. The parents of the child who died from leukemia not only want their child to be remembered, but they also want that child to be remembered in a particular way. These parents told stories about a child, who in a very short lifetime gave a great deal to the people around him, who touched many people and left his mark on the world. And that seems to be the most important story to tell. The parents of children who died from leukemia shape their claim not in terms of a narrative and a counternarrative but in terms of acknowledging a reality. Sharon Boyer and the other parents in Parents of Murdered Children insist on a counternarrative of all murder as tragedy to counter the narrative that constructs some children as innocent victims and others as somehow at fault, if not complicit. For these parents, the valid story is one that does not require that the child was good for the murder to be considered bad.

These two responses to tragedies work at different levels in response to available narratives. The parents of children who died of leukemia negotiate what can be told and to whom. Their insistence on a story about a child who left a large legacy in a short time works against the story of the tragedy of cancer taking the life of a child. The parents of children who have been murdered negotiate what the story they tell means. Both kinds of story are constructed in a cultural political context in which tellability and untellability are part of particular social contexts, both the personal and immediate contexts in which the stories are told or not told in everyday life, and the public contexts in which one person's story is told as representative of a larger social situation.

Whereas the meaning of a story is always situated within a particular cultural context, the claims people make to legitimate their stories as meaningful or true often extend beyond those local contexts. This can work by countering a universal claim with a personal narrative as the exception that disproves it; by universalizing the personal experience as representative of something larger than that singular experience and therefore worthy of note; by setting the local apart from the global as meaningful only within the context of its use and as distorted when taken out of context; by representing as personal, experience that has been concealed or overlooked by the dominant discourse and then identifying the practices of exclusion used by a dominant group to protect its interests; or by identifying a general pattern of accepted discourse that renders a particular local story untellable or not meaningful within its strategies of interpretation. Each of these examples (and I will discuss all of them in detail in separate chapters) involves a different relationship between the local and whatever is larger than local. Each of them locates both the situated and the generalized a little differently and uses different names for these, and each of them has a different motivation, a different rationale for insisting on the importance of either the local situated construction or the global universalized one.

Storytelling is part of cultural modes of communication and social relationships, and no story is told de novo, outside of these modes and relationships. Stories are told not only to reflect on events and to communicate with particular listeners but also in response to other stories about other similar or dissimilar events and in the context of existing ideas and the entire system of communication, including who speaks to whom, about what, in what circumstances, in what form, and with what consequences.[29] The legitimacy of any account depends on who tells it, what is the teller's relationship to the experience, who counts as a "participant" and who counts as a "witness" (and which of those is held to be more likely to have accurate information), and how the form in which the event is recounted helps to shape the way the experience is understood. In other words, the legitimacy (import, ethical charge, or authenticity) of a story depends not only on its relationship to the experience but also on the web of interpersonal and intertextual relationships in which the story and the experience are entwined.

As Boyer and other members of her group know, the recategorization of their stories in newspapers is a marketing strategy, designed to sell more newspapers, just as the packaging of Pearl Bryant's story was designed to sell the ballad broadsheet. Repackaging is one of the ways that stories travel. On one level, this is a matter of recontextualization, providing new contexts for stories as they travel to different situations; on another level, repackaging is a particular kind of strategy in which identities are manufactured and sold in a capitalistic marketplace. Boyer and the Parents of Murdered Children object to the use of their stories in the newspapers, but when I met the group, they were attempting to repackage their own stories, as part of the Memorial to Our Lost Children project. Many such groups learn to repackage their stories to persuade a larger, removed audience to adopt a position more sympathetic to the perceptions of those who have experienced a trauma. In their book *Troubling the Angels: Women Living with HIV/AIDS*, Patti Lather and Chris Smithies describe the repackaging of HIV/AIDS stories: "One doctor says, ' . . . we live in a racist society where the health problems of whites are considered to be more important. So we have to package this disease as a threat to the white middle class to get funding for it, to get attention, to get support'" (1997: 116). Stories can belong to more than one category at a time. HIV/AIDS belongs to both "trauma" and "scandal" categories, as do the stories of murdered children. The women who participated in Lather and Smithies's study, like the Parents of Murdered Children group and many other advocacy groups, hope that telling their stories will interrupt and thus subvert the dominant narrative.

People who have suffered often see the media appropriations of their stories as a problem of representation: their experiences have been represented inaccurately by people who, they believe, have no right to represent because they have not experienced the trauma and cannot possibly understand. In this book, I will suggest that although the question of who is entitled to represent whose experience is a problem, the larger problem is the packaging of suffering as sentimentality. In an explanation of the organization of their book, which gave primacy to the women's texts and placed metacommentary on separate parts of the page and in intervening chapters, Lather and Smithies write, "These women deserve better than sentimentality, and part of the work of the angels is to interrupt the kind of easy empathy or 'downward directed sympathy' that readers often fall into when reading about the tragedies of others. The hope is that the very fragmentation of the book, its detours and delays, will unsettle readers into a sort of stammering knowing about the work of living with HIV/AIDS, a knowing not so sure of itself" (1997: 52). Lather and

Smithies try to avoid packaging suffering as sentimentality; they provide a critique by creating awareness of the danger of making personal stories into marketplace commodities.

People make valiant efforts to correct what they perceive to be misappropriated or inaccurate representations, and these efforts can be more or less successful in shaping public thought and perceptions and creating forums for citizen action, and in more personal therapeutic claims for knowledge or self-realization. However, even if the particular meanings attached to experience change, that does not interrupt the commodification of identities in a marketplace. Temporarily, the "good guys" can prevail in their efforts to promote a particular story, but personal identities are still made into poster children for a cause. I use the image of the poster child quite deliberately because disability is perhaps the best case for understanding how empathy works in narrative. The poster child is a real child whose real experiences are used to persuade others to care about his or her predicament. But the poster child's narrative is overdetermined by the plea: "If you invest in this child, you invest in a narrative of hope, and possibly even triumph over adversity." The child's predicament must be seen as an adversity, and his or her life must be seen as unlivable. Efforts to "correct" this representation or to reappropriate it do not necessarily undermine or change the relationship of "easy empathy." The problem is not the accuracy of representations but the relationships between listeners and tellers produced by those representations. In this book, I describe that problem, and efforts to address it, as the critique of empathy.

The critique of empathy is a place to begin to see narrative as a relationship between tellers and listeners and their cultural, political, and historical contexts. I begin with the critique of empathy in order to understand narrative in the context of the politics of memory. Narrative creates chronologies and invents origins, crystallized moments in the past made to appear more significant than ongoing life in the present. Narrative creates the person as a character who can stand for a larger human experience. Narrative invents testimony as truth, as if only the past can provide meaning for the present. I begin with the critique of empathy because it offers a way to observe what happens when stories travel from tellers who claim experiences as their own to tellers who claim stories as representative.

My focus in this book is on storytelling as communication, an approach built on research on narrative in sociolinguistics and folklore. Several different disciplines study narrative, and although their topics are similar, ranging from the formal properties of narrative to the politics of narrative, they share few conversations and there is little evidence that they are aware of each other's work. In this study, I am primarily interested in how each of these fields examines the way the personal narrative interrupts or subverts the dominant narrative. In literary scholarship, I find the work on what is called "trauma narrative" particularly helpful in its understanding of the ways that narratives about personal and historical trauma obligate both the listener (the person who "collected" the story) and the reader to be a witness to the account (Caruth, 1995). Trauma narratives interrupt the complacency and distance of historical narrative.

They obligate us to situate ourselves in personal relationship to the account. In other words, not only do they insist on the personal in terms of the personal experience of the person who suffered the trauma, but they also hold the witness accountable. Psychological discussion of narrative is also interested in interrupting dominant narrative to help individuals challenge what they accept out of awareness as "normal" (White, 1995). When narrative is described as a story line, the goal of therapy is to interrupt a patient's pathological story line and replace it with a healthy one. The danger, of course, is that the dominant culture determines what counts as pathological and what counts as healthy. To some extent, this procedure reinforces, rather than interrupts, dominant narrative. At the same time, the therapeutic process of self-redefinition is at the heart of recategorizing and reshaping dominant cultural narratives. As individuals refuse their inherited narratives and replace them with revised understandings of the world, the world changes. As Arthur Frank argues, "In stories, the teller not only recovers her voice; she becomes a witness to the conditions that rob others of their voices. When any person recovers his voice, many people begin to speak through that story" (1995: xii).

Wherever sociolinguists and folklorists have been interested in the politics of narrative, they have helped to trace the conditions in which the process Frank describes occurs or is suppressed. Folklorists, interested in the ways that traditions are named, negotiated, invoked, and revised, have attended to the ways that personal narrative shapes collective cultural ideas. It is easy to oversimplify the categories of storytelling and attribute to each a social function. But we can easily make the mistake of attributing wisdom to traditional folktales, of blaming media appropriations of the personal for sensationalizing and scandalizing people's personal traumas, or of imagining that personal stories always provide a way for persons to speak and break down the cultural barriers to understanding their experiences. More productively, by observing the travels of personal stories beyond the personal, beyond local contexts, we might recognize the multiple roles assigned to the personal.

In this book, I offer several different kinds of examples of how people construct realities through the stories they tell about their experiences. A chapter on what I call "small-world stories," the coincidences of everyday life, looks at the way in which coincidence or synchronicity is constructed in such stories and how these, sometimes trivial, accounts differ from stories about destiny and fate. Several chapters concern the construction of self. One chapter examines a collection of "junk mail" that uses personal stories to convince readers of the actuality and seriousness of particular social problems. The book continually moves back and forth between the ordinary stories told casually in conversation and the ways these stories can achieve larger-than-life status. Chapter 3 concerns the relation between personal stories and parables and looks at how stories in everyday life become allegorical. I suggest that we replace the idea of stories as fundamental or natural with the idea of stories as both ordinary and at the same time larger than life. This book is an examination of the strategies for negotiating the relationship between the ordinary and the allegorical.

All of the chapters in this book discuss instances of rejected and accepted stories. I refer to the accepted stories as tellable and the rejected ones as untellable. Although the stories told in everyday life are "personal" stories, because the teller either claims some personal knowledge of the events recounted or makes other claims to authority on the subject, the question of authority, in the sense of who is authorized to tell what, can always be challenged. In one sense, stories belong to the person who had the experience, but in another, stories are never unique. Instead, for a story to be understood at all, it must be recognizable as a shared experience. The recognizability of experience is evident in remarks such as "that happened to me, too," as JoAnn Bromberg has observed.

In an examination of how political groups appropriate the same narratives for different purposes, I discuss the relationship between the story and the experience it reports. I ask, who owns the experience, and how does an individual's experience come to represent the experiences of a group? In order to better understand how stories work and what the basic components are, I look at stories told by adolescent girls about fights. What all of those who promote the liberatory possibilities of personal narrative seem to be suggesting is that personal narrative puts the listener in a position to better understand others' experiences. What I propose that we need, in order to understand both those claims and the failed promises of personal narrative, is a critique of empathy.

1   *"Get Outa' My Face": Entitlement and Authoritative Discourse*

The metaphor of voice, especially disparate voices, silenced voices, minority, and marginalized voices, has become a familiar part of political discussions. The too-easy solution, to let all voices speak, ignores the ever-present condition of interested voices with competing concerns. This chapter explores one aspect of the use of voices to protect interests: how authoritative voices are manipulated in reported speech. Throughout my discussion, I shall insist that although people challenge one another on the accuracy of their reports, the issue at stake is not accuracy but the appropriation of authority.

In exploring the interaction of competing voices, the concept of entitlement is as fundamental as that of turn taking. Indeed, the conventions of turn taking depend on conventions for defending or determining the right to speak at all. If "a speaker's right to be sole talker is a claim to a turn to talk" (Moerman, 1988: 19), entitlement concerns the right to make that claim. Challenges to entitlement raise questions about the ownership of experience. Any claim to the authority to report on experience; to disclose, withhold, or conceal information; to be an author of events; and to repeat another's remarks is an entitlement claim.

Entitlement is more often challenged than explicitly claimed. It is not a speech act but rather belongs to culturally specific conventions of metacommunication. As part of a discourse on rights, extending from political discussions about who can speak on behalf of whom[1] to the adolescent fight stories discussed here, entitlement concerns the distribution of knowledge. More precisely, entitlement challenges are one way of shifting attention from issues of knowledge and accuracy of information to issues of distribution and relationships between people.

Whereas studies of turn taking rely on a concept of shared understandings, or "what everyone knows," discussions of entitlement concern differential knowledge.[2] Probably the most familiar example of how conversation works to distribute knowledge and power in a community is research on gossip and rumor (Haviland, 1977; Goodwin, 1982), and the data presented here are similarly concerned with secondhand reports in which "the principal character in the story is a party who is not present," as Marjorie Goodwin characterizes similar exchanges (1982: 804).

The concept of entitlement applies not only to gossip but also to ownership of experience and information generally (or some might want to claim that gossip also has larger implications).[3] To assert or deny one's entitlement is to assert or deny one's identity of one's responsibility. To claim entitlement in the name of one's position is to appropriate power. Entitlement claims involve a contest about contexts, whether the "I was there" context of personal experience or the proprietary context of "it takes one to know one." In appropriating the floor, one also appropriates the context, and the contexts can be multiple and intersecting. The entitlement disputes discussed here involve problematic boundaries between the context of talk and the context of the events discussed.

The boundaries between challenges to authority and challenges to accuracy are never distinct; rather, there are interests at stake in resorting to one or the other in particular situations. Uses of reported speech call attention to some of the gray areas in challenges to accuracy and authority. Some of those explored here are the separation of talk about experience and experience as distinct categories, threats as a particularly interesting example of that separation, the role of the witness as a reporter of what can be claimed are someone else's experiences, the companion category of firsthand experience, varieties of referentiality (including misquoting), other means for concealing or revealing information, and finally, the problems of appropriate context and point of view. This discussion concerns the entitlement to appropriate another's voice as a means for borrowing authority, whether in an act of complicity or resistance to that authority.

All of the following narratives, excerpted from lunchtime conversations in an inner-city junior high school, concern challenges to entitlement. While entitlement is a basic part of turn taking in conversation, it is rarely as foregrounded as it is in these adolescent disputes in which entitlement is without a doubt the most frequent kind of challenge. The narratives provide a negative example of entitlement in which entitlement challenges are always a potential threat rather than an opportunity to appropriate power.

Challenges to entitlement as part of ongoing disputes present particular problems in the relationship between responsibility and evidence. Since the disputes are ongoing, the narratives themselves shape the course of events, and what counts as evidence is constantly changing and renegotiated. Most significantly, in the adolescent disputes the accuracy of the evidence reported is far less important than the propriety of who reports it to whom. Individual speakers rarely take responsibility for their own reports but, rather, using reported speech, assign authority to some prior speaker.

In the adolescent conversations, entitlement was negotiated at two levels: at the level of saving face, or reputation, and at the level of narrative presentation, or the use of reported speech and first-person accounts. In constant switching among these levels, participants readjusted affiliations and reframed the topics of dispute. Entitlement was not based on a set of shared rules such as the novelty of the information, the accuracy of the information, or the status of the speaker; rather, calling attention to entitlement was a means of shifting the topic and parties of the dispute. The central components of this shift in the relationship between the responsibility for speaking and the topic of discussion can be discussed separately as (1) the problem of the relationship between narrative and experience in the recounting of ongoing events; (2) the distinction between spreading and containing the flow of information in a community; (3) the uses of reported speech and the status of the narrator; and (4) the consequences of either erasing or calling attention to any of the above relationships involving the status of speakers in relation to one another, to their experiences, to the accuracy of their accounts, or to the original speakers quoted in reported speech.

Narrating an Ongoing Event

The narratives discussed here were told by a group of African American, white (Polish American and Irish American), and Puerto Rican inner-city junior high school students between 1979 and 1981. The texts were not elicited but were told in conversations and tape-recorded as a part of a larger study of the adolescents' use of writing and speaking (Shuman, 1986). If classified by topic, the narratives could be called "fight stories," but as will become clear, the stories were not always about past fights. The storytelling situation was itself always potentially part of what was an ongoing dispute. In the world of junior high lunchtime discussions, fights did not matter unless they were recounted.[4]

These stories are useful for exploring the shaky relationship between accounts and experience central to discussions of responsibility and evidence. In any discussion of accounts, but particularly accounts about purportedly actual events in which the account can be part of the ongoing experience, it is important to recognize that accounts do not duplicate experiences and that experiences are only constituted as events through some representation of them.

The relationship between fights and fight stories in the adolescent community implicated a whole system of shared and exclusive information. While challenges to fight began over insults or efforts to save face, actual fights were more often battles over control of information. Far more fight stories were told than fights fought, and a fight need not have occurred for a fight story to have been told. Thus, the relationship between fight and fight story, event and narrative, is not a direct mapping. Narrative and social conventions for appropriate communication together inform and constrain the relationship between event and narrative.

The conventions for entitlement—the right to tell or hear a story—require respect for the privacy of information and depend on narrative conventions for controlling the form of appropriate disclosures. In particular, in telling fight narratives adolescents manipulated the sequential ordering of events, the use of reported speech, and claims of authorship in order to ascribe unentitled information to other speakers or to leave information to inference.

The key to understanding the uses of entitlement in adolescent fight narratives is the relationship between talk and experience. First, adolescents talked about fights differently than they experienced them. Second, talking about fighting was a part of ongoing experience; talking was a part of fighting, not just a report of it.

The adolescents assumed that fights followed a pattern. Since they knew how fights proceeded, they did not need to articulate each action in stories about particular fights. A narrator who told a story without outlining each sequential step could appear to know both more and less than was being told.

The adolescents' narratives were inextricably connected to the situations in which they were told: to the immediate storytelling occasion and to the larger situation of ongoing relationships between the people involved in an incident.[5] The storytelling occasion often became a part of the ongoing dispute. Participation, either in listening or telling, implied involvement, and entitlement to involvement could always be challenged.

The stories represent a modification of Erving Goffman's concept of "replaying"; they were "couched from the personal perspective of an actual or potential participant who is located so that some temporal, dramatic development of the reported event proceeds from that starting-point" (1974: 504–6). The stories could consist of threats of future hostilities as well as accounts of past minor hostilities.

The following narrative recounts a threat.[6] The telling was itself the means for communicating the threat to someone who would perhaps retell it to the antagonist. In the adolescent community, threats were not made directly to one's antagonist but, rather, belonged to a chain of exchanges that could be interrupted, as it was in the following case, if the listeners did not do their part to retell the threat. Especially significant for the problem of entitlement was that in each step of the chain the teller's responsibility for the accuracy of the evidence shifted:

Richard:	Me and her boyfriend gonna fight?
	cause I was sittin' over on the table?
3	Eatin' my potato chips?
Irene:	I don't go wi' him
Richard:	And he asked for some, right?
6	I'm givin' him some
7	I took 'em outa' the bag
8	And he walked past and smacked 'em outa my hand
9	And I told him if he do it again
10	I'm gonna punch him in the face
Ellen:	And that's how it happened?
Richard:	And then he say
13	If I punch him in his face
14	He was gonna stab me, right?
15	And I told him if he do that
16	He better never come to school
17	Then he just walked away.

Three people spoke in this exchange (though a larger group, including myself, was present and, to a certain extent, paying attention). Richard narrated the event; he addressed his remarks to Ellen, and he referred to Irene, who was also present and to someone he identified as Irene's boyfriend, who was not present. As was typical of such threat narratives or previews to possible physical fights, the narrator addressed an audience that spread the news of the impending fight to both the antagonist and others. Whether or not a fight actually occurred, Richard established his reputation as someone willing to stand up for himself. His choice of Ellen as the explicit audience, and Irene as what Goffman called an "unaddressed recipient" (1971: 565) was important for managing the flow of information. Richard was threatening a fight with a boy whom he identified as "Irene's boyfriend." Irene protested, "I don't go wi' him." By her disclaimer, Irene was effectively refusing to become involved in the dispute and to carry the news of the challenge to the antagonist. Ellen was merely a vehicle for indirect communication with Irene.

Most of the adolescent stories could be categorized as fight previews rather than retrospective accounts of past fights. Fight previews reported a presumed offense, but unless the challenged person responded or the challenger persisted, the matter was usually dropped. The fight preview raised problems for its listeners in terms of entitlement. Often, as in Richard's story, the listeners were affiliated with the antagonist and felt obliged to communicate the challenge. Of course, this message would have to be reported as someone else's story and as such would be a potential breach of entitlement. It carries the additional problem of being the bearer of someone else's bad news. In this case, the difficulty was compounded, since the challenger could disavow all statements of challenge from the message bearer for not getting the facts straight. In many cases, the message bearer was held responsible for instigating the conflict, and the antagonisms shifted from the original offense to a challenge against the person who was not entitled to talk about someone else's offense.

Threats can be categorized in Searle's classification of illocutionary acts as commissives (1976); they commit the speaker to some future course of action, in this case, a fight. However, the intention of the threat—what Searle identifies as a sincerity condition—was always questionable in the adolescent stories. The point of the storytelling may be simply to assert one's reputation as someone who fights or to complain about the offense. One way to understand the problem the storytelling creates for the listener or witness is to see it as a transfer from a commissive into a declaration. A commissive has what Searle calls a "world to word" fit in which one wants to make actions fit the words. A declaration works in both directions—world to word and word to world—and has no sincerity condition. The transfer of the story from the person making the supposed threat to the person telling the story of the threat changes the point of view. The first can be challenged in terms of its sincerity; the second can be challenged in terms of either entitlement to tell it or the accuracy of the information.

Spreading and Containing the Flow of Information

Harvey Sacks discusses entitlement in terms both of rights to tell a story and of the related rights to have a certain kind of experience. An obvious aspect of entitlement concerns who has the right to talk about what. Sacks extends this concern to include entitlement to experiences. Further, the storytelling occasions are themselves experiences that can be replayed; hearing a story is itself a way of having an experience that one may or may not have the right to tell. Others have approached the topic in terms of gossip and rumor (Abrahams, 1970: 292; Goodwin, 1982).

Sacks says, "It is a fact that entitlement to experiences is differentially available." The witness to a car-accident scene (Sacks's example) can claim to have suffered through the resulting traffic jam; he or she is entitled to an experience. But, Sacks asks, "Do stories like this become the property of the recipient as they are the property of the teller? That is, the teller owns rights to tell this story, and they give their credentials for their rights to tell the story by offering such things as that they saw it, and that they suffered by it." He answers that a recipient of a story, who merely hears it, does not come to own it in the same way. Adolescent fight narratives demonstrate that the claim of firsthand experience is also negotiable (and not only in cases in which one can claim to have suffered through hearing a story so many times that it may be appropriated for telling). The negotiation of entitlement involves a combination of social and literary conventions: social conventions for what counts as a witness and for what topics are tellable on what occasions, and literary conventions for how to insert one's self into a story.

For the adolescents, storytelling was not a means for gaining unlimited information about others. When false accusations were made, the accusations were simply denied, and little, if any, attention was given to substantiating the details reported in a narrative. The limits of entitlement to talk were stretched to include entitlement to observe or to know, and adolescents accepted fight challenges as the expected consequence for having trespassed the boundaries of acceptable transmission of information. Challenges were directed at the offense of speaking behind someone's back or about someone else's business rather than at communicating inaccurate information.

Certain categories of information were considered private; thus, little was known about them and what was known was guarded in terms of rights to tell. Pregnancy was one such category; to say that someone was pregnant was slanderous whether or not it was true.

For example, one Puerto Rican eighth-grade girl was absent from school for a long time. Her close friends talked about her having cut school without permission. None of them had seen her in the neighborhood or around the school, and they assumed she was going to her older sister's house every day without her parents' knowledge. One day when I was walking through the neighborhood with some of the girl's Puerto Rican friends, we met the absent girl on the street. Her friends asked her where she had been and said, "Oh you're gonna be in trouble when your mother finds out you haven't been in school. Mr. A [the teacher] was askin' about you." The girl told us that she had married her boyfriend and that she was going to have a baby. She said that the husband was 19 years old and that he had a job, so he made her stay home all day. He wouldn't let her go to school anymore because, she said, "He don't want to hear about me messin' around." A few days later, when some of the same girls from the classroom and two other girls were sitting in the school lunchroom, one of them, Leona, mentioned that Luisa, the married girl, was lucky to be home having a baby. The next day, a rumor spread that an old friend of Luisa's was going to fight Leona, the girl who had "talked" about Luisa. Leona was not entitled to report about Luisa's pregnancy.

The determination of a category as off-limits or as potentially volatile and subject to challenges of entitlement was in part a matter of the relationship between the tellers, the listeners, and the characters in the story. When the listeners were totally unfamiliar with the characters, and when the tellers could safely believe that the tellers and characters would never meet, the field was potentially open for communication of details about family life. But even then, although the stories about family life were not challenged, they should be understood as entitled tellings in which entitlement was not challenged.

Depending on the context, almost any story can be challenged as transgressing entitlement. Similarly, almost any experience can be claimed as one's own. One can claim the right to tell a story one has heard, since storytelling or story hearing is itself an experience. However, it is one thing to claim entitlement to an experience as a witness and another to claim entitlement to a story as a hearer. Ownership of a story can imply ownership of experience.[7]

The position of the narrator in relation to the events recounted is not a simple distinction between participant and witness to a fight. Since the fight stories were part of the ongoing quarrel, the narrator who began as a witness could develop into a disputant. Fights about a minor offense often became fights about entitlement to talk about the supposed offense. And as in the example of Leona's report of Luisa's pregnancy, breaches of entitlement were an offense.

One incident at the junior high school dramatically illustrates the complexity of maintaining the boundaries of experience ownership and of containing the transmission of information. In one of the few serious incidents of physical violence at the school, one girl stabbed another. The stabbing was reported in the local newspapers, some of which portrayed the event as a racial conflict, even though both of the combatants were African American. The students objected to the news accounts, and some wrote letters to the local congressional representatives and the newspaper editors.

Letter 1:

Dear Mr. ———
I am very disappointed because of what the new and the newspaper
about my school which is Paul Revere. On March 8, 1979 there was a
fight on the 4th floor. One girl was persuing another girl. One of the girls
was stabed and she fell backwards. As teachers and students tryed to
take the knife off the girl. Other people helped the stabed girl, to get to

the point on March 9, 1979 The News had in bold type BLOODY WAR. That makes it look like there was a war at my school and in my three yars in Paul Revere I have never seen or heard about Anyone beeing stab. In my Three years I have made lots of friends like Steven who is Black, Pedro who is Spanish, and John who is white. I was hoping you would help us by calling Channel six News. It would help us a lot.

>   From
>   Chip
>   and
>   Thomas

Letter 2:

Her how it happen two girl was figthing in the room one name is Cindy and the other girl name is Sharon the one try to get the knife from Cindy so Sharon try to get it with the trash can so the trash can roll over and she ran down the hallway so Cindy ran up to Sharon and stave her on the backside our some way elese and Sharon went to the nurse and then the nurse told the principle about it. then they to called the Policeman came and lock here up and took Sharon to the hospitol and she was crying was bad she could not breathe got and then it was time to go home the First bell Ring veryone went home and told theire mothe about it so thier mother say this is a Bad Schoal so you will be get auttheir be fore April because it is so bad. School but it is not a bad shool it is nies it because the fight to much mot their this the first time some one got stave went I was theire some Paule Revere sould not be calorized for that every one like Paul Revere. Some white people like Black peole and Spanish peo- ple and black like but the dont now how it is some poeple like people color matter what color are you Black White or Spanish and some dont like I I like any color long I got Frient with me to play Color dont matter what color are you. Because dont got the same color dont go the same color But the inside is the sam we are sister and Brother to the leader . . .

Letter 3:

Dear Mr. ———

There was an article written in the paper March 9, 1979 about our school Paul Revere Junior High. The article was about two fourteen year old girls who were in a fight and one of the girls got stabbed.

We the kids of Paul Revere feel as though you have stretched the truth about the fight and out school. You have not only given our school a bad name but, other kids are no longer allowed to come here anymore because their parents feels that Paul Revere is a violent and dangerous place to go. You have taken away all the pride we had. We are very disappointed.

> Sincerely
> ~~Paul Revere~~
> ~~Bloody war~~
> Paul Revere
> Good School!

In their letters, the students charged that the newspaper accounts "stretched the truth about the fight," but more important, the students charged that the newspaper accounts misrepresented the school as a place of racial animosities. The author of the second letter presented what she claimed to be a more accurate version of what happened. The first and third letters charge that the newspaper accounts "stretched the truth" and that they tarnished the reputation of the school. Other letters and comments about the event criticized the newspapers' reliance on third-person accounts, since the student interviewed by one of the newspapers was not a witness to the stabbing.

In effect, the news accounts claimed entitlement to the experience as a community event worthy of reporting, and they claimed their entitlement through what they had heard rather than what they had seen. The students objected that it was not a community event, and further, to portray it as a racial incident suggested that such incidents were typical at the school. The student's primary objection was that the newspaper accounts did not mention that this was the first stabbing to occur in recent memory. The failure to include this information suggested to the students that the newspaper had not presented the whole story. In other words, a secondhand report was partial, lacking both the status of an eyewitness and the knowledge of what aspects of the event should be included in the account.

All of the letters concerned ownership of experience. The first and second letters were an attempt to set the story right and were oriented toward accuracy. They both began with an account of what happened and ended with a statement about racial harmony. Their point was that the newspaper misrepresented the story both by failing to mention that such violence was rare at the school and by not understanding that students made friends across racial groups. The third letter, written by a much better student than the first two, directly challenged the newspaper for hurting the reputation of the school.

If taken in the context of reports about fights, the letters to the editor can be seen as efforts to save face in response to the challenges to one's reputation. The first two letters, in this context, were not just reports of facts oriented toward accuracy; rather, accuracy was at the service of reputation. The issue at hand in disputes about accuracy, in context of adolescent reports about fights, was which person has the right to speak about an event. According to the students, since the newspaper reporters had gathered information from a girl who had not seen the incident, the facts were not correct and, more important, the story was not hers to tell. In Sacks's terms, the newspaper reporters could claim to be representatives of a community that, while not directly experiencing the events, has "suffered by it," and this is the basis of a reporter's right (newspaper reporters often insist on the stronger word, "duty") to report it. Alternatively, the students argued that the reporters were unentitled listeners, and further, they had listened to unentitled tellers.

My concern here is not the question of the rights of newspapers to report on events nor the boundaries between private and community experience. Obviously, the community can claim an interest in violence in schools; rather, I am concerned with the confusion between getting the facts straight and ownership of experience, and as awkward as the students' letters are in presenting their case, they provide an example of a subtle shift from the accuracy of evidence to the responsibility and ownership of evidence. In the simplest sense, the students claim that, without accurate information, the newspapers cannot make the claims that they do about the school. In a more complex sense, the connection between information and reputation depends not only on relative points of view but also on a preestablished hierarchy of vantage points based on ownership of experience. The hierarchy in the case of the adolescents begins with the proximity of the person to the event but also includes the questionable distance of the reporter from the event. What looks like a challenge to accuracy is, in the context of the adolescent fight stories, a challenge of "says who?"

Reported Speech

Quotation is a way of reclassifying a message. As Gregory Bateson writes, "[A]n effect of the metamessage is in fact to classify the messages that occur within its context" (1979: 116). He refers to the classical paradox, "Epimenides was a Cretan who said, 'Cretans always lie,'" as a quotation within a quotation. "The larger quotation becomes a classifier for the smaller, until the smaller quotation takes over and reclassifies the larger, to create contradiction" (Bateson, 1979: 117). Reported speech, as a particular kind of metacommunication, raises questions of authority, referentiality, and entitlement.

The following story reports several layers of offense in which the antagonisms between the original disputants (Ginger and Rose) shifted to a fight between Rose and Mary, who had supposedly started a rumor that she wanted to fight Rose. After the fight, Rose told the story to a group of classmates standing in the hall outside the classroom. Rose had just returned from an absence following the fight, and this was the first time some of the listeners had heard Rose's version of what happened. Her account refers to the rumors that preceded the fight (quotation marks indicate reported speech):

Rose: Ginger and Allen were talking
2   and Ginger said, "I better not be around you
3   or Rose will get in my face"
4   Mary said, "If Rose is bothering you
5   I'll kick her ass"
6   So people started saying that Mary wanted to fight me.
7   So I went up to her
8   and said,
9   "I hear you want to fight me."
10   And she said she didn't say that
11   and that if she wanted to fight me she'd tell me personally
12   That's when she slugged me.

In order to portray herself as the victim, Rose had to condense several events into one scenario. First, the account refers to the report of "talk" between Ginger and Allen in which Ginger suggested to Allen that Rose might be offended and retaliate ("get in her face") for talking with him. (Among the adolescents, "talking" between the genders could imply a romantic interest. A common retort to someone making a threat was "get outa' my face.") Second, the account refers to a separate conversation in which Mary threatened to retaliate against Rose for Rose's presumed threat against Ginger. (How this threat was communicated is unexplained.) Third, Rose heard about the threat against her. Fourth, Rose confronted Mary; Mary denied the threat and then slugged Rose.

The entire account was based on things that may or may not have happened and that, in any case, involved talking or reports of talking. Talking itself was a potential offense among the adolescents, and this case involved two of the most often contested offenses: talking with a potential romantic partner and talking about others in their absence "behind their back." The account assumed shared knowledge and "information state" of some facts, for example, that Rose considered Allen to be her boyfriend but omitted crucial conversational links. One of the crucial missing pieces here was how Mary learned that Ginger was concerned about complaints from Rose, since, supposedly, Ginger addressed her remarks to Allen privately.

All of the reported speech used direct discourse except (6) "People started saying," and (10)–(11) Mary's comments to Rose. If we can exclude "people started saying" as a separate case because it does not identify a particular speaker, we can note that Rose used direct discourse for her own speech and for speech between others but not for discussion between herself and another person. Rose quoted Ginger's prediction of a future antagonistic conversation with her, what Sternberg calls "prospective discourse" (1982: 138).

If told out of context, the final line, "That's when she slugged me," acts as a (literal) punchline in which Mary's actions contradict her words.[8] In the context of the storytelling occasion, the contradiction, reinforced by the use of reported speech, allowed Rose to present herself as the only person in a long chain of hearsay who was willing to confront someone face to face. Therefore, although Rose initiated the confrontation, it can be seen as a positive act, as speaking directly to an antagonist rather than speaking "behind her back." Rose reinforced her position by claiming that she did not initiate the physical fight; she further minimized the physical fight's significance by excluding a blow-by-blow accounting of it from her story.

Rose's story involved a typically convoluted set of minor offenses in which all messages were communicated indirectly (and reported as a direct discourse in the narrative) until the final face-to-face confrontation, which was represented with indirect discourse. The supposed initial offense was Ginger talking to Allen, and Ginger, not Allen, was the offender. Rose let the encounter between Ginger and Allen stand as a fact, complete with a quotation of what Ginger said, but did not substantiate the possibility that she (Rose) might have been offended. She let Ginger's remarks stand as prospective (indirect) discourse and left herself out of the course of events except by reference. By beginning the story with an initial offense against herself, Rose offered an alternative to the possibility that she started the fight with her (also unsubstantiated) challenge. Rose's account presented the fight scenario as a shift from an antagonism between Rose and Ginger to one between Rose and Mary. The first offense was talking to someone else's boyfriend. The new offense was the accusation that Mary threatened Rose indirectly rather than face to face. Rose, in her own account, was a twice-offended victim who had never threatened anyone.

Rose reported speech from situations in which she was not present. Her story was about talking behind people's backs, or what Marjorie Goodwin calls, "he-said-she-said stories":

> The speaker, as author of her own actions, has a right to monitor descriptions others make of her. The accusation is a challenge to the hearer about whether the hearer in fact made such a statement about the speaker. The structure of the utterance further locates the statement about the speaker as having been made in the speaker's absence. The act of the hearer at issue thus constitutes what the participants describe as "talking behind my back" and this act is considered an offense. (1990: 199)

In Rose's story, everyone (Ginger and Allen, Ginger and Mary, and other people) is talking behind her back. The listener is left to interpret the apparent contradiction between Mary's disclaimer:

10   And she said she didn't say that

and her slug, but in either case (talking behind someone's back or giving the first punch), Rose is the victim. The adolescent girls always presented themselves as victims who fought only because they had been pushed too far (Shuman, 1986: 128). The story is a "he-said-she-said" story, a story about who said what to whom. Rose's story, her turn at talk in the conversation, ended at the point at which her retaliation would be justified. By recounting a series of conversational excerpts of reported speech, she successfully presented Mary's slug as an unreasonable instigation.

The offense of using reported speech can focus on a lack of correspondence between original and reported remarks (a problem of accuracy) or on an unauthorized use of those remarks (a problem of entitlement). In Goodwin's discussion, reported speech is one kind of "talking behind someone's back." The potential offense is less a matter of accuracy than of entitlement. In John Hewitt and Randall Stokes's terms, "Issues of substance have been transformed into issues of participants' identities" (1975: 9).

The offense of "talking behind someone's back" is very often not an error of inaccuracy but an infringement on the rights of entitlement. Sternberg suggests that constraints of mimesis, of accurate reporting, of "whatever discrepancies there may be between original and quote" (1982: 153) are central to the social contracts of reporting; that is, the greatest challenge would be that one has been misquoted. He allows that a quotation might reproduce the actual words but still manipulate the "original meaning," but this point, too, insists on misquotation as the primary concern. The adolescents and, I would suspect, other groups as well were concerned with entitlement, not only with the faithfulness of a copy in relation to an original but also with the right to use someone else's speech at all.

The significant difference between questions of accurate retelling and questions of entitlement to retell is in the ways in which tellers manipulate the relation between the retelling and the supposed original. The larger question of concern here, and one addressed by Sternberg, is that of frames of referentiality. Reported speech has several possible referents, including the situation in which the quoted speech was first uttered, and other contexts in which it has been, or could be, used. The referentiality of reported speech is further complicated by the fact that retellings are used both to reveal and to conceal information. In other words, reported speech involves questions of accuracy and questions of control of the flow of information, that is, questions of entitlement.

The relationship between the storytelling situation and the events described is especially complicated in the narratives of everyday life because the storytelling can be part of the ongoing experience. It is important to point out that the stories about everyday experiences do not replicate experiences; they construct them. The clarity of an account, the accuracy of the portrayals, and the presentation of events in chronological order are conventions for concealing as well as for revealing information.

The girls talked about fights more than they fought, and talking was a way of avoiding fighting. If a girl could shift the focus, as Rose did, from an initial offense to some other offense, usually talking behind someone's back, she could successfully divert antagonisms away from herself.

The easiest way to shift antagonisms is to insert a predominant claim (one that supersedes other claims) such as entitlement. Reported speech refers both to something someone else said and to the present context in which it is repeated. In a discussion of how tellers "smooth the way, as it were, from the conversation," Livia Polanyi refers to the problem of "demonstrating the relevance of what has gone on in the storyworld to concerns outside of the storyworld" (1985: 164). The difference is that, rather than smooth the way, adolescent tellers, hoping to divert antagonisms, called attention to storytelling. Boundaries between the story realm, "the recounting of events and acts in narrative discourse" and taleworld, "a realm of unfolding events and enacting characters" (Young 1987: 24), are always complicated by reported speech but are especially complicated by relations between fights and fight stories.

Reported speech in the adolescents' stories served more than a descriptive purpose for telling what happened. The "he-said-she-said" sequence was a resource for retrospectively inferring a causal sequence. Rose may not have known exactly what Ginger said to Allen (and it is unlikely that she did), but she knew how to present their supposed conversation as reported speech. Statements such as "Rose will get in my face," and "If Rose is bothering you, I'll kick her ass," were so common in the everyday speech of the adolescents that they could be easily claimed as anyone's exact words.

The relationship between experiences and reports of experience, in this case, fights and fight stories, can be understood in terms of what H. G. Gadamer has called "temporal distance" (1975: 124). Gadamer states that understanding requires temporal distance, the "filtering process" that allows one to stand back from experience. Reported accounts imply temporal distance, but this distance is not an "objective" stance that allows one somehow to perceive a situation more accurately; rather, Gadamer states, "We define the concept of 'situation' by saying that it represents a standpoint that limits the possibility of vision" (1975: 128). The limited vision belongs not only to the listener, who hears a story without the opportunity of firsthand experience, but also includes the firsthand experience as a limited perspective.

"Firsthand experience" is a negotiated category of reported experience rather than an observable "fact."[9] Among the adolescents, the claim to firsthand experience was often disputed as only partial knowledge, and people often claimed hearsay as a firsthand experience. These contradictory claims contributed to a climate in which disputes could escalate far out of proportion to the incidents that prompted them.

Use of the category of "firsthand" makes a claim based on the presence of a person in a situation. The fact of presence is often used to assume firsthand knowledge as though presence were responsible for the knowledge. In the case of adolescents' narratives about prior conversations, a speaker asserted as a firsthand experience statements made by another person.

Reported speech is part of the larger category of transmitted words, or any discourse that refers to another source (including written sources, supposed sources such as "it is said," and authorized statements). Transmitted speech, whether described or reported, places the author in the position of recontextualizing others' words.[10] This is one of the primary means for establishing distance between author, teller, narrator, and reader or listener. In reported contemporary speech, a recognized part of the speech of the teller and listeners, the source, and the narrator and listener belong to the same speech community. Greatest proximity exists when all three share speech. Distance begins when the teller asserts shared speech with the source and excludes the listener, or the teller excuses himself or herself from an association suggested between the source and the listener. One means for creating distance between the text and listener or reader is what M. M. Bakhtin calls "authoritative discourse":

The authoritative word is located in a distanced zone, organically connected with a past that is felt to be hierarchically higher. . . . The degree to which a word is recognized by us or not—is what determines its specific demarcation and individuation in discourse; it requires a *distance* vis-à-vis itself (this distance may be valorized as positive or as negative, just as our attitude toward it may be sympathetic or hostile). (1981: 342–43)

Authoritative discourse is not necessarily lodged in persons as speakers and could include sacred words, beliefs, or other fixed texts. Bakhtin contrasts authoritative discourse, which "permits no play with its framing context" with internally "persuasive discourse," contemporary shared speech, which includes "retelling a text in one's own words, with one's own accents, gestures, modifications" (1981: 342). In the adolescent world, the school, the church, and family, adults represented "authorities": their discourse ranged from the contemporary and shared to the authoritative. The "he-said-she-said" stories rarely reported the exact words of these authorities; rather, they described them. Reported speech conveyed both the words and a sense of their performance: described speech did not insist that words were repeated exactly as heard.

Reported speech was one of the main means available to an author for manipulating the distance in time between author, narrator, and listener or reader. Reported speech afforded the possibility of multiple voices traceable to distinct time frames. In addition, reported speech could rely on shared understandings of the way something would be said in order to imply what someone had said. The pregnant girl—Luisa's—use of the phrase, "He don't want to hear about me messin' around," implied that her husband had said, "I don't want to hear about your messin' around." Just as proverbial sayings ascribe statements to an authoritative potential speaker, the adolescent familiar jargon provided quotable phrases, convincingly ascribed to other speakers.

The report of a past conversation located an event in time, and the narrator, as a mediator between the past conversation and the present storytelling, had the option of further distancing the narration by not accounting for his or her own position in the events. In the adolescents' oral narratives, the narrator almost always placed himself or herself within the events as a first-person witness or antagonist. Only in reports of television soap operas and a few accounts of the nonadolescent world did narrators omit their positions as witnesses. In fight previews and stories told during an ongoing dispute, the "fight" consisted entirely of words; reports of what people said to one another; and reported speech consisted primarily of description of offenses, accusations, and threats.

Reported speech is one device for recontextualizing. The teller not only claims entitlement to use words from another source but also entitlement to recontextualize or reframe the words as part of a particular perspective, point of view, or stance.

The Consequences of Entitlement

Entitlement can be approached from many angles: as an author's right to produce or perform a text; as an addressee's privilege to repeat what has been told; or as a way in which texts can be embedded, self-referenced, cross-referenced, and otherwise legitimated. In any case, a discussion of entitlement in narrative exposes cultural conceptions of the categories of author, text, and reports of experience. Framing a discussion of reported speech within the larger concern of entitlement calls attention to reported speech as a literary device but, more important, as a cultural convention subject to cultural negotiations for its appropriate use.

Challenges to entitlement are a means of bringing about a shift of focus from the accuracy of the evidence to the responsibilities of the speaker. One way of understanding this shift is in terms of the "double-directed" speech created by reported speech. Reported speech is a way of maintaining two voices and of manipulating the distance between them. In some models, for example, that proposed by V. N. Voloshinov and Bakhtin in their discussions of reported speech, the question of whether the voices are in solidarity or in conflict is crucial. Voloshinov differentiates reported speech on the grounds of whether it adopts the dogmatism of the authority quoted or confronts and attempts to challenge that authority (1973: 120, 138).

The adolescents' fight narratives present a different problem. The person quoted in the fight narratives was not an authority in Bakhtin's sense, and the adolescent speakers were not concerned with confirming or denying the status or authority of the prior speaker; instead, reported speech was used to deflect responsibility. In Voloshinov's terms, the speaker was a narrator rather than a character in the events recounted. While Voloshinov does not discuss the problem of the entitlement to report another's speech, the issue is not irrelevant to his argument. As an extension of Bakhtin's concept of authoritative discourse we can consider the possibility of both nonauthoritative sources and alternative ways of creating conflict between sources and reporters.

Any use of reported speech indicates a distance between the quoted source, the current narrator, and the listener-audience. The significance of the distance is not only a matter of the formal configurations among participants in a speech event but is also a determinant of cultural categories involving, for example, the authority to present a point of view and ways participants represent events. Bakhtin's model places all of the burden of distinction between uses of reported speech on the creation of distance between the source and the reporter. However, in the case of the adolescent fight narratives, distance did not have the consequence of undermining authority.

The adolescent fight narratives were characterized by the changing perspectives and positions of the participants in the ongoing events; by a precarious relationship between loyalty and responsibility in establishing a speaker's credibility; and by categories of offenses, such as spreading information considered private. Each of these characteristics corresponds to issues addressed by Bakhtin. Although conflated in Bakhtin's model, the first characteristic corresponds to the choice of solidarity with, or resistance to, an authoritative source; the third problem, concerned more directly with the entitlement to knowledge, corresponds with Bakhtin's general category of authority. Since Bakhtin's discussion focuses on the novel, he quite understandably limits his concern to the relationship between the quoted sources and the narrator. The entire concept of authority changes when considered in terms of ongoing communication in everyday life in which, for example, a witness can compete with a prior speaker for authoritative status. An examination of the differences between Bakhtin's examples from modern novels and the uses of reported speech by the adolescents is helpful to understand what is at stake in Bakhtin's claims for reported speech as a way of undermining authority. Bakhtin's central issue, solidarity with, or resistance against the authoritative source can be broken down into components more relevant to the adolescent fight narratives, and each of these components represents a different kind of claim, a different kind of responsibility, that a speaker can claim or deny in relation to the experiences reported.

The problem with phrasing the issue in terms of competing points of view is that it focuses on the perspective of the participants as if the experience remains a static thing represented differently only because it is seen differently. Telling a story always involves conventions for ensuring a point of view, and one aspect of the entitlement to tell a story is the question of entitlement to a certain point of view. However, the phrase "everyone is entitled to his or her own point of view" (though it is said as if quoted from authority) is not entirely accurate, especially if it implies that everyone is entitled to *express* that point of view without taking responsibility for the consequences. As soon as one takes a stance, one is a participant and not an observer and must take the consequences of involvement.

Point of view is one convention for manipulating expectations and for persuading the listener to adopt certain ideas and attitudes. In an issue of *New Literary History* devoted to the topic, Margaret Gilbert describes convention as a coordination problem in which common-interested parties perceive at least two possible solutions to a single problem (1983: 225–51). In the case of the adolescent narratives, the coordination problem occurs when a person relates a story about a conflict or a potential conflict with an absent person. The listeners must decide whether they are entitled to report what they have heard or whether they will be accused of talking behind someone's back if they repeat the story. E. D. Hirsch has argued, "[C]onvincing discussion of convention and context has always implicitly recognized that the real function of context is to supply probabilities of intent, nothing more" (1983: 392). And indeed, I did find that the shifting status of the adolescent fight stories, both as reports of events and as part of ongoing fights, could be understood as a problem of point of view, or a kind of switch in intent among the status of the disputant, the offended person, the challenger, the witness, and the conveyor of news. However, whereas Hirsch's purpose in making this statement is to discredit interest in context and particularly social conventions for reading, I see his equation of intentionality a convention as argument for the inextricable relatedness of point of view and entitlement, authorship, and authority.

In literary studies, problems of intent are often connected to problems of allusion (Wimsatt and Beardsley, 1987: 112–13). The attempt, in literary studies, to recover an author's intent by tracing the allusions in the author's text raises the same questions of authority and authenticity that are raised in any use of reported speech; only the process and roles are reversed. The author who does the alluding becomes the authority, and instead of questioning the speaker's right to quote, critics use the "original" reported texts to bolster or challenge their own and one another's authority as interpreters. In both cases, reported speech involves explicit challenges or claims to truth regarding the integrity of some original and often covert claim to entitlement.

Recounting an experience in narrative form fictionalizes the experience and personalizes it. In each telling, the teller or author authorizes a particular version of the experience. Any question of the authorization to take a particular stance challenges entitlement. The question is, does the experience belong to the author? It is not a question of accuracy but of authority and agency (P. Smith, 1988a).

Harvey Sacks was correct to approach the matter of entitlement in terms not of privacy of the topic of a story but of ownership of experience. What looks like privacy is actually a way of controlling information, of protecting the authority to assert a particular point of view.

If narrative genres could be identified by the way in which knowledge was organized in a story, then adolescent fight stories could be identified by their embedded patterns of concealment and their narrator's shifting point of view. An epistemological approach to conversational narrative would demand attention not only to the text itself but also to the distribution of knowledge in the adolescent community. What might appear to the outsider and the adult to be ill-formed narratives that fail to decontextualize, to provide listeners with the contextual information necessary for understanding the story, could then be better understood as appropriate concealments. By appropriately withholding some information and by using reported speech to ascribe evidence to other speakers, the tellers of "he-said-she-said" fight stories could hope to escape entitlement challenges.

All of the examples discussed here concern ways in which texts become permeable to social worlds: the fight preview shows how quoted speakers can be constituted as allies or cast as objects of ridicule; the pregnancy story raises the issue of restrictions on knowledge about others; the letters to the editor raise the issue of unentitled accounts; Rose's fight story demonstrates how focus is diverted from an initial antagonism to an antagonism about speaking. In part, these texts are permeable through what appear to be the shifting positions of their narrators as firsthand witnesses or thirdhand retellers, as characters in their own stories or as ancillary persons, and, more generally, as implicated or not in the consequences of the events. The appearance of shifting points of view can, and often does, disguise another set of relationships. Points of view in the sense of proximity to an event are sometimes used as an index to the accuracy of a narrator's account (a witness would be deemed more credible than someone who learned of the event secondhand, although see Philips [1993] on the cultural specificity of such indexes). However, the issue of accuracy based on proximity also can be used to conceal the interests of speakers. In this sense, the issue of accuracy conceals the problem of agency, or who gains from distributing or withholding information and knowledge. As long as some authority could be invoked as a source of accurate information, as long as a speaker could appeal to the fact that something had been said by someone else, the focus could shift to the accuracy of the reporting and could hide the complicit relationship between speaker and source.

Challenging entitlement and using reported speech together provided a complex way of shifting the relationship between speakers and the information recounted by the adolescents. They challenged a narrator's proximity to an event as a question of entitlement rather than accuracy, and they used this challenge to deflect attention away from the topic of the account itself. Narrating an event involved attention to both saving face (an entitlement problem) and reported speech (a way of appropriating someone else's proximity to an event).[11] They conflated these two strategies, combining the social problem of reputation with the narrative problem of reported speech.

While the adolescents were masters of shifting the focus of accusations from an antagonist to the bearer of messages about the antagonism, they became trapped in their own metacommunicative moves. They engaged in metacommunicative shifts in discourse for their own sake or for the sake of shifting from the topic of conversation to conversation as a topic, rather than toward the purpose of understanding disputes as a category of behavior; that is, they did not, as a result of mastering "he-said-she-said" routines, become reflexive about the assumed sequence of fights. They considered fights to be the inevitable result of people talking about one another and other daily offenses. Or even when they were reflective about fight routines, and there is some evidence that they were, "he-said-she-said" routines did not necessarily lead to diplomacy but more often became incorporated into the fight sequence.

The alternatives of resisting or complying with authoritative discourse are only two of many possibilities for the appropriation of reported speech. At the very least, another possibility exists that the reported speech may not be constituted as authoritative. Rajeswari Sunder Rajan and Zakia Pathak offer a dramatic example in their discussion of the case of Shahbano, a divorced Muslim woman who appealed to the (Hindu-dominated) Indian courts for a larger divorce settlement and found herself in a situation in which she was asking for protection by Hindu men from Muslim men. As the author points out:

> "Protection" can confer upon the protector the right to interfere in areas hitherto out of bounds or the authority to speak for the silent victim; or it can serve as a camouflage for power politics. An alliance is formed between protector and protected against a common opponent from whom danger is perceived and protection offered or sought, and this alliance tends to efface the will to power exercised by the protector. Thus the term conceals the opposition between protector and protested, a hierarchical opposition that assigns higher value to the first term; strong/weak, man/woman, majority/minority, state/individual. (1989: 566)

I have suggested that the concept of entitlement concerns the ways in which texts are permeable to social worlds. But much more is at stake here than the use of frames or what Gilbert (1983) calls a "co-ordination problem." At the very least, entitlement claims and challenges are one of the ways in which texts are constituted by contexts. Rather than identify points of view as orientations within texts, or within readers or social communities, and rather than set up an opposition between authorities and those who are dominated, we can consider the problems in terms of claims of ownership and appropriation and can understand discourses as framing particular kinds of subjectivity. If conventions are, as Gilbert suggests, a coordination problem, then the problem is not to coordinate realities but to comply with or resist the particular coordinated conventional discourse.

Entitlement is not just another name for either mismatches or fits between texts and contexts; rather, entitlement is one kind of metacommunication concerned very specifically with situations that call attention to the relationship between text and context. Unlike the concept of perspective, which places the burden of mismatch or fit on the spectators and leaves the object in view intact, and unlike the concept of double-directed voices, which calls attention to an opposition between authorities and those who would be dominated, the concept of entitlement does not depend on the possibility or problems of fits and mismatches. Quite simply, entitlement concerns ownership of experiences and the right to represent those experiences. For some groups, such as the adolescents discussed here, entitlement became an explicitly addressed issue, but this is not to suggest either that entitlement is only a factor when it becomes explicitly discussed, or that entitlement is ever present in all communication; rather, it is a part of those communications involved in disputing the rights of speakers to represent others.

Both discussions of competing points of view and discussions of authoritative discourse involve entitlement. In discussions of competing points of view, the problem is phrased as one of potential misunderstandings between people with different perspectives. The distance between their points of reference or horizons of understanding is said to account for lack of shared knowledge. The argument is that people take a stand based on their biases, their points of view; thus, they cannot be objective about the knowledge at hand.[12] The concept of entitlement enters into such arguments only as a problem of taking a stand.

In discussions of authoritative discourse, the distance is configured differently, and rather than a problem of the impossibility of objectivity, it is one of the displacement of original meaning, appropriated by new speakers. The entitlement question is, who appropriates whom in whose name for whose benefit?

The concept of entitlement helps to do away with frameworks that leave original knowledge intact and instead calls attention to particular agents' interests in controlling knowledge. However, identifying these interests does not in itself resolve any problems. The concept of multiple perspectives and that of authoritative discourse are both emancipatory concepts that provide their own sorts of resolutions to misunderstandings. Bakhtin's proposal, in which multiple perspectives are maintained in a dialogue that undermines any monolithic authoritative discourse, is an example.

The concept of authoritative discourse implies both the possibility of nonauthoritative discourse and the probability of conflict between discourses. In Bakhtin and Voloshinov's description of varieties of combined discourses in the novel, one kind of conflict is preferred, that in which plurality of voices maintain their identities in a dialogue. Bakhtin praises this plurality of voices as a means for undermining authoritative discourse.

Another way to describe the appropriation of authoritative discourse is the concept of displacement, the idea that an original discourse has been borrowed by a different discourse which bears traces of its source (see Derrida, 1973: 156). Bakhtin's concern is the way the original discourse is represented, whether by adhering to its original integrity (in solidarity with authority), or by parodying its authority. The crucial question in borrowing, displacing, or appropriating discourse is whether the *distance* (Bakhtin's term) or *difference* (Derrida's term) between the presumed original and current appropriation has been effaced. Bakhtin phrases this effacement in terms of monologic discourse in which there is no apparent distance between an original and a quotation, and Bakhtin's project is the description of the tracks left by various forms of appropriation, specifically in reported speech. The preferred representation is one in which the tracks of appropriation are still visible, in which both the voice of authority and the voice of the person quoting are maintained.

Derrida questions the whole concept of disjunctures and displacements as a concept in which representations are always supplements to "nature" (1974: 144, 163) and in which the act of appropriation, the supplement, potentially transgresses some prohibition. (For Bakhtin, however, this transgression is what enables a narrator to undermine authority.) According to Derrida, speech is always already supplementary, always already imitations and substitutions (1973: 224). The sign and the signified are always already displaced rather than traceable.

Derrida's position has two implications for the appropriation of reported speech. First, in keeping with Bakhtin's model, the conflict between the original and the appropriated discourse does not concern the validity of some original signified truth but instead concerns the path or trace posited as a relationship between them. Second, in contrast to Bakhtin's model, Derrida's position erases the difference between monologic conformity to authority and dialogic resistance to authority. The larger problem is appropriation and the role of the agent who represents someone else's words. In Bakhtin's model, monologic discourse, in effacing the distance between the authority and the narrator, effaces the agent, the narrator. Uses of reported speech become a game of presence and absence in which, by acknowledging the presence of authority, the speaker can make herself absent. An absent speaker takes no responsibility for the words said.

However, is it really the case that keeping both voices present, creating dialogue, is a special sort of accomplishment? Why not acknowledge the alternative strategy of making a present voice appear absent as equally dialogic? An absent voice isn't, after all, an emptiness but is a placeholder for a missing voice. In many systems, only those missing voices that acknowledge their own absence count. But what happens when an absent voice is acknowledged in retrospect?

The adolescent uses of reported speech can be seen as an example of speakers who manipulate their own absence and presence to manipulate taking and denying responsibility for their words. According to Bakhtin's model, the fight stories might be considered monologic in the sense that they do not disrupt the authority of the quoted speaker. However, this isn't sufficient to explain cases like this in which a speaker has invented the original quote in order to absolve herself of responsibility. The distance in this case lies not in a lack of conformity to an authority but in leaving the marks of the trace. The speaker effaces herself from time to time but rather than efface the traces between hers and another discourse, she makes them apparent. It is this relationship, between apparent and effaced tracks, and not the one between present and absent speakers, that is crucial in shifting attention from the question of the accuracy of the account, from the knowable or unknowable signified, and instead, toward the tracks themselves.

The study of entitlement is a study of a particular kind of appropriation. Any claim to knowledge invokes claims for a relationship whether between knowers and known, knowers and deceived, or knowers and those who do not know. The concept of entitlement provides one way of investigating how appeals for accurate accounts of reality couch and conceal the questions of whose reality is recounted.

2   *Collective Memory and*
     Public Forgetting

Collective narrative is both powerful and unstable. By establishing or confirming a shared version of events, a collective narrative shapes normative, hegemonic, or overdetermined worldviews. Personal narratives can confirm, subvert, appropriate, or otherwise disrupt or assert the power of collective narratives and vice versa. As I have argued, nothing makes a narrative more contested than the dispute over ownership of experience and the rights to interpret it, but implicit in that dispute can be the question of whether or not the experiences one claims are really one's own. Nothing makes narrative as a form more suspicious than the observation that it is a culturally constructed means for interpreting, rather than reporting, experience. Individuals contest the rights of a larger public to tell or interpret their stories, as I discussed in chapter 1. Listeners also contest the veracity of a story they have heard before. The story that is too unfamiliar, too exotic to be believed, and the story that is too familiar are both subject to suspicion. The familiarity of shared stories presents both obstacles to credibility and opportunities for shared understanding. Discovering that one's own story is not singular or idiosyncratic can help to provide a way to speak about what might have felt unspeakable. In this chapter, I discuss several dimensions of personal and collective narrative, including challenges to the veracity of collective narrative in political domains, the often formulaic structure of narratives told by people who claim to have shared similar experiences, the collective memories of trauma victims, and the mythic or allegorical status of collective narrative.[1] In a close examination of the collective memories and life histories of an artisan community, I ask about the role of collective narrative as a critical practice. The central question guiding my inquiry is the one posed by Walter Benjamin in the epigram for the introduction to the book: Is the possibility of critical practice overpowered by conformity to a shared collective memory?

Examples of the tensions between the personal and the collective are familiar in political discourse. Refugees petitioning for asylum status in the United States or Canada are sometimes denied because their stories sound too much like stories heard before (Barsky, 1994, 2000; Robertson and Camerini, 1999; Shuman and Bohmer, forthcoming). Jews hidden during the Holocaust who were previously reluctant to tell their stories (because they did not suffer in concentration camps) find the validation of their experiences in group meetings in which they share both the stories of their experiences and their experience of not being able to tell their stories. Persecuted Hutu are astonished to learn that other groups of people have experienced genocide and are comforted by the thought that they are not the only targets of destruction (Malkki, 1995). Finding others with similar experiences can be an affirming event that offers a framework for understanding or expressing cataclysmic as well as ordinary experiences. Not all stories begin as personal; some are understood from the beginning to be collective narrations, belonging as much to a shared group experience as to the individuals involved. Both the personal and the collective story can be legitimizing categories that provide meaning and pattern to life, but traversing the terrain between the personal and the collective can be fraught with obstacles to understanding.

Often, the personal and collective are positioned in relation to each other, either against each other as counternarratives or with each other as allegories.[2] Refugees petitioning for asylum status whose requests are denied because their stories sound too similar are an example of the former: personal stories mistaken as a collective one.[3] Hutu and Tutsi survivors in Rwanda who discover that others have also been victims of genocide are an example of the latter: a collective story that allegorizes a personal one. Entitlement claims are a significant source of the instability of collective, larger than life, narrative. As I discussed in the introduction, many stories travel beyond their tellers, beyond the people who claim to have had the experiences that their stories describe. Once a story travels, it is open to several kinds of challenges, including entitlement claims (discussed in chapter 1) that challenge the rights of new tellers to tell or interpret others' experiences and challenges to veracity that suggest a person removed from an experience might not portray it accurately. Any effort to untether the relationship between teller and experience complicates ownership and the right to interpretation. Stories about personal suffering are particularly subject to this untethering and retethering in which outsiders claim an interest in the suffering of others, and those who suffered the experience reclaim the rights to tell and interpret what happened.[4] Telling a personal story as a collective story requires making the claim to be able to speak for others. (The opposite is also true, a problem I address in chapter 5.) Collective narrative is produced at the intersection of memory and history, both as a record of events and as an interpretation representing shared and disputed ideas.

Kai Erikson's *Everything in Its Path* (1976) and his later discussions of that work (in Caruth, 1995) provide an example of a collective narrative in which the similarity of tellers' stories prompted outsiders to question the tellers' credibility. Erikson was hired by an insurance company to find out why all of the people who were victims of a flood in West Virginia seemed to be telling the same story about what happened to them. Surely, thought the insurance company, they couldn't have all had the exact same experience, suffered in the exact same way. What Erikson found is that the flood was such a catastrophe, wiping out all vestiges of the communities along the valley, that people were left homeless and without any sense of how to account for the consequences of what had happened. They had nothing left, both materially and socially, and as they searched for a way to account for what had happened, they constructed a narrative scenario that started with how each family had been taken by surprise, continued with how they had made futile efforts to save each other, and ended with a sense of becoming a bewildered survivor.

By selecting the same basic structure for their reports, the tellers of the flood stories called attention to the constructedness of their narratives, which were then challenged by the insurance company.[5] In their efforts to create a coherent picture that makes sense of the fragments of experience, narrators sometimes overlay their experiences on a familiar or available structure. I argue that such "available narratives" are a fundamental feature of narrative in everyday life and that, for the most part, such narratives are extremely useful to people either making sense of their personal experience in recognizable terms or resisting available interpretations. In some cases, using available narratives can make the stories appear less personal, more formulaic. Formulaic stories are not necessarily less valid as personal testimonials, and in some, especially religious, contexts, formulaic testimonials are accepted as valid. But in some cases, calling attention to the fact of constructedness makes the stories open to challenges of credibility. This is the case of both narratives told by asylum applicants in the United States and by the survivors of the flood. In both cases, tellers were challenged for telling formulaic (and thus potentially borrowed) stories.[6] As Erikson explains, trauma can have a "social dimension" (1995: 185).

> In places like Buffalo Creek, then, the community in general can almost be described as the locus for activities that are normally thought to be the property of individual persons. It is the community that offers a cushion for pain,

the community that offers a context for intimacy, the community that serves as the repository for binding traditions. And when the community is profoundly affected, one can speak of a damaged social organism in almost the same way that one would speak of a damaged body. (1995: 188)

The "first person" experience of such community traumas does not require eyewitness presence. Erikson points out that even people who were far from home experienced the injury nonetheless and became "ratified tellers" of the narrative.[7] One of the shared characteristics of many survivor narratives is the attempt to construct the survivor as a beneficiary of fortune rather than as a hero. In some situations, as in Buffalo Creek, the impossibility of an individual heroic narrative (since no one was able to do enough) makes the shared narrative the only possible story to tell. Whereas all narratives create coherence out of fragmented events, trauma-survivor narratives additionally recount experiences that are not only fragmentary but also inexplicable; the stories are about things that should not have happened. The mere effort to tell them cannot help but call attention to the difficulty of making coherence out of fragments.

As Ruth Ginsberg's discussion of the Holocaust narratives of Christa Wolf demonstrates, such stories are not a straightforward effort to represent the past but are torn between the obligation to remember and the desire to forget. If the victims share their stories, it is not because the experiences were the same or because the perspectives are the same or even because the shared representation is therapeutic and perhaps a safe way of acknowledging that individuals are not alone in their horrors. The problem is not to construct a unified "we" that represents individual experiences. Rather, discourse and especially narrative inevitably relies on what Ginsberg calls "a collective point of view embodied in language," and the problem is to create, discover, invent, a coherent "I." The problem that a trauma survivor faces is to integrate the self of the past with the self of the present, a problem complicated by "gaps in the story, gaps of the 'unsaid,' or perhaps the 'unsayable,' spheres of silence. The 'I' is unspoken as its components are partially said but still rejected, partially unsaid because still unsayable" (Ginsberg, 1992: 438). What is interesting here is that shared representation, steadying both remembering and forgetting, helps individuals to create coherent narratives (which is not the same as integrated selves).[8]

Writing about the modernist invention of the self, Charles Taylor argues, "our being selves is essentially linked to our sense of the good, and that we achieve selfhood among other selves" (1989: 51). Personal narratives implicitly speak not only on behalf of the self but also on behalf of shared experience, on behalf of others. Personal narratives are tellable to the extent that they successfully negotiate the tension between the person and the shared meaning that is "there for all of us" (Taylor, 1989: 492). The personal as allegorical is one way to negotiate that tension. Further, the invention of any particular coherent self relies on the larger cultural allegories of self (Clifford, 1988). Here, I am suggesting that the concept of self is itself allegorical. The question is not only who is this coherent self and how is it invented out of the fragmented selves of experience, but also how is the self situated in a community that recognizes and shapes it?

The factuality of narratives that appear to be just too similar has become a problem in the assessment of refugee narratives. In a study of the legal proceedings to determine refuge status in Canada, Robert Barsky found that the similarity of stories made them less credible (1991, 1994, 2000). Refugee status in Canada requires proof of a political rather than an economic rationale for seeking asylum. Potential refugees speak before a judge who decides whether or not they qualify for such status, and in these hearings, the narratives the refugees tell are the basis for evaluation. Since many of the refugees have resided in camps or other way stations before arriving in Canada, they have had a lot of opportunity to share stories with and hear advice from other refugees. Some of this advice includes stories that purportedly will pass inspection, but the judges are particularly suspicious of stories that sound "stock" or formulaic. At the same time, many of the refugees have experienced similar difficulties, and their stories are alike. According to Barsky, who collected these narratives in the Canadian hearings and in interviews, many of the refugees have long since destroyed all written documents since until asylum is granted, such documents constitute a threat to anyone who truly is a political refugee (1994). So, all that these refugees have is their stories, stories that have been communally shaped by experiences of recounting events in the camps. The communal stories are additionally motivated by a desire to please the interlocuters and give them what they are looking for (Ginsburg, 1992). In its most general sense, this is the problem of generic narratives, of how people come to tell the same story about their experience, of how one person's narrative can typify other's experiences, and of how that narrative can not only represent but also legitimize the experience.

The narratives of shared experiences are most similar on a structural level; the tellers have selected similar experiences to recount, and they have constructed a familiar sequence of events. I have suggested this is one way that narratives create a relationship between the coherence of narrative and the fragmentation of experience. Personal narratives often propose the integration of fragmented selves into some coherent person (Linde, 1993). It is important to point out here that the narratives invent rather than reflect coherence or fragmentation in the world. Narratives create their subjectivities and position them in a point in the past constructed as the true locus of the self. Each alignment, each positioning, changes the context in which the self (coherent or fragmented) can appear.

Claiming more-than-personal significance is one way of proposing that one's story is worth telling. William Labov and Joshua Waletsky discuss the problem of tellability in their basic formulation of the components of everyday life narratives. They make two central claims: (1) that narrative recapitulates but does not necessarily reproduce the sequence of events reported, and (2) that narratives depend on what Labov and Waletsky call evaluation, the nonsequential parts of the story that answer, among other things, the question, "so what?" and thereby justify the telling. What begins for Labov and Waletsky as an examination of narrative and temporality turns into a discussion of purpose and meaning, in which recapitulation is aligned with purpose, and evaluation is aligned with meaning. In framing gestures such as, "this is where it happened," the context expands beyond the events described to include both the larger social context in which those events are meaningful and the context in which the story was told. The difference between these two types of contexts is crucial for understanding how narratives work by excerpting events from everyday experience that are then represented as significant beyond the immediate group of people who were present during an experience. Framing devices cut out a territory in the world of ongoing experience. By making the claim that something is worth noting and excerpting from the stream of ongoing life, the teller marks the experience as important and separate and at the same time connected—the experience is both part of ordinary life and worth noting as apart from it, part of life and what I am calling allegorical, or larger than life. A second kind of framing device claims similar experience, as in "the same thing happened to me." The second kind of frame, though also making allegorical claims about the relation between ongoing and particularly noteworthy experiences, is also about the context of storytelling and thus is about both the experiences recounted and about the relation between the teller and the listeners. The first link, between the context of the experience and that of the larger ongoing life, is the more clearly allegorical of the two; it is a familiar problem that has been discussed as the relation between myth and history or individual and community. The second link, between the context of the experience recounted and the context in which the story is told, or what Katharine Young calls the taleworld and the storyrealm (1987), works against allegory at the same time as it insists on it. It works against allegory because any explicit claim for larger meaning undermines the authenticity of the personal disclosure. It insists on allegory to the extent that the story is a "me too" story, something that calls attention to shared meaning.

Granting mythic or legendary status to personal experience challenges its status as personal. At the same time, one could argue that collective narrative inevitably lends mythic proportions to experience. The narrative form with its causal sequences affirms and establishes relations between events and categorizes those events into paradigmatic units such that, for example, every departure evokes the hero-leaves-home motif. Joseph Campbell insists that it works the other way around when he writes, "In the absence of an effective general mythology, each of us has his private, unrecognized, rudimentary, yet secretly potent pantheon of dream. The latest incarnation of Oedipus, the continued romance of Beauty and the Beast, stand this afternoon on the corner of Forty-second Street and Fifth Avenue, waiting for the traffic light to change" (1956: 4). I would like to suggest a caution here; it isn't as simple as Campbell would have it. Rather, in our personal narratives and our life histories, we sometimes resist making examples of ourselves; it is not that we lack an effective general mythology and that dream becomes a substitute. The fact is that for the most part our lives have not been written yet, and narrative provides one of the few means for identifying suitable paradigms in which to categorize experiences. Rather than see the act of narrating as an act of filling in already-familiar slots in an already-familiar sequence, we will find it more often to be an act of searching for a way to integrate received motifs, seemingly uncategorizable experiences, and events that do not immediately make sense. It is a struggle, sometimes, to find an acceptable sequence that remains true enough to the events and persons and is still tellable or even thinkable.

The relationship between the personal narrative and its allegorical counterpart, its mythical script, is easily confused by writers such as Campbell who look for and easily find simplistic functional relationships supporting assertions such as that narrative shapes community or identity or gives meaning to otherwise undiscriminated events. Personal storytelling is often about naming the categories that define experiences, a project compromised by the fact that not only does the category exceed the experience, but the experience also exceeds the categories. Walter Benjamin's proposition is the opposite of Campbell's. In Benjamin's terms, the mythologizing or allegorizing of experience points not to coherence but to fragmentation. The seemingly fixed and coherent allegorical text is an illusion in the modern world; it is a sign of what is not possible; it is a record of catastrophe. Judith Butler defines allegory "as a kind of narrative in which one speaks otherwise than one appears to speak" (1997: 177). This double speak works in several ways, between the actual and the appearance, between the personal and the more than personal, and between the illusion of coherence and the actuality of fragmentation. Drawing on Gershom Scholem's work, Benjamin understood that in the process of "becoming allegorical . . . something loses its own meaning and becomes the vehicle of something else" (quoted in Buck-Morss, 1991: 235). It is archaeological (Buci-Glucksmann, 1984: 7) rather than utopian. As a response to catastrophe, it offers redemption not by creating coherence but by observing the hope and promise still evident in the fragmented ruins of the past.

One argument would claim that all we have is a hermeneutic circle in which our meanings come to us in recognizable forms and in which we search for some degree of, in Charles Taylor's terms, shared intersubjective meaning. Consensus, then, occupies the dual position of received traditional knowledge, values, or assumptions and of shared understanding. Following this line of thought, we can observe that it is no wonder that our stories seem to be the same, for it is only through familiar structures that we are able to recognize and portray our experiences as significant.[9] By shifting the focus of our inquiry slightly, we can ask under what conditions a personal story can have more-than-personal significance and then, turning the question of shared meaning around, ask at what point the collective narrative reveals its failure to provide a coherent narrative? I have described an ongoing tension between the personal and the allegorical based on issues of entitlement and credibility. These tensions point to a slippage between signifier and signified, involving questions such as whose story it is and what really happened. The personal and allegorical meanings are supposed to match, and the problem begins whenever they do not.[10] Beyond these problems is a critical issue, the danger that indebtedness to the collective memory can obscure the ruins of the past by imagining coherence. If Benjamin was right, the redeeming possibility of allegory is the vestiges of hope in the ruins, in resisting the aura rather than lamenting its loss, then the imagined coherences of collective memories damn the future even as they redeem the past.

The life-history narratives I consider here provide an example of that problem.[11] They are the collective memories of a community of artisans who regard their past as a lost legacy. The artisans of Pietrasanta, Italy, have been carving marble for the past two hundred years. The town is located at the foothills of the Massa-Carrara marble quarries and has always had the marble industry at its center, first as a quarry site and later as a production site. The carving work includes sculptures for cemeteries or private collections, but the biggest client, for most of the past two centuries, has been the Catholic Church. Today, the artisans continue to copy Classical, Renaissance, and Romantic sculptures for export to private collections around the world, and in addition, hundreds of foreign artists bring clay models and carve them themselves or give them to the artisans to be enlarged in marble. The artisans of Pietrasanta built many of the large cathedrals of the Americas and furnished them with carved altars and baptismals and with saints carved in marble and cast in bronze. This type of work was at its height in the early part of the twentieth century. The work was disrupted by the two world wars, by the Depression, and, finally, by the decisions of the Ecumenical Council of Vatican II (1961–62) to discontinue both the embellishment of churches and the proliferation of figures of minor saints. The town has seen many booms and falls in the marble market—whether for architectural works rather than marble sculptures and whether bronze or marble is in greater demand—but of all of the stories that could be told, whether of booms or falls, the period of the early 1900s, when artisans worked in large studios employing hundreds of workers, has become idealized as a golden age.

Italian artisans tell their stories in relation to (whether conforming or departing from) what they consider to be the ordinary, expected sequence of events. By setting up the story of the ordinary artisan, a sort of Ur story of the way things used to be, the artisans both construct the past and set up what counts as change in the present. Their stories are nostalgic reminiscences that glorify a lost past and lament the present state of events. These include stories about their education and early apprenticeship, stories about the kinds of mistakes that everyone makes at some point and that become a kind of initiation into the field, and stories that dramatize the ways in which things have changed. For example, Mauro, an artisan sculptor, begins his life story by saying, "Well, my life is like this, you know, I started like everyone else. I attended the artisan school. [He goes on] This is the story: I was lucky because I quickly found the right studio where marble was worked properly and they taught."

In the artisans' narratives, certain stories have become emblematic; there is a story that is like everyone else's, and there is a proper way to have been taught. These shared understandings of the right story are central to the image the town has constructed of itself and its lost history. Emblematic stories are allusions to an idealized period that the stories dehistoricize and resituate in a particular relation between the present and the lost ideal. The ideal becomes an origin to which all changes in the present can be traced, and only those changes that illustrate the relation between the present and that ideal count. This is the invention of the problem of discontinuous selves, of fragmented understandings, or of a lack of coherence. There can be no coherence because the story of the idealized past period is not a literal, historical story but instead points to something larger than the period itself: it houses all of the meaning needed to understand the present; it is allegorical. The idealized past is the authentic period against which contemporary life is measured as fragmented. The following story illustrates this almost too well. Ledo Tartarelli told me the story more than once in the eight years in which I frequently returned to his studio to learn more about him.

> When we went to school, they would say, "Tomorrow morning, bring a rose, design *dal vero* [from the real] for four hours." Understand? . . . Once I dropped it, and this rose became all ruined. They made me make it as it was. (Interviewer: Ruined?)
> All ruined, and they made me reproduce it exactly. Ah, but when we went to clay, which was four hours, in plaster, then they would say, "Bring," for example, "a lily," and they would have to make that. Also frogs, lizards. So do you know what the professor would do to the frogs? He would put a bit of tobacco in its mouth and it would fall asleep. Cigar tobacco, no? He would make it eat that tobacco, and then it would be a bit, it would be still. It's true. It's not a story. When it woke up it would jump.

Although the director of the current art school (that replaced the school where Tartarelli studied) claims that the artisans still design *dal vero* or from live objects, Tartarelli's point is that carving from real-life objects is a sine qua non of training for an artisan. Tartarelli would say that even if they still do a bit of this kind of training at the new school, they certainly do not do it for four hours a day, and it is definitely not a centerpiece of the education offered today. By remembering not just the regular occasion, the fact that artisans designed *dal vero,* but instead a particular incident in which he dropped his vase and had to copy a ruined rose and in which the frogs were so very alive that they had to be numbed by tobacco, he is able to portray just how important designing *dal vero* was in his training and how different it is from the token variety of the exercise offered today. The example depends on personal knowledge, and the story has become an apocryphal symbol of the traditional educational system.

Stories such as Tartarelli's describe what has been inscribed in Pietrasanta as an authentic moment. The true artisan has to have studied in this way. Conveniently, Pietrasanta's image of authenticity is the representational, figurative sculpture. Michelangelo's *David* is the ideal figure, not because it looks like an ideal man (and in any case the local people argue about whether Donatello had the right idea in depicting the biblical David as a younger boy) but because carving the *David* requires using the skills that are most valued in the community. Tartarelli's story glorifies not only his past but also the unquestioned realism that pervades Pietrasanta's aesthetic. What is more authentic than carving from a real rose than carving from a real rose that has been crushed? Stories such as these create allegories of experience in which some particular event, period, or moment stands for a larger reality. Of course "realism" is itself invented. Michelangelo and his associates defined what sort of illusions would count as realistic through much of the modern period.

The use of exemplary narratives is crucial in constructing Pietrasanta's lost past. Pietrasanta's artisans are making themselves into a culture of memory. They are creating a nostalgic golden age precisely in order not to perpetuate the present. They are making examples of themselves, not seeking resolutions.

The artisans lament the past, rather than simply note it, because they see particular changes as irreparable. No one ever suggests that the Catholic Church should again begin building cathedrals. And in a largely nonreligious, communist town such as Pietrasanta, the building of churches is no more desirable than would be a marketplace reinvigorated by a fascist Mussolini desiring monuments to the Republic. Instead, some of the artisans place blame on the school, and while they insist that one cannot become an artisan at school, they recognize that the school provided an opportunity for young people to choose artisanry. On the other hand, stone carving is hard work, and few of the artisans choose it for their own sons, so that although they lament the changes, they never lament the choices of their own children.

Explanations of change are themselves constructions, and when people select particular moments of their past to call "the time before change" or the golden age, they are performing the same acts of construction that any narrator does in constructing a story out of the fragments of experiences. The explanations for change provided the context for understanding and constructing community for the artisans, but they did not justify the choice of particular features of the lost past in the construction of the golden age. The golden age was the one in which their grandfathers worked, when Pietrasanta was producing the architecture and sculpture for the cathedrals of the world. In this period, artisans were trained as specialists, and the training matched the work required. In contrast, today, one worker often executes an entire sculpture, from start to finish, and when specialists are needed, they are hard to find. The categories have blurred, between the specialists and between the roles of artist and artisan.

Today, the artisans see their world as disappearing. They are constructing this scenario of disappearance by determining what counts as continuation and what deserves to be lamented in change. The community has constantly changed, but only the contemporary situation is characterized as a disappearance. The community is defined in terms of the skills of the specialists, and as long as particular people die without passing on their skills to others, the community is perceived as disappearing. What stronger case could be made for confusing the authenticity lodged in individuals with the loss of a golden age? The imaginary golden age is stored in the embodied skills of the authentic artisans. Alternatively, the community could have been defined in terms of the kind of work done, and the artisans could celebrate a triumph of the artistic over the commercial, the continued reproduction of Michelangelo's *David,* and the demise of cemetery and cathedral saint reproduction. But this would require a more critical appraisal of the golden age.

The construction of the golden age is particularly evident in the artisans' life stories. The artisans almost always responded to my request for a life story by beginning a generation or so back, often with their grandfathers. The responses to the question were brief, as if the story were already familiar because everyone shared a similar experience, and all of the tellers soon launched into discussions of how things had changed. For example, Mr. Menchini begins his story:

> The story of my life is an old story. Our grandparents started 80 years ago. They started . . . they lived on the mountains in Serravezza, then they came down here, bought some land and started to work the marble. They started with two workers, then, slowly, their business grew bigger and bigger.

Sergio Cervietti, an artist and artisan in his twenties, also begins his story with his grandfather's:

> I am the son of an artisan. My grandfather was an artisan who worked with wood; he made the crates for the marble sculptures. My maternal roots are from Modena, of Emilia, and I think they came down about 1850. Then the great-grandfather of my father, the head worker, was assassinated with a knife. My grandfather was a carpenter. My father started to work with marble at the age of 11; now he is 70.

In beginning a personal story with the story of one's grandfather or father, the artisans articulated their shared ideal of how one was supposed to inherit skills and positions, or more particularly, the idea that one should be able to account for one's heritage. Each story becomes an example of the larger heritage of the community; each story insists on not only the inheritance of an individual but also the legacy of the community. The allegorical scenario is firmly in place; the tellers need only insert the particulars of their circumstances into it. Not only are they not troubled by being examples of a larger story, but they also demand it. Here, the problem of incoherent selves is instead a problem of anachronism.

The elder Palla brother shares proprietorship of what was one of Pietrasanta's main institutions. The Palla studio, located in the center of town and continuing to display the plaster models of saints and famous sculptures, even though they are no longer reproduced there, is in a sense the story of Pietrasanta. I asked Mr. Palla to tell me his life story, and this is how he began:

> It was about 1870 when my grandfather founded the studio; he died in 1943. He came here with the passion for sculpture, from Pisa. We have a few pic-

tures where you can see that there was nothing here; he was a real pioneer. He came here because he knew that there was white marble. He started here, in the piazza, out in the open, where the marble used to be cut like wood with hand saws. In order to cut a block, you needed a month. Then since 1900, my father also became interested. When he was young, he went to America, about 1902–3. He went to see some Italian-American sculptors, Piccirelli. He returned and developed the studio a little more; then there was a boom about 1915 because the church, especially the fast growing American one, had a tremendous demand for white marble. A studio like ours used to have 100–115 workers. But then everything was done by hand. Through great crises, difficulties, and wars, we have survived. Once the war was over, we already had some orders. And then it was easier for us—technological advance. Today the work is much less physically difficult. Once it was a work for slaves. There have been firms that have fallen and that were reconstructed, but we have always kept going.

Palla's studio is an institution in the sense that a particular place of business can come to represent and institutionalize an entire community. Palla represents the community in more than one sense, both in the ways that all of the studios represent themselves as examples of a tradition and in the larger sense in which Palla exemplifies the tradition. Ironically, as so often happens with our exemplified, institutionalized representations, since that discussion, the Palla studio closed the artisan sculpture part of its business and later briefly opened a school for foreigners. I interviewed Mauro, the last sculptor to work at Palla's, just after he was "let go," a week before he would have begun to receive his pension. He reminisced and told what has become a familiar story about how men would flood out from the studios at the noon bell:

> When I worked at Palla's, we were fifty or maybe more than fifty, and even there were twenty people who made sculpture; there were twenty who made architecture, and others who did the cleaning or generic jobs that the firms required. Then little by little . . . but in Pietrasanta, I remember when the noon bell rang, there were two thousand people who went out of the laboratories; there was Luisi, who had two hundred people; there was the Montecatini, which is now the Montecatini Edison, and in Pietrasanta there were hundreds of people.

Mauro's story is one of the stock stories of the community. Everyone recounts the days when people poured out of the studios to go home for the noon meal. Why the large studios should be the ideal, in contrast to the small studios where one could claim personal success, can only be explained by the role this piece plays in the construction of the lost golden age. But it is clear that some people consider that any story other than this one is not worth telling. One artisan literally protested about telling his personal story. After a bit of discussion about the work being done in the studio today, my assistant, Massimo Pasquini, asked him to tell "the Blasco story."

> Mr. Blasco replied, "No, not the Blasco story."
> Massimo asked, "Why not?"
> He responded, "It's the story of the artisanry, not of Blasco. What does Blasco have to do with it?"
> I explained, "Your studio never had 100 workers, like Palla's; it is something different, very interesting. It is a way of working that is very important today in Pietrasanta, that there is such a studio, which does classical sculpture and also modern sculpture."
> Mr. Blasco said, "But look, nowadays, we are,—the artisans are reduced to having to do everything on their own because the specialists [can no longer be supported]. We are everything; once there used to be . . ." and he continued his story, always told in the context of the way things used to be.

There was far more commentary than storytelling in these life histories; stories were told to punctuate, to emphasize, and I heard many of the stories repeatedly. For example, in a discussion of reputation, and how the Palla studio had achieved its renown, Mauro told the following story:

> Once a sculptor who worked for the Vatican came; he made portraits of the cardinals. He was quite known. He came to Palla's, and this artist was very annoying and picky, and he had his work retouched more than it was necessary. To have it retouched by a worker was very expensive. The children [of Palla] were a little angry about this man; the father told them that to gain his reputation it had taken 150 years, and he didn't want to lose it for 200,000 lire. Isn't this right?

Stories such as this one are overtly allegorical; they have a lesson to tell. In all of the stories I collected in Pietrasanta, the larger message overtook the particulars of a personal story; every personal story became a story of the community. The mention of where one had gone to school became a discussion of how the school no longer provides the kind of training the artisans found there; the discussion of apprenticeship became an explanation of how current labor laws require employers to pay apprentices too soon; it takes years to be able to earn one's salary as a marble-carving artisan.

The artisans did tell longer stories, most often to illustrate the contrast between the current situation and the lost past. The investigation of the past as disappearing or changed always invites questions concerning who sees the changes and who claims them in whose interest. These simple points alone, the idea that tradition is invented and that the invention involves judgmental assessments of value, are a starting point, but in the end not sufficient, to understand the lamentation of the past in an artisan community such as Pietrasanta.

Any discussion of tradition and change must come to terms with the whole romantic idea of lamenting a lost past. The Industrial Age in the West has been characterized throughout its history by glorification and promises of a wondrous future and accompanied by lamentations of the lost old ways. Of course, these discourses have also been accompanied by critiques—measures of one benefit against the other loss and also concepts of change and tradition themselves.

Personal-experience narratives, such as these, set up a series of arrangements or configurations between the personal and the more than personal, the present and the lost past, the fragmented and the coherent, the constructed and the seemingly natural. I have been naming this problem in its larger sense the problem of the relation between the personal and the allegorical, and I have insisted that this is a necessary relationship. Not only can we not do away with the allegorical to find some unproblematized pure representation of sincere and personal experience, unencumbered by the problem of speaking on behalf of others, but also we cannot do away with the personal to achieve the mythic, unencumbered by its roots in and relevance for personal life; the encumbrance is on both sides of the balance. To attempt to separate them is impossible and undesirable: the personal would lose its relevance to others, and the allegorical would lose its relevance to the self. It would be nothing but splintered selves without social worlds.

The Italian artisan's life-history narratives are nostalgic inventions that acknowledge the fragmentation of the present, in which all we have is our memories. It is usually against the coherent allegorized past that we assert the present as fragmented. The artisans present themselves as fragmented selves, torn from their heritage and from the possibility of reproducing themselves in future generations. Their narratives invent rather than reflect coherence, traditions, and consensus. They invent the relationship between disparate selves, between self and other, and between person and community by being inescapably allegorical.

The range of relationships between the personal and the allegorical in personal-experience narrative includes both the collective trauma narratives and the emblematic narratives of a community lamenting a lost golden age. Each alignment with the collective narrative sets up a different construction of the self. Claims for the authenticity of the personal, as a representation of a unique experience naturalize the subject and obscure the relationship between the personal and the allegorical as complicit inventions. In the case of the Italian artisans' narratives, in which persons are explicitly measured against conformity to an ideal scenario, it is the allegorical that is naturalized and granted authentic status.

At one end of the spectrum, we find narratives that naturalize the person, and at the other, we find narratives that naturalize the allegorical. If we un-critically accept either the authenticity of personal experiences or the authen-ticity of a lost past, if we fail to see the ways the relationship between the per-sonal and what I am calling the allegorical is constructed in personal-experience narratives, then we miss the gap that makes critical practice possible, what Benjamin describes as redemption.

To create allegories of experience is, in Derrida's terms, to create a rela-tionship between nature and its supplement. The represented experience is assigned the status of the natural, and the representation is supplementary. There is no way around allegory, no way to make an account exist only for it-self and not become an allegorical statement about something else. The ac-count, especially the personal narrative, is always an example of something, always a supplementary representation. And the example is always potentially a dangerous supplement in which what appears to be personal appropriates the personal to claim a more-than-personal truth, and in which, in order to monitor accountability (in the sense of the right to speak on behalf of another), challengers make the sometimes strategic but mistaken maneuver of debat-ing veracity.

In other words, the important question is not whether the artisans have represented the golden age accurately, and in any case, their accounts are for the most part consistent. The easy correspondence between personal and col-lective memory naturalizes and overdetermines a story of loss of authenticity, located forever in the past but recoverable through narrative. The construct-edness of that narrative is obscured by investment in it. The only tellable story is the one represented in the collective memory.

This problem, in which memory confronts tellability,[12] is only partially de-scribed by claims to the ownership of experience, or what I call the problem of entitlement. The concept of entitlement is useful for complicating the rela-tionship between memory and experience. It begins, as I have said, with Har-vey Sacks's observation that "in this world we own little else but our own expe-rience." Which experiences are properly one's own and how those experiences are translated into memories, replete with claims to ownership, is a question about the obligations between listeners and tellers. But implicit in claims to en-titlement to one's own experiences is another claim, or actually, a demand or request. We ask others not only to grant us our experiences but also to re-member them for us and, at times, quite selectively, to forget them. I refer to forgetting here primarily as a social, rather than a perceptual, process, in which parties to an exchange participate in the erasure of a category of experience so that that experience is no longer marked as memorable and, instead of being remarkable, attains the status of the ordinary. In this chapter, then, I have explored how experience becomes ordinary, normal, and forgotten, as well as re-membered and remarked. I see the production of the ordinary through for-getting as a relationship between tellers and listeners just as testimony and wit-ness, processes of remembering, describe a relationship incurring obligations, negotiations, promises, protections of privacy, acknowledgements of intimacies, and disclosures between participants in an exchange. Forgetting, too, describes such obligations. Indeed, I suggest, forgetting intensifies these obligations, es-pecially when forgetting is understood as an action, as a deliberate and binding commitment to the present as ordinary.

In the simplest, and most obvious, sense, I am describing forgetting as a kind of suspension of disbelief in which the day to day can obliterate the past, if only temporarily. But this simple generalization falls apart when put to the test of particular social circumstances. The ordinary is no more generalizable than the profound or the extraordinary. The ordinary is attained through cul-turally specific modes of forgetting. The Pietrasanta artisans' stories could be described as examples of culturally specific public forgetting. These acts of for-getting call for a public face-saving gesture to restore or acknowledge the ordi-nary. Forgetting, in this public sense, recasts the suspension of disbelief as a so-cial realignment. The ordinary, in this case, requires a kind of solidarity among all participants. Unlike remembering or commemoration, that very public form of remembering, which invokes a sense of loss, a desire to retrieve what re-mains, public forgetting depends on reclaiming and redefining the moment of loss as a moment of realignment that revises what counts as normal. Public for-getting is no less celebratory than public mourning over loss, but it celebrates in a different way. Public remembering produces empathy and guilt. Public for-getting resists empathy and works to realign participants in a shared experience of a different reality. Public forgetting, then, requires a different sort of collu-sion. In the most instrumental terms, the collusion of public memory plays it-self out in scenes in which people who did not commit mistakes or atrocities take on the guilt of the privileged and make apologies and sometimes repara-tions. Colluding to forget is a more deliberate sort of collusion in which the play-ers must avoid offending each other and at the same time level the playing field. Reparations are framed as ordinary acts of politeness. Most blatantly, when pub-lic memory is an act of recovery, in many senses of the term, from memory to repair, recovery itself is anathema to public forgetting. Public forgetting is com-pletely antagonistic to the *lieux de memoire*, the second order recovery of mem-ory (Nora, 1996).

3   *Allegory and Parable as Subversive Stories*

Allegory is a primary trope for translating experience. Allegory in personal narrative is remarkable because although it is deeply contextual, depending on its occasion, listeners, and larger communicative situation for meaning, its meaning is not restricted to or even accountable to the experiences described. Of all the personal narrative genres, it pays least attention to the ownership of experience. In my terms, allegory is a form of narrative that travels beyond its owners; moreover, it is intended to travel. Allegory is designed to be translated across contexts and across experiences, all within the framework of multiple, unrelated, but nonetheless particular, "performance arenas" for interpretation.[1] Allegory is also, not surprisingly, one of the means by which people empathize with others.

By allegorizing experience, people distant from an experience draw their own meanings from it and claim some mutual understanding. Empathy, then, depends on the sort of translation that allegory provides. At the same time, allegory, when understood as the use of one's personal story to create meaning for others, is the kind of appropriation that tellers, claiming ownership of an experience and its interpretation, sometimes reject or resist. Positioned at the intersection of the personal and more than personal, allegory in personal narrative is an important site for understanding the limits of empathy.

Personal narratives align the self to the world. And because a story can be told as not only personal but also as representative of a larger, collective experience, this alignment makes it possible for stories to have meanings beyond their contexts. However, the alignment between the self and the world is a point of negotiation, if not contest, requiring constant reassessment of both the concept of self and the larger categories a personal experience might represent. Personal narrative as allegory is a means for representing personal experience in larger contexts, invoking, in Jameson's terms "the collectivity itself." Each negotiation is a way of understanding personal experience as more than personal. As I have discussed, personal stories can be understood as more than personal in several ways:

- because they create persons whose identities and claims to interpretive rights extend beyond experience;
- because they recount experiences recognizable by others, even others unfamiliar with the persons or experiences;
- because the stories travel beyond their original tellers to be told by tellers who were not eyewitnesses to the experience or who did not suffer the experience;
- because the meaning of the story addresses issues beyond the particulars of either the persons involved or their experiences;
- or because from the beginning, the story is told as belonging to a collective, shared experience of which the person is just one representative.

Personal narrative works both to contain persons within experience and to expand representations beyond particular experiences. In this chapter, I address two ways in which personal narratives extend their alignments between the self and the world. First, I consider the ways that personal narrative can be allegorical, that is, the ways that the narrative represents something other than the particular experiences recounted. Second, I discuss the problem of alignment in personal narrative. When one reconsiders the construction of self in the light of the problem of representing a particular relationship between the self and the world, one sees that personal narratives are inevitably about more-than-personal experiences.

I begin with a story that is deliberately allegorical. Told by an Orthodox Jewish woman teacher to newly Orthodox Jewish women, the story was presented as a lesson with a message larger than the particular circumstances described. The speaker, Rebbetzin Tzipporah Heller, told the story in the context of a larger explanation of Orthodox Jewish positions on feminism. She argues that Orthodox Judaism and feminism are not necessarily incompatible. In answer to those who might argue that women are excluded from religious public life and are therefore not equal members of the community, Heller offers the distinction between an exemption and an exclusion. She explains that Jewish law says that a person who is already performing one obligation or deed (mitzvah) is excluded from performing another obligation. As an example, she tells the following hypothetical story, an "illustration" in her terms, in which she has to make a choice between saving a drowning man and getting to work on time. The question, she says, is which deed to perform, to save the drowning man or arrive at work on time? Of course, the protagonist chooses to save a life rather than be on time, and she compares her decision to a woman's experience of conflicting obligations between family and public life. Conflicting obligations require one to choose between deeds, and one choice exempts obligation to the other. The woman, she explains, chooses to raise a family because "that's where the saving the life would be." Heller situates her argument both within her own hypothetical personal narrative and within Orthodox Jewish law. Her use of personal experience as allegory allows her to speak as if from personal experience but always in reference to the purportedly comparable experiences of her listeners.

> You have a rule that works like this: Ha osek b'mitzvah, patur b'mitzvah. If you're doing one mitzvah already you can't be expected simultaneously to do a whole other mitzvah. Let me give you an illustration.
>
> I teach at Neve Yerushalaim. Suppose I'll live out my fantasy—not that Neve moved to Netanya but Netanya Beach moved to Jerusalem. If it's a fantasy, I might as well do it all the way. Netanya Beach is in Itan Nof somehow.
>
> So I'm walking to school on the beach and I see someone drowning. So of course I have a tremendous moral problem. I'm supposed to be at school at 8:30. Saving this person will take oh 15, 20, maybe even a half hour, yah? I'll be late. That's not right. So, ah, what do I say to myself? I say, "Self, you have to know the priorities. Which mitzvah is more important: the mitzvah of keeping your commitment to your employer or the mitzvah of saving a life?"
>
> Being very insightful and scholarly both, I'll say, "Oh, saving a life, right? That's the one, yah?" So I'll jump into the sea, save the person do all the—you know, I can do all of the first aid maneuvers that I learned when I was fourteen, which of course I remember like perfectly clearly. I save the life; then I have to like call authorities, go home and change my clothes. I've missed three classes.
>
> OK, suppose I would have made the opposite decision. I would say, "Well, Sweetheart, you have your problem and I have my problem.
>
> "It's my responsibility to get to work on time. I didn't tell you to go swimming.
>
> "It's your . . . I don't own this problem."
>
> Remember this from pop psychology?
>
> "I don't own this problem you own your problem; I can't take responsibility for your drowning. Goodbye."
>
> To which you'll reply, "Shma," and go under, yah? That would be incorrect. It wouldn't be the right way to do things, right?
>
> So the rule is if you have more than one mitzvah to do, you have to know which one comes first, and if you choose to do the one that should come first; of course you're exempt from doing the other one.
>
> In the same way often there are life conflicts when you're raising a family. Often there are not—most women don't spend their whole life raising a family, right? Very few people marry much before they're twenty; very few peo-

ple continue having children after they're in their early forties, so you're talking about not your whole life, right? But during that time that you are raising
a family there will be—and being here or being there on one hand and taking care of things the way they really should be taken care of on the other hand
can't always be juggled.

Sometimes they can, and sometimes they can't. The situation of exemption
is that human roles are more self-expression for a woman than the full—that's
where the priority would be. That's where the saving the life would be. (Heller,
n.d.)

Heller's story is an account of her own hypothetical experiences, but it is potentially anyone's story. By extension, the meanings the story imparts are not
only her own but also those purportedly shared by the group. How Heller accomplishes this shift from the personal to the more than personal can be ex-
amined both in terms of rhetoric and discourse. In terms of rhetoric, the use of
the allegorical form to persuade listeners of a shared truth depends on their
willingness to accept the comparison she offers. In terms of discourse, we can
observe how she uses pronouns to shift the alignment from her own (hypothetical) experiences to her listener's (purported) experiences.

This story, told to an audience of Orthodox Jewish women already persuaded by Heller's position, reports a personal experience in which the protagonist makes a choice that the listeners, too, would make. By asking the audience to share her choice, Heller asks them to share her larger rationale and
judgment. As Heller explains, this is not just one individual's choice to save a
life but any choice to save a life, or any choice that recognizes "where the saving the life would be." The use of the allegory, in which there is no real question about whether or not to save a drowning person, helps the speaker to create a shared community narrative, larger than any one individual's choices.

Allegory, sometimes defined as "the translation of ideas into images" (Frye,
1957: 90) creates a narrative that is larger than the personal experiences recounted. By using narrative as an example of her central idea, that a person
who performs one deed is exempted from another, Heller provides an image
of herself making a choice between deeds. She then draws a parallel between
her own (hypothetical) personal experience and any woman's personal experience of raising a family. This move, from the particular person to anybody,
is the crucial move that allegory strives to make. On one hand, an expansive
gesture, encompassing not just the person's but the community's experience,
allegory is, on the other hand, a restrictive trope that controls the categories
for understanding personal experience. The speaker's shift from the hypothetical personal narrative to its application in the everyday lives of the addressees is a typical pedagogical strategy in the Orthodox Jewish community.

Further, the speaker reformulates the example (the personal narrative in this case) and restates the lesson she is teaching. Her lesson, that a society that encourages women to raise families rather than participate in religious public life exempts, rather than excludes, women from that participation, requires the shift that her narrative accomplishes, from the personal to the collective experience. Her personal experience, choosing to save a life, becomes an example of women's experiences generally, of choosing to raise a family.

Allegory requires the listener to locate the message in the figural, instead of the literal, message. The genre conventions of allegory require the listener to recognize the comparative relationship between a specific taleworld described in the story and another world, in this case, the world of women attending to their families. Persuading the listener to think allegorically is a rhetorical problem requiring, first, that listeners recognize and share the conventions of the genre and, second, that they accept the terms of comparison offered. In order to accept Heller's position (that women are exempted rather than excluded from public religious practice), the listeners needed to accept the relationship between the choice to save a drowning person and the choice to raise a family. The listeners and speakers in this conversational use of allegory do not judge the allegory on its literary merits. Unlike literary critics, who might evaluate the merits of the form (for example, by generalizing allegory to include all criticism and metacommentary [Frye, 1957] or redeeming its complexity of language [Quilligan, 1979]), conversational audiences measure their reception of the genre by the wisdom conveyed.

If literary critics understand each genre to contain its own type of judgments, participants in conversational narrative use the type of message to define the genre. Allegory's message is wisdom gained by examining the literal story to identify its figural message or by comparing the circumstances of a story to another, usually real-life, circumstance. Other genres, too, are recognized by the participants according to how they convey a particular type of message, located in a particular configuration of time and sometimes space. Rumor, for example, is a temporally and spatially restricted genre, meaningful only to people within an already determined sphere of familiarity and within a time period defined by currency (Abrahams, 1970). Rumor provides information, which has value only as long as it is new. Life-history narrative, which can be understood allegorically to contain wisdom, or as part of rumor, to expose scandal and thus convey information, can also present a message in the form of knowledge. The recognition of a genre signifies, in part, reception of a particular kind of message, whether, for example, wisdom, information, or knowledge.

Genres of personal-experience narrative hold different possibilities for securing and developing the relationship between the self and the world. Those genres that overtly proclaim the significance of their message beyond the story itself, such as cautionary tales and parables, insist that the message transcends the particularities of both person and experience. Genres that contain persons within their experiences, including genres as disparate as rumor and historical narrative, maintain an attachment to particular persons and circumstances. Some genres, such as trauma narrative, are at the center of controversy about the contradictory requirements of familiarity with or detachment from the particular contextual circumstances. The trauma victims might claim that only those familiar with the context can understand, whereas others, remote from the circumstances, might claim to be able to gain wisdom or understanding from the stories because they are not enmeshed in the circumstances. Of course, the wisdom gained is not necessarily, or even rarely, the wisdom claimed by those who have suffered the experience. The question, in the consideration of genres and their relationship between self and world, is the translatability of the message. Each genre offers its own conditions and conventions for translation.

Another genre that purports to have translatable messages is the cautionary tale, the story of one person's difficulties told to caution others against making the same mistake. The cautionary tale works by analogy, suggesting the potential similarity between circumstances but offering the listener the chance for a different outcome. Clearly stating the difference between the person who experienced difficulties and the person who might avoid them, the teller of the cautionary tale marks a boundary between persons. The listeners are invited (if not explicitly asked) to recognize the shared circumstances and are invited to draw a clear boundary by making a different choice. The whole point of these stories is that recognition. If listeners recognize themselves in the cautionary tale, they might apply the message to their own circumstances; this is the premise of the cautionary tale. But translatability depends on many more factors than the recognition of oneself in another's message. Even when the message is rejected, when listeners refuse to see that another person's experiences could be their own, they still understand that the story was told with a larger purpose than the recounting of particular events. Listeners may recognize the genre and still reject the message. Since the "message" is never restricted to the content of what happened but always includes the relationship between tellers and listeners (and, when they are relevant, others described in the narrative), accepting or rejecting the message is always contingent on considering those relationships. For example, listeners may reject a cautionary message on the grounds that the teller had no right to "interfere," or they may welcome the suggestion of shared experiences.

Since any narrative can be read allegorically, a major arena for contesting narrative is in negotiating the limits and possibilities of translation across experience. When people distant from an experience read wisdom into someone else's traumatic experience, that is, when they perform an allegorical reading of the experience, they can be challenged as violating the intended genre. The challenge is rarely put in those terms; more likely, the challengers argue that the distant readers have no right to interpret the experience, that the distant readers are too distant to understand. Essentially, the challengers are saying that the narrative is personal and not allegorical. Allegorical reading shifts the grounds of understanding from experience-based knowledge to larger categories and ideas. Experience-based conversational narratives contain the message within specified relationships and grant individuals in those relationships all rights to interpretation.

Allegory in its most basic definition addresses the double meaning of texts that do not mean what they say. Beyond this definition, the genre is more difficult to pin down, because any narrative extends meaning beyond the text and because important distinctions can be made, for example, between meaning that goes beyond the literal, and meaning that plays tricks with the conventional (Quilligan, 1979: 47). Beginning where Angus Fletcher leaves off ("allegories are the natural mirrors of ideology" [1964: 368]), Stephen Greenblatt argues for a historical understanding of the use of the genre, which, he points out, emerges "in polemical atmospheres" (1981: 28) and contains an "archaeology" of original meanings (1981: 30). The archaeology of allegory points not only to origins but to the multiple speakers within the text, creating what Michael Holquist refers to as a "dialogism," using Bakhtin's term for the appropriation of multiple voices in conversation with each other (1981).

Fletcher describes the "potential weaknesses" of allegory as "anesthesia," which he attributes to "the ritual order of enigma and romance" and "a diffusion of inner coherence, since the typical allegory threatens never to end" (1964: 367). Maureen Quilligan agrees, adding that "mere aesthetic commentary seems not only insufficient, but impertinent" (1979: 290). This contrast, which positions fiction as inventive against allegory as conventional, does not necessarily translate to a discussion of personal narrative, which though not considered anesthetic, would still fail to measure up to the standards Quilligan and Fletcher address. Nonetheless, I find the concept of the anesthetic useful, especially as it implies a distinction between aesthetic and anesthetic, corresponding to complacent or compliant and creative or unfettered. The unlikely pairing of aesthetic and anesthetic provides a critique of the distinction between the mere copy (the allegory, which is always a citation, if not, in fact, presented as already used material) and the creative original (in both senses of the work tied to its author and the new work, never seen before). The allegorical has provided a critique of modernism by unseating the hold of the aesthetic, and although this critique is more familiarly described as the antiaesthetic rather than the anesthetic,[2] the concept of the anesthetic is useful for calling attention to the deadening, numbing dimension of decontextualized and recontextualized fragments of already-used material. Gregory Ulmer explains Walter Benjamin's observation, "Allegories are, in the realm of thoughts, what ruins are in the realm of things" to say "something becomes an object of knowledge only as it 'decays,' or is made to disintegrate" (1983: 97). Allegory is, as Fletcher notes, unfinished, a dimension I would suggest can be in part attributed to its translatability as endlessly reusable: a story continues by becoming another person's story.[3]

As Hal Foster suggests in his introduction to *The Anti-Aesthetic* (1983), and as James Clifford argues in his essay on ethnographic allegory (1986b), allegory has been particularly useful to the critique of modernism because allegories acknowledge their inadequacy as representations. Jameson's claim that "the telling of the individual story and the individual experience cannot but ultimately involve the whole laborious telling of the experience of the collectivity itself" (1986: 86) sidesteps the possible failure of the allegorical enterprise. Jameson makes his claim within a larger lamentation of the loss of collectivity in the modern world, but the changing configuration of the collectivity, whether tribe or nation, cannot fully account for the failure of allegory to match personal experience. The collective narrative is not only laborious but also precarious. It guarantees neither liberation nor conformity.[4] The question is, which way does this failure run? Are people unable to read themselves into allegory, to make it personal? Or is allegory unable to do justice to the personal experience it's an allegory of? Each cultural genre system has its own means for negotiating the precarious relationship between experience and representations. The instability of the anaesthetic unfinished allegory provides both the possibility of seemingly inflexible authoritative discourse and an opening for critique of the authoritative discourse as a ruin.

Heller's narrative is seemingly unfinished in its pretense of an offer to permit the listener to make ch oices. Her allegory is unfinished, in Fletcher's sense, because it is reusable; it exceeds the limits of the particular plot. Heller has rigged the game. By making the alternative work in both cases, she has created a false equivalence between saving a drowning person and raising a family. However, although the speaker presents worlds with alternative possible scenarios, they can have only one outcome (Greimas, 1987: 117). The story of choosing to save a drowning person becomes the story of taking care of a family. The alternatives are a foil made possible by the narrative form, which points to a road not taken. There is no acceptable alternative to the choice Heller makes; it is presented as inevitable fact. Whereas there might be an instability in a narrative traveling beyond its owner, in an unfinished story that completes itself in someone else's narrative world, or in the translation between supposedly comparable domains, allegory instead introduces stability, agreement (even complacency), and alignment in both worlds, the allegorical and the real.

Alignment is what Roman Jakobson called a "shifter," a code that depends on its context to determine its meaning (1990: 386–92). As Jakobson points out, all pronouns are shifters. Of course, the "I" of the personal-experience narrative necessarily depends on who is speaking. In personal-experience narrative, the "I," the speaking self, is often promoted as a stable, coherent subject, referring always to the same person. Indeed, one purpose of personal narrative is to establish the stability of the subject by suggesting that a person is the sum total of his or her experiences or by claiming that however diverse the experiences, the person, by virtue of inhabiting the same body, however changing, remains the same. What is remarkable is that this coherence is claimed for personal narratives told in conversations where they are a site for constantly shifting alignments. If personal narratives do produce coherent selves—and this is questionable—they do so while at the same time readjusting and repositioning fragmented and shifting selves. As Erving Goffman points out, "A change in footing implies a change in the alignment we take up to ourselves and the others present as expressed in the way we manage the production or reception of an utterance. . . . [P]articipants over the course of their speaking constantly change their footing, these changes being a persistent feature of natural talk" (1971: 128).

Heller's narrative is addressed to both her audience of observant women and to an imaginary audience of feminists who might challenge women's lack of participation in public religious life. Her argument, that women are exempted, not excluded, matters not to the observant members of the community but to the feminists. Preaching to the converted while also addressing the critics is an example of multiple alignments, achieved by managing a change in footing.

Demonstrating multiple alignments, especially potentially contradictory alignments such as feminist and observant Jewish woman, is one way to persuade others to realign. In blurring the voices of the "I" who claims to have suffered the experience with the "you" whose experiences can be considered comparable, allegory strives for a collective story of shared meaning. The territory that can be so contested in personal narrative, the right of the person who suffered the experience to claim the interpretation, undergoes a shift in allegory so that the speaker claims the right to interpret a much more general realm of experience. Rather than dispute the validity of the experience, which is, after all, hypothetical, in this case, we can only dispute the validity of the comparison. Is choosing to save a drowning person like choosing to raise a family? Is choosing to raise a family "where the saving the life would be"? The argument that both cases are choices between two obligations is persuasive, so it follows that one choice exempts the other. By enlisting narrative to illustrate the central premise, that undertaking one mitzvah exempts the other, the speaker is able to do what might otherwise be contested; she is able to provide an interpretation for other people's experiences.

At the level of discourse, we can observe the changes in footing in the use of the generalized "you" in Heller's narrative. She begins by addressing "you," the listener. Then, while she is describing her walk on the beach, she refers only to herself, "I," and to the drowning person, who sometimes appears as "you." As soon as she has finished telling the details of that event, she switches the subject of the action to you, the listener.

> So the rule is if you have more than one mitzvah to do, you have to know which one comes first, and if you choose to do the one that should come first, of course you're exempt from doing the other one.

Continuing to use her audience as the subject, she describes the woman who chooses to raise a family as "you" when she turns to the situation she proposes as parallel to saving a drowning person: "when you're raising a family." After referring to "most women" who "don't spend their whole life raising a family," or "very few women" and "very few people" in her description of the years devoted to raising children, she returns again to the "you" of her audience as the subject:

> so you're talking about not your whole life, right? But during that time that you are raising a family there will be [conflicts or choices]. And being here or being there on one hand and taking care of things the way they really should be taken care of on the other hand can't always be juggled. (Heller, n.d.)

In a study of conversations in a prison, especially conversations between herself and prisoners, Patricia O'Connor describes how the generalized "you" is used by prisoners to distance themselves from the act of their crimes. She describes several functions of the generalized "you":

> When the speaker switches to "you" yet still indexes the self, several activities are going on: (1) the speaker is distancing himself from the act by dropping the "I" and using a "you" that indicates the self as generically or commonly like others in that position; (2) the audience is being involved through the positioning as a fellow agent in a situation commonly experienced or, cu-

riously, as participant in an act not ever experienced; and (3) the speaker, by using the "you," also is addressing the figure of the self in his own past and is perhaps closing up, not distancing, the "space" between the past act and the current understanding of that act. (2000: 77)

As O'Connor points out, in the use of the generalized "you," "the speaker's linguistic choices show he is making sense of his experience through such generalizing involvement in his teller's world by creating a co-construction of the situation. His actual experience is being tied to the generalized possible experience of the interlocutor and others. He seeks and gets empathy" (2000: 102). Heller does not distance herself from her act of choosing to save a life, but like O'Connor's subject, she uses the generic "you" to create a sense of commonality, of like-minded people sharing a choice. Kenneth Burke's concept of consubstantiality is also useful here as a means of describing how a speaker relies upon commonality to establish mutual understanding with an audience.

When employed in personal narrative, the rhetorical move to establish consubstantiality and the use of discourse strategies such as the generalized "you" have as their central task the attempt to translate across personal experience and to create a more-than-personal framework for interpretation. (This task is, of course, central to the creation of empathy.) Telling personal narratives is often an attempt to create a match between a particular experience and some larger human story, but often the larger human story is unstated. The personal narrative is an example, but what it is an example of is often left open to inference and interpretation. The problem that the use of examples, especially present-tense, first-person examples, sets up is that while the example announces some past historical event, interpretation is not directed toward the factuality of the past. In Benveniste's terms, the personal narrative as example is not *histoire* but *discours*. The present-tense example is always allegorical; it is always about the relation of the particular to some larger whole. This is something that all students of personal narrative discover sooner or later, though they often mistake that larger whole for genre. Thus, personal narrative research often examines themes, such as birth narratives, abuse narratives, or other life-story categories. Not surprisingly, these themes often identify trauma or life-cycle experiences in which one person's experiences can be seen as representative of a more general experience. This move from the personal to the generalized occurs as if naturally.

Heller's hypothetical personal experience is what Jacques Derrida called "a dangerous supplement," an example that exceeds the argument. Rather than provide a logical argument for why women are exempted from participation in religious ritual, she tells a story about choosing priorities. The issue becomes not the exemption but the priorities, which, we are to understand, also shape the rationale for the exemption. Being exempted from religious ritual becomes the same as choosing to save a life, and more important for her later argument, being a mother becomes the same as saving a life.

Using a personal example to make a larger point can be praised as a pedagogically sound means for grounding an abstract concept or it can be criticized as overgeneralizing a particular experience. Personal examples use the same strategy of generalization as the ethnographic monograph (in which observations of particular events are translated into descriptions of how people in a culture typically behave), but when the particular is used "for example," the allegorical move is explicit. The point is not only the match between a particular experience and some larger human story but the noncontingency of the relationship between specific and generalized experience. Whereas all attention has been drawn to the specific experience as the opaque signifier, all that attention, we find out, is a ruse, as the example is always a ruse to persuade us of the noncontingency of some larger story.[5]

In everyday conversation, and in the context of Heller's seminar, allegory is often used to persuade us of the noncontingency of the relationships it proposes. If the listeners, the ratified audience (to use Goffman's term), hear the allegory as persuasive and noncontingent, then why do outsiders (folklorists, anthropologists, sociolinguists, or other academic listeners) insist on the instabilities of the form? I think the answer lies in the questions of social critique that inform these fields. For the social critic (defined as one who resists aligning with the "you" in stories such as Heller's), allegory provides an occasion to destabilize worldview from personal experience and thus to identify opportunities for reflection and change. The allegorical is itself contingent; it is a placeholder for worldviews and ideologies and thus is always open to the question of what holds it in place.[6] The contingent example is always a ruse to persuade us of the noncontingency of the allegorical. It elects, in the postmodernist gesture, what to hold steady discursively.

The following story, from a completely different cultural context, presents some of the same issues of allegory as a placeholder and opportunity for reflection and change in social values as Heller's story. Heller's story represents a moment of repositioning between Orthodoxy and feminism and reframes what might otherwise appear to be an exclusion from public life as a choice. Heller's willingness to position Orthodoxy within a feminist discourse acknowledges an instability, brought about in part by the presence of the newly Orthodox Jewish women who come from secular backgrounds. Not surprisingly, Heller's story reconsolidates the Orthodox position within the new questions. Similarly, in the following story, the narrator struggles to reconsolidate (and, in her case, reevaluate) her position within a new context. Both narrators work allegorically to position themselves on a changing map, stabilized in part by allegory, which claims the preexistence of foundational knowledge. In both cases, women's changing roles or reevaluations of their roles are at stake. Although we (academic feminists) might be tempted to celebrate these reevaluations as evidence of women taking power over their lives in the act of reevaluation (and Heller, at least, might agree with that position), the narratives do as much to reconsolidate and reaffirm existing ideologies as they do to provide an opportunity for reflection and change.

Personal narrative and allegory compete for noncontingency, and in so doing, they destabilize each other. The personal narrative appeals to the authenticity of experience and says, "this happened to me." The allegory claims the authority of a distant voice, true for the ages and not dependent on particular circumstances. The following story intersects personal narrative and allegory (in the form of a parable).[7]

Mrs. L. told her story within the context of an open-ended interview, part of a lengthy conversation about social services available to Latina women in San Jose, California. She followed her husband (to whom she was not legally married) from Mexico to the United States where she worked with him on the migrant labor circuit. When she got pregnant, they returned to Mexico, where she stayed, and he returned to work in the United States. Mrs. L.'s friends told her he would not return, and both friends and family members treated her as an abandoned woman, with neither the status of a married or a single woman. She describes living with her husband's family where she felt like "flour in another sack." The husband did return, but he left again after the birth of their second child. After several years, she took the two children and made her way across the border to join him. They lived together and had a third child, but then he left again, and she knew it would be difficult or impossible to find him again. She lived as a housekeeper for a while but was assaulted by her employer and then was on her own, dependent on social services and a few friends. A few years later, when she was interviewed, she was still living illegally in San Jose, where she cleaned houses and exchanged child care with a neighbor. She was describing her difficulties in getting the proper immigration papers to be able to work legally in the United States when the interviewer asked, "How are you trying to achieve these things that you want?" She responded:

> I have done many, many things, but how shall I say, when I was small and I went to school, there was a lesson in a book about a pair of little frogs that were jumping jumping around near a window. They were in the garden in a basin. So, they were looking around to see what there was outside the garden. They jumped, jumped up to the house, and fell through the window onto the dining room table. And they fell into a bowl of *natas* [cream]. Then they were

scared because it wasn't mud, it wasn't water, it wasn't grass, it wasn't—, they didn't know what it was, no? They were,—they were,—they were drowning. So they started to kick their legs, kicking, kicking. And uh one of them got very frightened, very scared and she began to drown. She drowned, she drowned in natas. The other one kept on kicking, kicking, kicking, kicking. And if you beat them a lot, if you beat them again and again, they turn to butter. So the little frog was kicking, kicking, kicking, kicking. And that stuff began to get hard underneath. She kept on kicking kicking until she could could could support herself on what was becoming hard. And she jumped out of the plate, you see? She wasn't familiar with where she was. And no one told her what to do or how to do it.

My situation is similar. There is someone who tells me what to do, what I should do. But I can't because I don't have—, I don't have,—in the first place, to begin with, eh? I'm in this country illegally, I don't have papers. There's no one who can tell me, "I can give them to you." I ask in one office, I asked in another. They say, "Ask that notary." I go there to that notary. They say in that place, "There's someone who works for the community who can give you guidance about immigration." And there I go to ask. They say in the welfare office, "There's someone who—who can tell you what to do." So I go to welfare. And it's like that, see? And nowhere has anyone given me the answer to that, everywhere I go, they tell me I can't.

But I've been like the frog. I can't—, it's not my environment, it's not my country, but I keep on kicking (laughing). I don't want to drown, you see? I want to get out, even if it's just out of the country. And that way, if I can't do anything, at least,—at least get out and say, "But I tried, no? I tried to do it, I couldn't do it, but I did try." And that's what I'm doing here, trying to—, trying to get papers.

Balanced against a life-history narrative of struggle, Mrs. L. tells a parable of survival. In the life-history narrative, she describes herself as a victim of circumstances, both the particular circumstances of trying to support three small children in a country where she cannot legally find work or speak the language, and the cultural category of "abandoned woman." In the life-history narrative, she is "flour in another sack," a person who does not belong. The parable provides a positive ending to her unfinished life-history narrative. She pictures herself as the frog who keeps on kicking until the cream turns to butter, and she has enough solid footing to escape her current dangers.

Personal narratives describe the speakers' and other participants' alignments within a particular interaction, but the narrative does more than report this past alignment. Additionally, the narrative proposes to establish an identity relevant to the conversation in which the story is told. Thus, Mrs. L. uses the parable to clarify her footing. She does not want to be understood as a mere victim of circumstance, as a drowning woman without resources. Instead, and perhaps partly as an appeal to the interviewer, she wants to be seen as a survivor.

So often, when people tell their life stories, they tell more than one story. They tell what has happened, and they tell what might have happened. Sometimes, as in Mrs. L.'s narrative, the story does not end with present circumstances but projects a future ending. It is not the case that unknown endings are just an easy place to revise the past or thwart inevitable destinies. Narratives may be told as retrospective, but they hardly ever are. Narratives are told from the middle of unfinished business; they negotiate the present as much or more than the past. Rather, the relationship between narratives and their possible trajectories is more complex and more a matter of mapping parable or allegory onto narrative or example onto experience than of opening up closings. Understanding the multiple trajectories and multiple footings narratives offer is one way to comprehend how narrative constrains or subverts cultural categories.

An alignment can force people into an untenable position. Mrs. L. reports several such untenable positions in her life-history narrative. When her husband leaves her, she has no economic resources, but to get a job would be a violation of her marriage. She says, "In Mexico, the situation of married women, it is very difficult. A woman marries and she has no rights, not even to work, not without the permission of her husband." Mrs. L.'s positions as wife, mother, employee (for the employer who assaults her), and citizen (in the United States where she does not speak English or have legal status) are all untenable, and her narrative reports her attempts to gain footing in these situations. Reporting on her relationship with her husband's parents, she recounts:

> At first . . . when they . . . understood that he had left me . . . I do not know
> if he spoke with them or because they saw he was not coming . . . I don't know.
> They began to help me in small ways, but yes, they were helping me. But later
> on . . . as the months went by, it was like they thought . . . that it was my fault
> that he had left me. Or maybe he gave them a powerful reason why he left
> me . . . The first thing was they stopped helping, you see?

Throughout her life-history narrative, Mrs. L. describes before and after scenarios marked by repositionings in response to her husband's abandonment. In describing her relationship with her mother, who was her constant supporter throughout, she says:

> Before I was with him, my mother and I used to go out together, you see. . . .
> I think she felt proud to go out with her daughter. . . . But afterwards, during
> the first year I was alone, and I tried to go out, even if only to the movies, my
> mother would say, "Why don't you take one of the girls?" . . . And she started
> to not want to go anywhere with me. She did not want people to see us out on
> the streets together. I guess she felt ashamed.

Mrs. L. describes her own reassessment of her situation as well. "My mother understood very well that I had been abandoned, even though in the beginning I would not admit it." Here, as in each of the incidents she reports, Mrs. L. positions her own understandings in accord with or contrary to the position of others. Using reported speech to articulate a dialogue, she re-enacts her footing in the situation. Most poignantly, when she describes her employer's assault, she reports his bold-faced lie as further evidence of the injustice. She reported the assault to her employer's wife, Elena, who says "Ay, you must have been dreaming." Mrs. L. continues:

> And when he came to bring his lunch box, Elena was there in the kitchen. She said to him, there in front of me, she said, "Listen, Mrs. L. says you frightened her this morning, that you went into her room." Then he said, "I thought you were in there." Why would he think that she was in my room and in my bed? We did not argue, nor did we clarify anything. Everything was left according to what he said.

Reported speech defers to the authority whose words are spoken (Bakhtin, 1981; Shuman, 1986), but in this case, Mrs. L. uses the force of that authority to describe the helplessness of her situation. In the face of an authority who has the last word, she can find no justice, and her own credibility is challenged. Recapturing her credibility through this narrative, she asks the question she did not ask at the time. The narrative gives her an opportunity to reenact the scene with a different footing. However, changes in footing are not only a feature of talk (as Goffman claims) but can also be a sign of a realigned relationship between self and world. When, as in Mrs. L.'s story, an alignment obliges an untenable position, changes in footing can be an effort to secure acceptable ground. Throughout her narrative, Mrs. L. uses images of being contained or seeking liberation from a contained space. In particular, she describes her present situation in terms of the possibilities of not being constrained by spaces and places. She says, "Maybe in five years I'll still be here closed in. . . . And well, I'm learning something and, and not staying stuck here in the house." She contrasts her wishes for the future with her mother's life.

> So my mother depended on my father all the time, depended on what he took home so we could eat and be clothed. And uh, well, in some ways my mother stagnated. . . . I'm doing something more than my mother did. . . . And I have to go out and get what I distribute.

The parable is also dominated by images of containers and spaces of containment. The frogs go into the house and jump into the bowl of *natas*. The second frog creates solid ground in order to jump out of the bowl.

In the end, Mrs. L. creates a different ending for her story than the one dictated for her by her community. She describes herself as a survivor under new terms of survival. Under the terms described by her community, she fails as wife, mother, and daughter; she is "flour in another sack," never able to occupy the right sack, always dependent on the wrong others. In her new version of her life, she still measures her success by dependence/independence, but instead of viewing the safe life of the wife supported at home by the husband who goes out to earn a living, she sees her own success in terms of going out of the home. This huge transformation is represented, interestingly, by a traditional parable, a story accepted in her community. The difference in her telling of the parable is that she aligns herself with the frog who goes out and successfully lives in the world. She assigns herself a position that her community assigns only to men. The parable provides Mrs. L. with a way not only to make sense of her current situation but also to predict a successful outcome.

Parables are always vulnerable to new uses (however monitored) and subject to subversion. When used as the vestiges of a lost past, as the historicized ruins of another way of thinking or being, they take on the authority of reported speech without any of the entitlement constraints that demand attention to the rights of appropriation. When used to create bridges between contexts understood by conversational participants to be traditional and modern, parable and allegory invoke an additional, archaeological dimension opposing the lived experience of the present to the wisdom of the past. This opposition between living present and appropriated past can create what Walter Benjamin has called "allegories of oblivion" in which the allegory is a ruin, separated rather than linked to its past completeness. At the same time, narrators can "work the ruins,"[8] not only to reconstruct and retrace a path and thus make a silence speak but also to subvert the connection. In Mrs. L.'s narrative, when the parable is respoken, it says something different than it might have been expected to say.

Allegory lives at the edge of sentiment, but some allegories are closer to the edge than others. Heller's allegory, insisting that a life be saved when no one is actually drowning, lives at that edge. Mrs. L's story, also about saving a life from drowning, presents hope at the brink of despair and cannot yet afford sentiment. In part, the difference is that Heller offers her listeners a chance to save another's life, and Mrs. L. attempts to save herself. But the stories are further differentiated by their investment in the past. Mrs. L. attempts to reconcile a past in which she cannot belong, in which, as I suggested, her alignment is untenable, by reframing her present. Heller is not interested in severing a link to past alignments; rather, she is interested in cutting off future contingencies, especially in the form of feminist choices. Both Mrs. L.

and Rebbetzin Heller offer redemptive narratives that are inspirational not only to themselves but to others and that rely on inspiration to revise a way of seeing the world. Both describe contingent realities in which the interpretation of the allegorical drives a proposed necessary outcome. Both conform to Christine Buci-Glucksmann's definition of allegory as an "archaeology of the imaginary of and in history" (1994: 48).

Allegory is memory without a signifier, the ruin without the trace of lived experience, the appropriated story disconnected from any former speaker. Not surprisingly, allegory is maligned for its cheap sentimental appeal and its too-easy claim to both authoritative wisdom and the reality claim of "this really happened." Derisive criticisms of allegory within art criticism are understandable, beginning with Goethe's famous pronouncement, quoted and discussed by Walter Benjamin:

> There is a great difference between a poet's seeking the particular from the general and his seeing the general in the particular. The former gives rise to allegory, where the particular serves only as an instance or example of the general; the latter, however, is the true nature of poetry: the expression of the particular without any thought of, or reference to, the general. Whoever grasps the particular in all its vitality also grasps the general, without being aware of it, or only becoming aware of it at a late stage (Benjamin, 1968: 161).

Ironically, the poet may seek to express the particular without reference to the general, but in "the particular" of everyday conversation, the particular often makes reference to the general. When speakers draw on their stock of allegories to explain everyday lives and events, they make the claim that their lives are more-than-personal, individual experience. At one end of the entitlement continuum are claims to ownership of an experience and its interpretation; at the other end are stories that travel so far from their owners as to become generalized and appropriable. In the two cases I have discussed here, the generalized allegory and parable were summoned to help resolve otherwise untenable alignments. These are not the stranded allegories of modern-day inspirational collections in which the reader is invited to invent the new mythologies of everyday life out of other people's suffering. Instead, this is the use of allegory applied to very particular contexts and circumstances. In both cases, the untenable alignments were the product of transported cultural values in conflict with new contexts and, more particularly, of women's reassessments of these alignments. Insofar as allegory marks a break and constitutes an attempt to resolve discontinuities, it can be considered subversive, as long as we keep in mind that subversion works in both directions, both to resist new and perceived threats to tradition and to find new ground.

Small-World Stories: Coincidence and Fate in Narratives of Everyday Life

All claims to the contrary, narrative can be a precarious form of communication. While the dangers of hegemonic or dominant narratives are by now a familiar topic in cultural studies, narratives told in everyday life are often claimed to be a communicative salve, a way to make meaning out of chaos and to show people that they are not alone, that they share experiences. The narratives I discuss in this chapter are, seemingly, the most innocuous of stories, claiming no special status in the making of meaning. They are stories about coincidental meetings in everyday life, and I refer to them as "small-world stories," since so many of them contain a coda commenting, "Small world, isn't it?"

The following is one of the most extraordinary small-world stories I collected, and its telling was prompted by an earlier version of this essay, presented at a meeting of the American Folklore Society. A member of the audience said to me, after hearing the paper, that I had to hear Hal Cannon's story. I found Hal Cannon, and this is the story he told:

> I have a man who's on our board of trustees. He's very wealthy. He's an eccentric person—the way he avoids, avoids doing too much business, avoids sort of being as wealthy as he is.
> He stays up in his jet all the time; he has a staff of people who keep track of where he is. And we're buddies. And he's sort of like a jet bag man. He opens his jet and beer cans fall out.
> Anyway, so we decided to go to Australia in his jet. And his staff said we think G is going to be in Palm Springs Saturday night, so if you want to go, just come to Palm Springs and we think he might be there. But I was getting a bit nervous, because earlier in the week they had said, "Have you seen G out playing hockey?"
> So on Saturday I had prepared to go, but I was really nervous about this trip. And a friend called me on the telephone and said, "You have to come to this estate sale." And she said, "There's a cowboy piano here for sale." And I

said, "A cowboy piano?" She said, "Yah, you've got to see this thing!" And I said, "I don't need a piano. I'm going to Australia tonight."

And I sort of collect cowboy things, because I study that. And, uh, so I went to this lady's home. And I went down into the basement. And sure enough, there's a piano that was made of knotty pine. And it had a carved longhorn on it, brands in the wood, and [a] leather bench with leather straps. And it was very cowboy. And there was somebody bidding on it right while I was there. And I got in a sort of bidding war with this guy. And I ended up spending $300 more than I was told it would cost. And I all of a sudden owned this piano. And I didn't know what to do with it.

And I told this lady, "I'm leaving town tonight. I won't be back for two weeks. Would you hold this for me?"

And she said, "Yah, sure. I'm not going to leave for a couple of months. Come and pick it up when you get back."

So I sort of forgot about it and I went home and packed, took the plane down. And I was very nervous about this situation. . . . G wouldn't show up and I'd be stuck in Palm Springs. But I got off the plane and I looked across the field and sure enough there's this beautiful white jet. And they were unloading hockey sticks, hundreds of hockey sticks. . . . So I went across the field and sure enough G got out of the jet. Actually we went an' unloaded the hockey sticks and we went and sang karaoke songs all night at a sushi bar. He mumbles a lot so I got him—he had never sung in public before, so I convinced him to sing "Polly wolly doodle all the day."

Why am I telling such a complicated version of this?

So the pilots called and said you've got to be at the airplane by 8, because we won't make the schedule. We're going across the Pacific Ocean. So about an hour later we got up and went on the plane, flew to Hawaii, refueled there. I remember we went in the jetport and looked in the guest book and Imelda Marcos had signed her name there. And, uh, then we started flying again.

Middle of the afternoon, I'd been looking down and it's just ocean for 4–5 hours. The pilot called back and said, "G, where do you want to land?"

And he looked at a map and saw the Marshall Islands. And there was a little island. I can't remember the name of the island, but there was a World War II landing strip there. And his brother apparently had fought there and he said, "I really want to see that little atoll down there." So we landed.

And there was one of those little Volkswagen buses with the top cut off. And we went to this village and it was really out there. And the next morning, the pilots said, "Okay, we'll get an early start to get to Australia." And we were driving back to the airport and G saw a little village square with a museum and a school. And he said, "Let's stop and look at the museum."

And we stopped and went in and there was an American behind the desk. And she was sort of showing people around and directing things. And I overheard her telling some other people who spoke English that she used to teach on the Navajo reservation. And I said, "You used to teach on the Navajo reservation, what brought you out here?"

"Oh I married a Marshalese guy. I was in the Peace Corps. I've been here for a long time."

And I said, "Well we're from the West too. I'm from Utah." And she said, "God, I'm from Utah, too." And I said, "Well, uh, where are you from in Utah?" And she said, "Salt Lake." And I said, "Well I grew up in Salt Lake, too." And she said, "Where'd you go to High School?"

And I said, "Highland."

And she said, "I went to East."

You know that kind of talk. And then . . . then I said, "Well where did you grow up?"

And she said, "Bryan Avenue about 23rd East."

I said, "I went to an estate sale in that neighborhood yesterday."

She said, "My mom had an estate sale yesterday."

And I looked at her and she looked at me and she said, "Did you buy my piano? That's amazing."

That was amazing. Her mother called her that week, and said . . . [she was] getting rid of a bunch of things . . . [and was] a little nervous about selling . . . [her] piano. "She was really hesitant about it, but she couldn't figure out how she'd get it to me, and I didn't want to sell it to someone I didn't know."

And then we went to Australia, went all over the outback. (Personal communication, October 1994)

This story is extraordinary in its reliance on the completely unexpected connection between two seemingly unrelated events, the purchase of a piano and the trip to Australia. It accomplishes the tale of extraordinary connection without reference to destiny and without reference to the possible significance of the events. Instead, it describes an unexpected purchase of a piano in the context of an unexpected trip to Australia. Of course, this particular telling was designed for an audience of a few people, including me, interested in what had already been categorized as small-world stories.

Not all stories about coincidental meetings are "small-world stories." Small-world stories recount a discovery that makes a large, unfamiliar, strange, and perhaps chaotic world seem at least temporarily familiar, ordered, and not so strange. These stories rarely travel beyond their owners, except as representations of the fantastic.[1] They are meaningful primarily to people already familiar with the participants and secondarily, when the coincidence is extraordinary, as in Hal Cannon's story, to others interested in a good story. Other kinds of coincidence stories travel far beyond the contexts of the people involved in the story and can become allegories for understanding the way the world is ordered, whether through miracles; divine intervention; or plan, destiny, or fate. This distinction between the small-world story and the allegorical coincidence story is not hard and fast; in this chapter, I use the small-world story to explore the difference between coincidence stories that travel and those that do not. I find the small-world story to be a useful way to understand the redemptive dimension of narrative. Allegorical coincidence stories are a good example of redemptive narrative; they offer the promise of meaning in a chaotic world. And, as I will argue, many of the most ordinary small-world stories also lend themselves to this redemptive promise. Here, I suggest as evidence not only the popular collections of small-world stories marketed as miracle tales[2] but also, in the stories I discuss, references to guiding angels, destiny, and fate.

Through the years, as I have worked on the small-world story, friends and students have offered many examples. Most of the stories people tell describe unexpected meetings. The more unexpected the meeting, the more fantastic the story. For example, one student told me the story of her roommate's discovery of her long-lost brother. When the roommate was a very young girl, her teenaged brother ran away from home. The girl went to a neighboring state to go to college (at Ohio State), and one of her professors asked to see her after class. After asking her a series of question, he revealed himself as her brother who had changed his name (but recognized hers). The story has many of the characteristics of the small-world story, especially the chance meeting and discovery of a connection away from home.

Not every story of meetings and partings is a small-world story, but it is helpful to examine reunification stories that have been accorded tremendous significance within a particular culture to better understand often less significant small-world stories. The biblical story of Joseph is an example of an allegorical reunification story that depends on a coincidental meeting. Joseph, whose brothers had sold him to the Ishmaelites, was living in Egypt, where his brothers went many years later in pursuit of food. At their first meeting, "he acted like a stranger to them," and "they did not recognize him," although he recognized them. Joseph put his brothers through several trials, including sending them back to Canaan to return with the youngest brother, and only then revealed himself, saying, "I am your brother Joseph, he whom you sold into Egypt." Joseph told his brothers not to "reproach yourselves because you sold me hither" and attributes the coincidence of their reunification to an act of God: "It was to save life that God sent me ahead of you." In this story, the consequences of earlier events (selling Joseph) are revealed only later. Further, the story is understood as the reunification and reconciliation of the brothers and as the restoration and redemption of the people of Israel.[3] It is anything but a simple coincidence. Unlike small-world stories, which focus on the improbability of the encounter, the biblical Joseph story asks readers to entertain the possibility of a master plan that reveals the meaning of events.[4]

The small-world story could be considered an everyday correlate to the fairy tale; they share some structural characteristics, and both refer to fate, although differently. Fate and the destiny of heroes and villains are commonplaces in the fairy tale; such claims are more precarious in the small-world story, which requires a more delicate balance between the ordinary and the profound. While feminists and other scholars challenge the worldviews and character stereotypes of fairy tales, the proclaimed smallness of the world in small-world stories usually passes uncontested, subtly insinuating a particular way of making ordinary events extraordinary. Small-world stories provide one more link toward understanding the relationship between personal narrative and the more-than-personal social narratives they reference and shape.

Some small-world stories convey the sense that an ordinary connection may have profound meaning. Often, moving beyond the discovery of an unexpected connection, they claim a second discovery: the profound claim to have experienced the world as small or as destined. By making a possibly profound story out of ordinary events, small-world stories exemplify the blurred boundaries between the everyday and the exceptionally meaningful. As part of their commonplace status, they carry the assumption that anyone can tell them in a wide range of contexts and that anyone might have one to tell. I have collected dozens of these stories in conversations (in which one story led to another) as well as from students, newspapers, and other media. The following examples are in condensed form to provide a quick sense of the category, but all were told with much more detail in conversation, and all of the tellers claimed them as personal, true experiences:

> Two men who meet in the army in the South Pacific find out they live in the same building in Brooklyn.
>
> A folklore professor discovers that a newly hired faculty member was his childhood pen pal.
>
> A family traveling to a family reunion gets a flat tire, and the man who stops to help them fix it is a long-lost relative.
>
> A student meets a friend from a British program abroad in a tour bus rest stop in France.
>
> Two friends in a church choir discover that their wives are old friends.
>
> A woman visits her boyfriend's apartment and after looking closely at the boyfriend's roommate's family photograph on the wall discovers that she and the roommate are related.
>
> A woman in a restaurant recognizes her waitress as one of her dorm mates from fifteen years ago.
>
> Three graduate students preparing course materials begin talking about birthdays and find out they all have the same birthday.

Any story in which someone finds someone in an unexpected place or in unexpected circumstances could be called a small-world story. Many of the narratives I collected describe how two people discovered that they had a friend in common or report people finding each other or themselves in unexpected places. The participants in small-world stories, however, are not in pursuit of their discovery; rather, the story is about finding something when one is not looking for it. The key element is an unexpected discovery, a discovery that is not part of a quest. In addition to the motif of the unexpected discovery of connections and coincidence, which defines the small-world story, these narratives have an additional shared characteristic. As told in everyday conversations, they are characterized by the interpretive, evaluative claim made for the small world.

In this chapter, after describing the characteristics of the small-world story and the ways that it organizes knowledge and asserts a view of the world as small, I ask: Under what social and cultural conditions is the concept of the small world claim possible? I explore the category of the small-world story formally, with particular attention to the "Small world, isn't it?" coda, and I consider the kinds of connection—especially between strangers who turn out to be associates—that constitute the core of the small-world discovery. I contrast these rediscovered connections, which reveal existing associations, with narratives that create new connections among fellow sufferers of similar experiences. I further contrast the small-world story of travelers who find strangers to be friends with stories of people living in diaspora, searching for loved ones they have lost. Each of these contrasts helps to describe the characteristics of the small-world story and to articulate the relationship between the ordinary and the profound in narratives of everyday life.

Here, it is useful to make a further distinction between small-world stories and what might be called fellow-sufferer stories. Fellow-sufferer stories consist of the discovery that events one experienced as unique are shared by others. What appeared to be idiosyncratic is, even in some small sense, generic. Narratively, it is the discovery of genre (and that others might offer a way to recount what felt unsayable or indescribable). Experientially, it is the discovery that the world is not random or chaotic but that it has pattern. The fact that what has happened to one person has happened to others, the sheer duplication of experience, helps to make meaning. Using Roland Barthes's model for charting the paradigmatic and syntagmatic dimensions of narrative (1996), we could say that people map their personal experience onto a plot structure and, in so doing, accept the themes that guide that way of organizing and relating the story. They recognize themselves as different characters in a shared plot structure. If the paradigm is fixed, its constituent elements are substitutable. The story is not exactly the same but is a variation on a theme.

In contrast to fellow-sufferer stories, in small-world stories, characters imagine themselves in two separate plot structures that intersect. The discovery is the surprise in finding that these two separate life courses are part of the same world. Unlike the fellow-sufferer story in which the individual moves from seeing his or her situation as unique to seeing it as shared, in the small-world story, the discovery is that one's unique world contains unexpected characters. The unexpected characters do not widen the horizons of the story but close it in (thus the small world). The unexpected people are characters from another story, and suddenly they appear in one's own story as well. In telling their small-world stories, narrators rarely recount all the circumstances (the other people's stories) that brought unexpected people together. Instead, the unexpected coincidence is an interruption. (Often, it is an interruption in a story about difference, about traveling to a different place—the story about difference is interrupted by an experience of sameness.) I will suggest that these characteristics also help to explain why the small-world story often does not travel beyond the context of the participants involved. Put simply, the small-world story does not represent something beyond itself but can only be collapsed in on itself and represent less than itself.

Small-world stories of the everyday are part of ordinary life; they are what Norman Bryson calls the overlooked. Bryson refers to Charles Sterling's distinction between megalography, "the depiction of those things in the world which are great—the legends of the gods, the battles of heroes, the crises of history" and rhopography, "the depiction of . . . the unassuming material base of life that importance constantly overlooks" (1990: 61). Bryson notes that the categories of megalography and rhopography are intertwined and that this is true for narrative as well. Bryson's topic is still-life paintings, which he describes as "the world minus its capacity for generating narrative interest" (1990: 60). "The whole principle of story-telling is jeopardized by the hearer's objection 'so what?' But still life loves the so what" (1990: 60–61). Bryson's characterization of still life as loving the "so what" is especially startling in light of William Labov's observation that narratives without evaluative devices to underscore the extraordinariness of the event recounted are likely to elicit a "so what" response. "If the event becomes common enough, it is no longer a violation of an expected rule of behavior, and it is not reportable" (1972: 370–71). For both Labov and Bryson, the contrast is between the extraordinary and the commonplace, and the commonplace is what elicits the "so what" response. Labov's discussion demonstrates how narrative evaluative devices can be used to attach significance to commonplace events. The coda, "Small world, isn't it?" at the end of the narratives is an example of an evaluation that locates significance in the commonplace. It expresses the idea that destiny can be experienced in the everyday. Using evaluative commentary, expressed emblematically in the

"Small world, isn't it?" coda, small-world narratives cut across the boundary between the important and the commonplace. Bryson uses a comparison between still life and narrative to call attention to the unusual properties of the still life, a genre in which "nothing exceptional occurs: there is a wholescale eviction of the Event" (1990: 61). Small-world stories, recounting the most mundane and ordinary of events, must do the opposite; they must evict their ordinariness and proclaim the extraordinary.

Small-world experiences are anything but ordinary. They are the disruption of the ordinary, and insofar as they claim to carry a profound message of fate or destiny, they claim to find that message in ordinary life. In using the term "small-world story," and in using this example to explore contextualized (nontraveling) personal narrative, I am calling attention to the smallness, rather than the ordinariness, of these stories. As Susan Stewart suggests in *On Longing*, miniature worlds are contained and offer the possibility of perfection. They describe an interior world, "diminutive, and thereby manipulatable . . . domesticated and protected from contamination" (1984: 69). The small-world story is often a contrast to the situation the narrator describes, traveling away from home in an unfamiliar world. Elaborating on Stewart's discussion, Katharine Young observes, "Reconstitution of the world as small, as more tightly connected and neat than we thought, returns us to the perfection of the miniature, to the already fated, the already coincidental, the causally tight, instead of our thrown-ness into the unaccountable, the open-ended, the fragmentary" (personal communication, November 2, 2002). It is not destiny in the everyday; it's the everyday revealed as destined. It is the commonplace turned perfect.

The protagonists of small-world stories often leave home and travel to unfamiliar places, only to find a connection to home. This is true of all of the examples I gave at the beginning of this chapter. A sister must travel from home to college to discover her long-lost brother; two men need to join the army and travel to the South Pacific to find out they live in the same building; a family on a trip meets a relative when he stops to help them fix a flat tire. The small world ontologically shrinks the global. Narratives accomplish this by beginning with a random universe and ending by finding people connected and in their proper places.

Characters afoot in a world larger than they are, one that escapes them, a gigantic world of incompletes, fragments of massive events they cannot get control over, fall through into a miniature world, the epitome of the controllable, *as if it had been there all along*, like Alice through the rabbit hole.

Unlike fairy tales or quest stories that begin with a problem to be solved (a lack to be liquidated in Alan Dundes's terms), in small-world stories often a resolution is provided without an initial problem. In small-world stories, the punchline is given away in the first line. To retrieve the punchline as the end, one would have to tell the story backwards, concealing its first move as its last element.[5]

As Alan Dundes explains in his introduction to Vladimir Propp's *Morphology of the Folktale*, the morphology can be usefully applied to other narrative texts. In the examination of a corpus of Russian fairy tales, Propp identified a core sequence common to the tales (and variations of this sequence are common to many folktale collections). First, the hero leaves home; second, the hero encounters a helpful being; third, the hero encounters problems which he or she solves with the help of the wisdom or materials provided by the helpful being, and so on. According to Propp's model, actions are tied to characters, and units of action and character are sequential, one predicting and necessitating the next. In small-world stories, for example, the morphology tends to be the following:

1. The protagonist travels to an unfamiliar place (and may need assistance).
2. The protagonist meets strangers.
3. The protagonist discovers connections with the strangers.
4. The connections assist the protagonist in some way.
5. The world is experienced as small.

In an alternative scenario:

1. The protagonist has a problem.
2. A stranger helps to solve the problem.
3. The protagonist and the stranger discover a connection.
4. The stranger is not a stranger.

In the first sequence of events, the protagonist is not seeking the discovery, although those narratives that present the need for assistance at the beginning forecast the possibility that the stranger will come to the aid of the protagonist. Both of these scenarios are complicated by the parallel stories of other characters. The point of the small-world story is the intersection of different characters' stories that collapse into one. In Hal Cannon's narrative, several stories coincide. Each of the protagonists has a different trajectory:

The piano seller has a piano to sell.
The piano seller's daughter has her reasons for living in the Marshall Islands.
Hal Cannon collects instruments.

Hal Cannon has been doing fieldwork in Australia.
A philanthropist acquainted with Hal Cannon is interested in visiting Australia.

Structurally, small-world stories follow the classic pattern of narrative in everyday life as articulated by William Labov and Joshua Waletsky (1966), elaborated by Labov (1972), and discussed by others, including Livia Polanyi (1989) and Charlotte Linde (1993). The narratives are constituted by a sequence of events and clauses that provide background orientation and evaluative description. Additionally, four elements are particularly important to the structure of small-world stories. First, the basic structure of the story entails a character who finds a connection when he or she was not looking for it. Second, this structural property is accomplished by setting up problems that turn out not to be the point of the story. The choices the characters make create the conditions for the connection, but the unwitting nature of those choices, leading not to a solution of a defined problem (a quest for the connection), are necessary for the unpredictability of the connection. Third, the unpredictability of the coincidence depends on strangeness (usually strangers) that becomes familiar. Fourth, the stranger's narrative becomes (sometimes only at the end) a parallel narrative that intersects with the protagonist's. (Strangeness may be the modality or symbol of the unaccountability, unnarratability, undomesticability of the real, the natural, nature, the gigantic in this genre of story.)

In Hal Cannon's narrative, two stories coincide: the purchase of the piano and the trip to Australia. The intersection of the stories begins as a potential time schedule conflict: Hal Cannon wants to go to the estate sale, but he also has a plane to catch. Both of these events are set up in the narrative as somewhat unpredictable. He does not know if he will find anything at the estate sale, and he does not know if the philanthropist will be in Palm Springs. However, these are cases of predictable unpredictability: either he'll find something or he won't; either he'll meet the philanthropist or he won't. The small-world coincidence of meeting the owner of the piano in the Marshall Islands presents an entirely different kind of unpredictability. As is typical in small-world stories, the coincidence is not just unpredictable; more important, it is not even an option.

Building on Propp's observations about the morphology of folktales, A. J. Greimas's work on narrative structure further complicates the necessary and predictable relationship between sequential narrative events. Greimas observes that at each juncture of the tale, the hero has a choice. These choices are not binary oppositions (to accept or not to accept the philanthropist's invitation) but part of a more complex classification scheme that defines both the characters and the action. Each category invokes a set of alternatives either by substitution of subjects, substitution of objects, or transformations (1987: 90). Cannon's decision about whether or not to accept the invitation from the philanthropist invokes several relationships and possible implications that characterize the philanthropist either as trickster or benefactor. In other words, Cannon must assess the stranger to make his choice. He postpones his assessment of the philanthropist's offer and decides to take a chance. Taking a chance sets up the possibility for the unexpected and creates the sense of his journey and his discovery as almost not happening. Just as in the story of Joseph and his brothers in which the ending is not about the consequences of selling a brother to traders, in Cannon's story, the purpose of the quest is only discovered retrospectively. Cannon's choice about whether or not to go is rendered arbitrary; his motivation is extraneous to the outcome. It is a quest story backwards, with the quest concealed from the seeker. With this concealment, coincidence is substituted for fate and the trivial for the mythical, the hero tale.

In this narrative, as in many small-world stories, the problems the narrative sets up initially are not, ultimately, the point of the story. Cannon articulates several choices clearly in his narrative. First, he wonders whether he should accept the philanthropist's invitation. Then, he wonders if he has time to go to the estate sale. When he buys the piano, he identifies the problem of figuring out what to do with it until he returns from his trip. Each juncture of the narrative sets up alternatives that predicate later action. If he did not accept the invitation, he would not have been in the Marshall Islands at the museum where he met the piano's original owner. If he did not go to the estate auction, he would not have found the piano. However, even though retrospectively these conditions turn out to be necessary for the connection that results, the point of the story, as a coincidence, depends on the unwitting and unplanned actions of characters not seeking what they find. They are making apparently "random" choices that turn out to be "destined." At each juncture in the story, the characters make decisions for reasons that are unrelated to making the connection that becomes so important at the end. In Cannon's story, the coincidence is completely unpredictable and is made more so by a complete lack of necessity in discovering it.

Protagonists in small-world stories are most often in the position of unwitting recipient of destined good fortune. The good fortune may be the meeting itself or some benefit from the meeting. The role of the stranger, who turns out not to be a stranger, a central element in the stories, varies, depending on whether or not the stranger/friend is also a benefactor or donor, someone who provides assistance. Sharing properties with stories about relying on the kindness of strangers, small-world stories in which the stranger is a benefactor or donor call additional attention to the importance of the connection. Stories about the kindness of strangers place additional weight on the good fortune of needs met, dangers averted, and problems solved. All small-world stories depend on a relationship between strangeness and familiarity. Stories about relying on the kindness of strangers additionally are motivated by the problem that necessitated the kindness.

The book *Small Miracles: Extraordinary Coincidences from Everyday Life* provides many examples of relying on the kindness of strangers (Halberstam and Leventhal, 1997). A comment on the back of the book makes its larger social message clear: "Have you ever experienced a moment when a seemingly random event also seemed strangely meaningful, or even miraculous? Whether it was as simple as anticipating a phone call, or as dramatic as rekindling a lost love, what you experienced may be more significant than you thought. It may be nothing less than a small miracle—possibly the work of angels, or a message from a higher power." The following example from the book combines a problem solved by a kind stranger with a small-world coincidence:

Queens, New York

A woman leaned out of her eighth-floor tenement window and screamed for help. She was trapped in her bathroom. The inside knob had fallen off when her youngest child, age two, had closed the door from the other side. Two of her other children, ages four and five, were in the kitchen, alone, as supper cooked on the stove. The woman alternated between trying to break down the door herself and shouting to be heard. Both courses seemed futile and she was beginning to give up hope.

Meanwhile, a young man who lived twenty miles away happened to be visiting the neighborhood that day. From the street below, he heard the woman's pleas. He waved his hand to catch her attention and screamed out, "I'm coming up to help you!" A short time later, she heard his voice from outside the bathroom door. "Listen closely," the young man instructed. "Put your fingers in the hole where the knob should be, pull it up, lift the door slightly, and then quickly pull it open." The woman followed the stranger's instructions, and within moments, the door was open.

Once freed from her temporary prison, she ran to check on the children. In response to their mother's screams, they had become upset and needed some coddling to soothe their cries. When all three children were safe within her view, the woman turned to the young man and asked in amazement, "How could you possibly have known how to get into my apartment, and how did you know how that door opens?"

"I know very well," he answered with a smile crossing his face. "I was born here. I lived in this apartment for fifteen years. I know how to get in the front door without a key. And the bathroom knob? It would always fall off, and we learned to open the door just the way I showed you!" (1997: 122–23).[6]

For the narrator of the story, it might have been enough to solve the problem of being stuck in the bathroom. For the collector of this story, who offers it to an audience unfamiliar with the characters, it is a miracle tale. A miracle is the necessary value-added that allows the story to travel, in this case, the intervention of a supernatural, revealing by magic that the world is fated, destined, that is, more perfect than we thought.

In this narrative, a stranger with just the right knowledge appears at just the right time. He is a stranger to the woman in the apartment, but the apartment is not strange to him. The stranger's narrative, told in fragments, only makes sense when the coincidence is revealed. First, we learn that he just happened to be visiting the neighborhood, and then, in the final lines of the story, he explains his knowledge of the apartment. In the narrative, he is a benefactor, and not unlike the benefactors in fairy tales, he has unexplained knowledge. For him, the coincidence is that he happened to be in the neighborhood when the woman got stuck in the bathroom.

What compromises small-world stories (and I use the term *compromise* also in reference to the compromised or failed promise of narrative) is that the story turns out to be about something other than the problem it describes. The princess is freed from her confinement by a passing prince who turns out to be anyone, a passerby, and not only a neighbor but someone from one's very own house, all at the same time. But the prince is not on a quest to save the princess; like rescuers everywhere he cannot take credit and most likely says, "Anyone in my position would have done the same thing." However, such stories are marketed as heroic (as in the *Small Miracles* volume), and to some extent they persuade us to settle for the perfection of small worlds rather than the heroism of large ones.

The role of the stranger in small-world stories can be usefully compared to the role of strangers in numskull tales. For example, in a well-known numskull tale from Shalom Aleichem's collection of Chelm stories, villagers decide to build a stone wall, and they go to the top of a hill to collect round stones for their wall. When they have carried all of the heavy round stones down the hill, a stranger comes by and asks why they have not rolled the stones down the hill. When the stranger leaves, they consult, and not wanting to appear foolish in the face of such wisdom, they carry the stones back up the hill and roll them down. In her extensive survey of numskull tales, Heda Jason identifies the stranger in these tales both as occupying a particular position in the sequence of events and as representing a spatial conception outside of the world occupied by the characters (1975: 209). The stranger "symbolizes the normal world as opposed to the numskull world. His being in the normal world of low social status and his 'wise deeds' being just ordinary common sense in the normal world set off the more the foolishness of the numskull world and of its leader" (1975: 221). The strangers in the numskull tales and in the small-world stories both display common sense; they are marked by their ordinariness. However, whereas the common sense of the numskull tale stranger is marked in contrast to the foolishness of the numskull villagers, the ordinariness of the stranger in the small-world miracle story is marked as an angel in disguise.

For the most part, small-world stories describe the intersection of onto-logically similar worlds, everyday contemporary worlds, not fairy-tale worlds in which beings transform between supernatural and human or plant and an-imal form. The appearance of an angel or other supernatural character in a small-world story ruptures the ordinary world, suddenly made permeable.

Both stories share another feature worth noting and useful for under-standing the relationship between the ordinary narrative and the larger social narrative. Jason briefly entertains but rejects the possibility that numskull tales provide political critique, "a kind of 'ritual of rebellion' which represents an in-stitutionalized way of expressing the antagonism towards the social leadership" (1975: 220). Arguing that numskull tales are rare and that sacred tales more effectively provide this sort of critique of the social status quo, Jason suggests that numskull tales comment more on relationships between the real and the imaginary than upon social status.[7] Numskulls could be understood as liminal beings. Small-world stories similarly occupy a liminal realm, between the or-dinary world populated by unexpected events and the supernatural, destined world populated by disguised angels. The stranger helps to mark the territory of these worlds. In the numskull world, the stranger represents the world of common knowledge; in the small world, the stranger, who turns out to have friendly connections after all, represents the extraordinary possibility that the ordinary world is small.

Numskull tales, like familiar joke genres, are structurally predictable. The listener does not know exactly what will happen but still that something will. The stranger, usually embodying the new perspective, brings that about. Small-world stories have far less predictability. The narrative does not pro-vide clues to suggest that the woman screaming out her window will be heard by someone who once lived there. If the moral of the story in numskull tales is that common sense is good, but too much common sense can be bad, the moral of small-world stories is the recognition that strangers can turn out to be friends or that coincidences can happen anywhere, if only one is paying enough attention to notice.

Small-world stories preserve both the ordinariness of everyday life and the extraordinariness of coincidence. They are widely tellable, whether as sto-ries told to people familiar with the stranger discovered to be a friend, as sequential, topical stories following the telling of another small-world story, as stories about travels or sometimes as simply extraordinary stories. Extraordinariness, produced by the unpredictability of the discovery, combined with the familiarity of the form, evidenced by the structural similarity of the narratives (everyone knows the morphology and constructs the narrative using the familiar pattern and order of events), contributes to their tellability. The least extraordinary stories rely on familiarity with the characters for their tellability and thus have a narrower audience unless the teller can claim destiny, providence, or some supernatural force at work, thus shifting the extraordinary from the events themselves to another realm. The most extraordinary stories, such as Cannon's, in which coincidence of stories is least predictable, have the widest audience, and, based upon my arbitrary sample, rarely make claims to destiny or fate. Indeed, as the postscript to Cannon's story indicates, the participants themselves are not even necessarily surprised.

Placing coincidental meetings in the category of "Small world, isn't it" creates two ontological worlds in the narrative: the ordinary world in which the events occurred and the small world in which, it will turn out, the events also occurred. Not surprisingly, people often report small-world experiences away from home. Away from home they can enter the different realm of the small world. Describing these narrative constructions as "ontological geographies," Katharine Young writes,

> Moving around in the course of everyday life, persons experience transitions from one set of ontological assumptions about the nature of reality to another . . . these other realms are separated from the ordinary by borders, barriers, interstitial spaces which are also thresholds to another world . . . [some realms are marked by] a path, a road, wilderness, barren regions. . . . Other realms are accessible only through altered states: time travel, space travel, changes of class or ethnicity, sleep, trance, fantasy, memory, hallucination, mediation, magical transformation, death. . . . Other realms are more or less akin to the ordinary. The realm of the past and the realm of the future are removed from the ordinary along a temporal dimension. The realms of the exotic and the extraterrestrial are removed along a spatial dimension. And perhaps the realms of the supernatural, the demonic, the angelic, the ghostly, and the dead could be said to remove themselves along a metaphysical dimension. The arrangement of such realms according to their kinship with the ordinary suggests hierarchies or fields of realities distributed from the familiar to the fabulous to create, as it were, an ontological geography. (1987: 188–89)

A common theme of the small-world stories is that the world is a chaotic, enormous place but that strangers can turn out to be friends after all. Sometimes, this point is pushed further, and events are explained not only as examples of order amidst chaos, or syncretism, but also as destined. Most generally, small-world narratives construct a sense of order by setting up the resulting coincidence as unpredictable. The particular construction of the unpredictable in each narrative is useful for understanding the claim the narrative makes for meaning. In some narratives, such as Cannon's, people's separate stories intersect. The only strangeness is the discovery of the intersection; we might wonder how often our lives intersect with others without our realizing it. Alternatively, the woman stuck in the bathroom reflects on a chain of events as destined. What seems arbitrary turns out to have meaning; that is, in the seeming chaos of life's events, some things are meant to happen. The woman's story argues for the syncretism of a patterned universe and suggests that what seems to be unpredictable is instead a lack of knowledge. Small-world stories provide retrospective explanatory accounts of the unpredictable. Narratives such as Cannon's, making no claim for destiny, place the burden on the observant life participants who recognize their intersecting paths.

Like all narratives, small-world stories construct a sequence of events that did happen and, by implication, a sequence of events that did not happen. The event that did not happen is that the people completely missed each other, that new acquaintances found no past friend in common, and that the situation continued to develop. For the most part, only the world of happy destinies or familiarity is reported. In an example of what might be understood as a failed small-world story, a television commercial depicts a man walking down a street while a voice-over says that he is about to meet the woman he is to marry, that they will have three children, and so on. Only he did not buy a particular Seiko watch, so he misses her by a few seconds and never meets her. This commercial, like other failed small-world stories, tells two stories, that which did not happen and that which did happen. Attention to the story that did not happen is what makes a failed small-world story remarkable. Whereas all narratives convey implicit alternative chronologies, few narratives make the alternative not only explicit but also more important than the story told. Further, whether successful or failed, both sorts of small-world story confirm a vision of a world in which familiarity and met destiny are possible. The failed small-world story, like the successful one, calls attention to the chance element in events—the possibility that the event might just have easily not happened. Saul Broudy tells the following story of mistaken, but recovered, connections:

> Back in 1975, I was in England. I was walking on Charing Cross Road, going to the Charing Cross railroad station to go on a commuter train to some club in the suburbs to do a spot, as they called it, walking down the street—I had my guitar with me and some guy from across the street who sort of looked like an American—I think he was wearing blue jeans or something—he came over—he looked at me a little strangely and he walked across the street and

says to me, "Excuse me, are you Shelley Posen?" So I said, "No, but I know Shelley Posen." Well, this guy's from Toronto and he saw the guitar and I wear a beard and I'm not bald—Shelley is partially bald—but I don't know. I had glasses and a beard and a guitar and for some reason he thought I was Shelley Posen and we spent about two days together. We went to dinner; we went out clubbing together; he was a nice fellow. I forget his name—David or something—from Toronto—where Shelley's from. Small world, isn't it? (Personal communication, March 13, 1983)

In Saul Broudy's story, a potential coincidence fails and is replaced by another. Saul Broudy and the person for whom he is mistaken, Shelley Posen, actually do share similar spheres of life. Both are folklorists, and both are musicians; it is not impossible that Shelley Posen would have been in London and carrying a guitar that evening. The narrative rests not only on the mistake but also on sorting it out. A story about someone mistaken for another is not particularly remarkable. The remarkable story is knowing the person for whom one is mistaken. For example, in a case remarkable enough to be reported in the newspapers and on talk shows, a young man transfers to a new college where many people seem to recognize him but call him by the wrong name. One fellow student who confronts him and asks why he is unresponsive tells him that he has a double at the school. The young man, who had been adopted as a child, contacts his double, and the two twins are reunited and invited to a television talk show to tell their story. The next day, one of the twins receives a phone call from another young man who says, "I believe I'm the third."

The following joke, with the same problem of mistaken identity, has a different effect and outcome.

A woman calls up her mother and says, "I don't know what I'm going to do. The little one has a cold, and I have to take him to the doctor. I think he has an ear infection, and the older one has to go to a skating lesson, and I don't know what to do."

And the mother says, "Well, look, I can come and watch the children."

"Oh," says the daughter, "that would be really wonderful. Look, I'll pick you up on the 7th Avenue bus."

"Why would I take the 7th Avenue bus? I'm going to take the midtown bus," says the mother.

"The midtown bus; why do you take the midtown bus?" asks the daughter. And they have a long conversation about the routes until the daughter asks, "Is this 752–8351?"

And the mother says, "No, I'm sorry, you have the wrong number."

And the daughter says, "Does that mean you're not coming?"

"Small world, isn't it?" is a coda; "Does that mean you're not coming?" is a punchline. Codas, according to William Labov's definition, "have the property of bridging the gap between the moment of time at the end of the narrative proper and the present. They bring the narrator and the listener back to the point at which they entered the narrative" (1972: 365). Punchlines, in contrast, according to Richard Bauman:

> achieve their effect by rekeying the situation, overturning the apparent direction of the interaction and the moral alignments and attitudes that have seemed to control it and establishing an ironic alternative, not as a substitute but as a coexistent perspective. The effect of the punch line is to that extent subversive, a breakthrough both on the part of the one who is reported to have spoken it and on the part of the narrator into a kind of skepticism and relativism that takes pleasure in refusing to take ideal, normative moral expectations too seriously—a "comic corrective," in Burke's apt phrase, "containing two-way attributes lacking in polemical, one way approaches to social necessity." (1986: 75)

These stories presume a scenario in which accidental juxtapositions lead to actual connections. The strange(r) turns out to have a familiar connection. The point of the story is the discovery of coincidence, though the grounds for connection in Saul Broudy's story are as spurious as in the joke. Saul Broudy meets a person who obviously does not know Shelley Posen well enough to be able to recognize him or differentiate him from Broudy, but the link is good enough an ocean away for an acquaintance. Sometimes in small-world stories, the characters discover no actual points of connection, but their shared travels are enough to make them friends rather than strangers. In the joke, the mother and daughter negotiate their relationship so successfully that the punchline asks, "Does that mean you're not coming?"; in other words, isn't the connection enough to pursue the relationship anyway?

The difference between the coda, "Small world, isn't it?" and the punchline, "Does that mean you're not coming?" is a significant difference that is instructive for understanding what sets the small-world story apart from other stories. The "small world, isn't it?" coda is evaluative; it comments both on the extraordinariness of the particular experience and on the nature of the world. The coda invites the listener to share a worldview. Additionally, Katharine Young points out, "codas construct continuities between disparate realms" (1987: 45). The coda belongs both to the world constructed in the narrative (what Young calls the taleworld) and to the conversation in which the narrative is told (what Young calls the storyrealm). While all codas sit at the boundary of these two worlds, most restrict their interpretations to events in the taleworld. The small-world coda conflates and compresses the storyrealm and taleworld. In a mythologizing move, the small-world coda transforms the ordinary experience of meeting friends in strange places into a profound expe-

rience of a shrunken world. The mythologizing move is a realm shift, the transformation of the ontological conditions, what Alfred Schutz called the "meta-
physical constants" of the world (1962). Occupying the transitional space between the narrative and the conversation, the coda invites the listener to share
the view that the world is small, and sometimes listeners take up the invitation
by telling their own small-world story, especially given the rhetorical convention of making the coda a question, "Small world, isn't it?" Instead of providing closure, the coda invites a response, often in the form of another small-
world story told by one of the listeners.

The following story was told told to me in October 1982 by a radio talk
show host who interviewed me for a program on small-world stories. After
the program, he told his own story of a coincidence that helped to solve a
problem. Many small-world stories recount a turn of events. People find themselves in the wrong place or in need of the kind of networks and connections
that a small world provides, and they manage to find a connection:

> I was in Dallas at a convention of radio broadcasters, and I was with my
> buddies and we were having a good time. Well, I lost track of the time and I
> missed my plane. I tried to reach my wife, but she must have left already and
> she was waiting for me at the airport. Here I was spending our money and
> having a good time, and I couldn't even reach her. So I tried to find a room
> for the night, and the whole city was booked solid with the conference. I
> couldn't find a hotel. My buddies had already left to go to some fancy party
> where they were eating caviar for free. So I went back to the hotel—it was a
> grungy kind of place with a bar. So I went into the bar, and plopped myself
> down on a bar stool—I still couldn't get ahold of my wife—I was really down
> in the dumps. The bar was full of reprobates—the kind of people who drink
> when they have nothing to do—and some guy came and sat down next to me.
> We said hello. I said, "My name's Thom McCane." He says, "Yah, I know you."
> He says, "I'm your cousin . . . My mother, Linda McCane McDonald, was your
> grandfather's sister. I'm a grad student at Athens. And my mother says I should
> look you up at the conference." I just looked at him and said, "How about if
> I slept on your floor tonight?"

McCane's narrative sets the scene of a dejected character who is in a most
unlikely place to find good fortune. Remorseful for missing his plane, not reach-
ing his wife, and spending money, he describes his situation as unlikely to produce a solution. He "plopped" himself on a bar stool in a "grungy" bar "full of
reprobates." Using a tension between opportunity and dejection comparable to
the tension in Hal Cannon's narrative between the familiar and the exotic, Thom
McCane's narrative creates a scene in which the coincidental connection will
appear most unexpected. As in other small-world stories, the benefactor's narrative and its point of overlap with the protagonist's narrative is told only at the

end. McCane's narrative ends within the taleworld frame, the solution to the problem provided as a punchline of surprise; the final lines, "I just looked at him . . ." shift the frame from the cousin's story and return to McCane's own narrative. The narrative makes no claim to destiny or providence but lets the frame shift the scene from misfortune to well being.

Narratives such as Thom McCane's, in which the coincidence solves a problem, sometimes suggest themes of fate or supernatural intervention. The following story, told by Jay Brodbur Neibur, also prompted by another teller's small-world story, makes a mythologizing move from coincidence and the discovery of connection to providence and destiny. This narrative introduces a problem, solved by the connection, but displaces the role of benefactor to an angel. Here, coincidence is a sign of divine intervention.

> The way I met Eileen—I went to a Washington conference and I got there early and I helped out. I asked if there was something I could do.
> "Sure," they said, "You can help with registration."
> So I sat down and started registering people. There were three of us. I was on the right, Eileen was on my left, and on her right was another person.
> To make a long story short, after a year, Eileen and I decided to get married. In fact Riv Ellen helped us to get a rabbi. We asked him to recommend a musician. He said, "Try this woman."
> It turned out she was going skiing so he said, "There's this other guy, but he's kind of expensive. His name's Jody Hirsch."
> Eileen says, "You know this name sounds familiar."
> So she looked up the conference register and it was the guy who had sat with us registering people. It's as if an angel would have appeared in December 1980 and said, "One year from now you'll be marrying the guy sitting on your left, and the guy on your right is going to be playing at your wedding."
> And none of us had ever met each other before. One of us was from Ohio, another from Michigan, and the third was from California. (Personal communication, 1982)

As is typical of small-world stories, Jay's narrative begins by setting the scene for a meeting with unanticipated significance. He just happened to arrive early at his conference, and he just happened to be assigned a task at the registration desk. The details are connected by a series of "and" clauses punctuated by "so" and "to make a long story short." Dell Hymes's discussion of ethnopoetic patterns in narrative is useful here. The "and" and "so" pattern describes the chronology of events, from meeting to marriage. This chronology, narrated in the third person by Jay, contrasts with the use of first person reported speech to report the "discoveries." Both the rabbi's and Eileen's voices shift the chronology from the orientation scene to the small-world discovery. Finally, shifting not only to present tense and reported speech, but also addressees, the angel provides the evaluative coda, naming the significance of the story. The coda has a complex frame in this narrative; the coda is addressed to Eileen, suggesting that while the story is Jay's, the destiny is hers:

> It's as if an angel would have appeared in December 1980 and said, "One year from now you'll be marrying the guy sitting on your left, and the guy on your right is going to be playing at your wedding."

Each of these patterns codes a different part of the meaning of the narrative. Jay's first-person, past-tense orientation establishes the reality of the setting and situation. The ordinariness of the events, neither planned nor anticipated, sets up the necessary contrast with the discovery of destiny represented in the coda. The use of present-tense reported speech reenacts the discovery and creates a distinction between the ordinariness of the scene and the drama of the small-world connection. The coda retells the story and, by shifting voice, tense, and audience, further creates a distinction between ordinary actions and destiny. The coda tells it in reverse, which is to say that the coda tells the story from the inside, from the perspective of the small world, instead of as a small-world story, which falls from outside in.

The narrative form is defined not only by a chronology but by a necessary chronology; the meaning, that is, depends on a particular temporal sequence. If the events were ordered differently, the meaning would change. Harvey Sacks argues that we assume the necessity of chronology and that unless we have information provided by phrases such as "before that," we assume that "the order of the sentences indicates the order of the occurrences" (1992: 331). Sacks proceeds to develop a framework to explain how these assumptions work. He introduces the term *category-bound activities* to describe how particular actions become attributed to particular categories of persons. Using this model, we could describe Jay's narrative as relying on several category-bound activities, including the categories of single, heterosexual, marriageable, Jewish, and strangers and the activities of meeting, marrying, and playing music at weddings. As Sacks points out, category-bound activities are often attached to norms, and we make the appropriate assumption about the link between chronological events by relying on our shared understanding of those norms. Jay's narrative does not describe himself or Eileen as single, marriageable, or heterosexual, and since he names Eileen but not the person on her left, we can only assume that they were strangers, a fact supported only later by the angel's description of Jay as "the guy sitting on your left." Small-world stories typically depend on retrospective joining of categories and activities.

In this sense, small-world stories can function like riddles, and riddles can use the small-world story as a motif. For example, the riddle: a boy and his father are in an accident. They are rushed to the operating room where the doctor says, "Oh, my son!" Who is the doctor? The boy's mother.

In Jay's narrative, delaying the couple's discovery that the guy on Eileen's right was a musician permits the formation of the final coincidence as a solution to the problem of finding a musician for the wedding. At this juncture, the narrative presents the possibilities of finding or not finding a musician, the first offering the possibilities of finding a musician who is busy (going skiing), finding a musician who is too expensive, getting help (from the rabbi or someone else) to find the musician, and the second offering the possibilities of having a wedding without a musician, finding an alternative to live music, not having music, and so on. The narrative introduces a new, surprise possibility: finding a musician who is already somehow connected. Finding the musician who sat on Eileen's right at the registration desk of the conference gives significance to this moment of the narrative. The alternatives available at these narrative junctures are not arbitrary; narrative creates the value that separates the significant from the insignificant. Of course, the most significant alternative created by Jay's narrative is the possibility that Jay and Eileen might not have met; a less central but still significant alternative would be that they might not have discovered that the guy on Eileen's right was a musician or that without the connection to that particular rabbi, suggested by another friend, Riv Ellen, that they would not have found him for the wedding, just when they needed a musician. In this narrative, the need for the musician is made explicit; it is a clearly articulated problem to be solved. Eileen and Jay's need for marriage partners is not made explicit and is instead left to normalizing values, larger presumably shared narratives that articulate a need for single strangers to find each other and marry. Narrative depends on sequences of what Alan Dundes called "lack/lack liquidated" structures, a problem identified and then, hopefully, solved. But the sequences are mere chronologies without the value placed on normative solutions.

Angels speak from a different ontological world than humans, and indeed, the angel is posited as having spoken during the conference (as is the nature of prophetic voices, whose speech is reconstituted later, often using reported speech). The complexity of these references marks the boundaries that needed to be traversed between the two worlds.

The characters in small-world stories are rarely either heroic or tragic. Rather—and this is a significant element of their claim to ordinariness—they are unwitting and unexpected beneficiaries of fortunes that do not necessarily change their status, either tragically or favorably. I have chosen several stories that are exceptions, involving marriage, acquisitions, and rescue. However, the benefits of the discovered connection are more often convenience or the immediate pleasures of companionship. Meetings and partings in small-world stories depend on what M. M. Bakhtin calls "random contingencies" (1981: 92) controlled entirely by chance. In these narratives, temporal markers are inseparable from spatial markers; the narratives rely on what Bakhtin calls "chronotopicity" (1981: 97), the overlapping of place and time. Bakhtin points out that many narrative forms, from epic to novel, rely on chronotopicity, and plots from marriage stories to road stories depend on the motifs of meetings, partings, escapes, and acquisitions. However, genres manage the sudden and unexpected differently, for example, chivalric romances normalize the unexpected so that "the whole world becomes miraculous, so that the miraculous becomes ordinary without ceasing at the same time to be miraculous" (1981: 152). Small-world stories sometimes attribute the sudden and unexpected to fate; moreover, in making this attribution, they claim the accidental as expected, as a perfect world just waiting to be observed. The fate of characters in the small-world story is rarely the shared fate of a tribe or nation, and this, more than any other characteristic, grants these narratives ordinary, rather than epic, proportions. The sudden plunge of the fated into the trivial or domestic, the personal and ordinary, prevents these stories from transcending themselves, expanding, lifting themselves into the mythic proportions of the similarly fated epic in which the hero's fate, already megalographic, becomes the shared fate of the tribe or nation, what we might call the mythographic.

The small-world story, or story about a coincidence, is a pervasive literary theme: "the unexpected discovery." Pervasive as this theme is, however, in both everyday personal-experience narratives and written literature, it has been criticized, in written literature at least, as a weak literary device, a not very subtle way to reunite characters. A guide written in the 1970s in the People's Republic of China specifically and explicitly alerted would-be authors to avoid using catastrophes or any fantastic events, natural or political, to bring an event to its conclusion by bringing characters together by surprising circumstances. This is exactly what small-world stories do. In Charles Dickens's *David Copperfield*, the hero fails to find people when looking for them. "I walked miles upon miles daily in the hope of seeing her," he says of Dora ([1850] 1977: 365) but then coincidentally learns that his friend is boarding with the Micawber family just when he most needs to reunite with them ([1850] 1977: 373–74). Dickens plays against a suppressed narrative of characters finding each other and manipulates the contrast between the absence and occurrence of small-world coincidences. His play with the small-world device tests the limits of plausibility and becomes a testimony to the fictiveness and craftedness of his stories. If, using Alan Dundes's formulation, narratives work by following a lack/lack liquidated structure, in which a problem is identified and then resolved in a coincidence (in which the characters might not even be aware that there was a problem in the first place), this is a weak form of resolution. Dickens defies this edict against coincidence and makes it pivotal in all his narratives. His genius is in lending his formulaic plots and conventional, caricatured characters any semblance of plausibility, usually by an extraordinary proliferation of the ordinary in his settings, of local detail, along with a dose of pathos. In some literary works, the small-world story is not only a vehicle for moving the plot forward, but it is also the central feature of the plot. Judith Krantz's *Emmeline,* for example, tells the story of a girl who, sent away from her home to work in a textile factory and pregnant as a result of being raped by her boss, gives up the baby for adoption and returns home to live a life of isolation and shame only to finally fall in love with a wonderful man thirteen years younger than she, who, of course, turns out to be the child she gave up for adoption. A story could plausibly turn on one coincidence; mysteries often do, giving them their one indecipherable point of entry, but a story that is nothing but coincidences can seem incredible. Of course, not all literary works try to pass off the credibility of small-world coincidences, and some, most notably *The Good Soldier Svejk,* use the small-world device ironically. Literary and conversational small-world stories do not share the same conditions for credibility, although some literary accounts, such as *Emmeline,* claiming to be "based upon a true story" borrow the conventions of the small-world conversational narrative.

Small-world stories are meeting and parting stories. In contrast to narratives in novels, in which characters learn something about themselves and we might then learn something about ourselves, small-world meetings and partings are more like epics, in which self-discovery takes a second seat to questions of destiny. Especially in stories that claim destiny and fate, small-world stories take on epic proportions. Perhaps the most famous example is Oedipus Rex. To call Oedipus a small-world story is to collapse the boundary between the important and the commonplace, the epic and the ordinary, but Oedipus is, in a sense, the quintessential small-world story in which the character discovers his relatives in unexpected places.

Oedipus is at all points a tragedy, whereas small-world stories are at best happy resolutions and more often innocuous in their resolutions. At their most dangerous, small-world stories tread close to incest and describe a world in which no one has enough distance to be marriageable. Oedipus, in the grip of coincidence raised to the level of fate and pierced to the core by his self-discoveries, becomes the quintessence of the reflective man, the man of interiority. The difference is that Oedipus is proposed as a member of the world of fate, not as some ordinary man who dropped into it by chance. To reduce Oedipus to this scenario is to trivialize the larger questions of destiny raised by the play, but my point is that commonplace small-world stories do not make the same destiny claims (though these can be made for them, as in the miracle claim) but, rather, suggest that oddly enough, against expectation, things sometimes work out *as if* destined. The difference between these two kinds of small-world representations is that some of them treat the small-world coincidence as an illusion, and others naturalize it; some acknowledge it as a fabrication, and others claim it as a truth. The question concerning these narratives, literary or conversational, grand or commonplace, is whether the coincidence is claimed as a truth larger than the particular events.

If we compare coincidence stories in which people are not searching for whomever they find with quest stories in which people are searching for whomever they have lost, we can begin to see what I will argue is the danger of the small-world story. The following story is part of a longer narrative told by a woman named Libe Gelt to a member of her family, Marcy Miller (1993). It is not a small-world story, but perhaps its opposite—a story of losing one's family. Gelt begins by saying that in 1938 she traveled from the United States, where she was born, to Poland with her parents and brother to witness the wedding of one of her father's six brothers to her mother's sister. On their way, they visited cousins in Berlin. Gelt recalls, "There was a procession of uniformed men whose synchronized steps reverberated through the Jewish neighborhood where my cousins lived. It gave me nightmares for months." Three months later, on their return trip, Gelt's family found their cousins' home abandoned, the shattered windows boarded up. The rest of Gelt's story is about her father's unsuccessful efforts to find the family after the war. He failed to find them, but one of them found him. One of his brothers, who turned out to have escaped from a train en route to a death camp, contacted him from Sweden in 1949 and after an enormous bureaucratic struggle, her father managed to bring him to the United States. But for the others, the quest was futile. Gelt says, "For the most part, the family was murdered, but there are some mysteries. I had cousins . . ." Whether these searches are successful or unsuccessful, the stories are about a real or large world that refuses to yield up a small world.

The stories of institutionally sponsored reunions of families separated by current events such as the Berlin Wall or the Korean War are instructive in their deliberate connection to a larger social political drama. Most of these narratives, as reproduced in newspaper accounts, begin with chaos that creates disruption and a lost loved one, followed by speculations, sustained or lost hope, and then, prompted by the political dramas that created the chaos, the reunions. Newspapers, obligated as they are by larger social narratives, provide different accounts than personal narratives, of course. But in these instances, the coincidence is not engineered by the choices or searches by family members but by the politicians. In one account of the political narrative: "This reunion is intended to be the critical first step in bringing the two nations together. As the two leaders acknowledged, without restoring the human bonds torn by the war, there would be little hope of cultivating the economic cooperation and reduction in military tension that would form the foundation for eventual reunification" (*New York Times*, August 13, 2000). Reporting that "the meetings have been carefully scripted," the newspaper account contrasted the fragments of personal narrative with the politically engineered narratives of reunification. These stories of reunions between lost loved ones are not small-world stories, but like small-world stories, they rely on existing alignments. Although the narratives relay the joys of rediscovery and many accounts of elderly parents reunited with children they had little hope of ever seeing again, these narratives also, inevitably, remind whoever might be listening that the reunion does not recompense the separation. These belated reunion narratives invoke alignments, neither to create a sense of fellow suffering, nor to promote new connections, nor to discover old ones. Instead, against the social narrative that frames a shared national story of separation, each personal story appears as fragmented and singular. These do not end, "Small world, isn't it?"

I offer these variations of narratives of meeting and parting to create a larger frame for understanding the alignments produced by small-world stories. Not all coincidence stories claim that the world is small. The question is, for whom is the world small, and to whom is this claim made? Perhaps offering the greatest challenge to the small-world story frame are narratives that rely on coincidence but do not claim the world to be small. For that discussion, I return to Ned Lebow's story, which I discussed in the introduction. The version Lebow wrote begins with the facts of the deportation:

> At 4 A.M. on 16 July (*jeudi noir*—Black Thursday), Paris police raided apartments and houses in and around the City in an attempt to arrest 27,388 Jewish immigrants from Germany, Eastern Europe, and the Soviet Union. Many of the 12,884 Jews who were actually arrested were sent to Drancy for subsequent deportation to Auschwitz. Children and adults with children were held at the Velodrome d'Hiver, a glass covered sports stadium in the fifteenth arrondissement. More than 8,000 people were crowded into the inadequately ventilated and suffocatingly hot stadium and fed only soup supplied by the Red Cross and Quakers. The water in the sinks had been turned off and the available toilets promptly jammed. Survivors, and there were only a few, remember an unbearable stench, constant noise, and a complete lack of privacy.
>
> The police had their hands full. Few Jews had illusions about their fate even before they were marched out of the Vel d'Hiv' to a nearby rail siding for trans-

port to Auschwitz in rank cattle cars. One woman went berserk and was hand-cuffed to a stretcher. There were several suicides, and one mother tried to kill her child with a broken bottle. Another lacerated her son's veins. Some of the police were sickened by the scene of wailing mothers, screaming children, and baton-wielding police. In defiance of orders, one contingent managed to pro-tect a handful of young children, including a several month old baby. That baby may have been me.

The police handed the children over to a group of well-placed, French-born Jewish women who banded together to provide refuge for them and other, mostly older children, who had escaped the roundup. Native French Jews re-mained at liberty until November, 1943, but risked their lives by hiding "for-eign" Jews marked for deportation. One of the women rescuers, Paulette Fink, was the daughter of the chief rabbi of France and mother of two young girls. Her husband, a reserve officer, was a prisoner of war, as were the husbands of several of the other women she mobilized to care for what were now almost one hundred children.

Madame Fink and her friends knew that it was only a matter of time be-fore they were discovered by the Milice (the national police). Something had to be done to get the children out of Paris, and better yet, out of France. A priest known to one of the women offered to hide them temporarily in his vil-lage. He told his parishioners that it was their Christian responsibility to pro-tect the children, and they did so for several weeks under the nose of Nazi oc-cupation forces. Everybody in the village knew what was going on and kept quiet. (2001: 264)

Lebow's narrative continues to describe the escape routes designed by Madame Fink and involving Zionist groups, the Portuguese Consul, Ameri-cans, and others and then returns to Madame Fink's story before returning to his own.

In *Le Nozze di Figaro*, Figaro is saved from marrying his mother, reunited with Susannah, and lifted from his station as a servant by the discovery of a birth-mark. Nothing quite so dramatic happened to me, but the catalyst for my dis-covery was a birthmark of sorts. I met Madame Fink in Palm Springs, Califor-nia, and over drinks and dinner listened to her describe her efforts to rescue children during the war and her subsequent difficulties in reclaiming many of them from the Catholic orphanages or homes where they had been stashed. I was naturally intrigued by her account of how she and her friends had managed to arrange the escape of a group of children from France in the summer of 1942.

No possible personal connection crossed my mind until she mentioned the name of the American group and adoption agency who had helped to arrange the passage and subsequently placed the children with American parents. It was my adoption agency. The timing was about right too. When I told the story to my parents, my mother told me that the agency had no children at all in 1941 and much of 1942. Then they received an unexpected call announcing that children were available and that they would be allowed to choose one from among them. My mother further remembered that some of the kids they met were older and spoke languages other than English. Former social workers I subsequently spoke to confirmed that the agency laundered a group of Jewish children from France and provided their adoptive parents with cover stories about their origins.

The circumstantial evidence seems compelling, but there is no way of ascertaining if I was indeed one of these children. For obvious reasons no official records were kept. . . .

My encounter with Madame Fink and other participants in the rescue operation has affected me deeply. I am awed by their courage, selflessness, and collective accomplishment. That all of these people, many of them not even Jewish, would risk their lives or careers for children with whom they had no personal connection says something wonderful about the human capacity for empathy and altruism. Their actions seem especially poignant against the contemporary backdrops of Yugoslavia, Burundi, Rwanda, and Zaire. One can only hope that similar stories of protection and rescue from these horrendous conflicts will come to light in due course. (2001: 266)

I have included this extensive excerpt from Lebow's essay because, even though as a written account it provides the kind of historical context that would be unusual in a conversation, it calls attention to issues significant for understanding my larger question about the conditions that make the small-world story possible. The small-world story is the meeting between Madame Fink and Lebow and the discovery he might have been one of the children saved by her rescue operation. Their meeting in Palm Springs, removed in time and space from their possible initial connection, shares the trappings of the typical small-world discovery. Like other unwitting characters who discover the intersections between their stories and others, when Lebow begins his conversation with Madame Fink, he has no knowledge of his own possible role in her story. Only when he recognizes the name of his adoption agency, does he place himself within her story. This story transcends the small-world genre, because instead of seeing his ordinary world collapse into a small one, Lebow sees his small-world story as part of a larger narrative. It is perhaps best categorized as a small-world story, reframed, or a small-world story framed by (not as) a fellow-sufferer story. Madame Fink possibly holds a piece of his story, a story that he does not himself know in its entirety. One fragment meets another, but the whole story is still not known. For Lebow, the point is that this is not a story that can belong to one person; instead, it is a story about how many people were necessary to create possibilities in the face of atrocities and about the willingness of people to help strangers. It is a story about strangers (Ned Lebow and Madame Fink) who turn out to be connected after all; the larger story is about strangers who remain strangers but this small-world story within the story is a redeeming exception. The kindness of strangers who put themselves at risk is the astonishing phenomenon of these stories. Although the story has elements of providence and an element of lives intersecting, it is not a story about the world as small. It is nearer a personal story that becomes an allegory of a larger story of tragedy and heroism.

Stories of reunited lost loved ones, separated by political or natural disasters, who find each other by chance or changes in fortune, could be considered quintessential small-world stories, but they are told differently. In their tellings, these stories and small-world stories are worlds apart, although stories of reunited lost loved ones report close escapes and chance meetings, both of which involve small-world coincidences. Although the tellers often report themselves to be lucky and often describe escapes and discoveries as unbelievably fortunate occurrences, they do not conclude by asserting that the world is small. Only for tourists, who travel by choice, or for mobile populations, who have opportunities to live in or visit new places, can the world be small. In the stories of reunited lost loved ones, the world is too large. It is dangerous, and escapes and discoveries remain at the edge of what happened, what could have happened, or what did not happen. Small-world stories depend on the intersection of parallel narratives: the tale of the unwitting protagonist intersects, usually with the tale of another unwitting character. In tales of lost loved ones, the characters also rely on chance, coincidence, and fortune (good and bad), but the relationship between character and coincidence is constructed differently. The dimension of the humorous, inconsequential, harmless, or unexpectedly fortuitous found in small-world stories is, instead, a dimension of tragedy or hope. This difference, evident in the structure of the narratives, requires a different relationship between the personal tale and the larger social narrative that it claims to represent.

The configuration of structure, subjectivity, connections, and claims to a larger social narrative make one kind of story different than another. This is the central premise of many collections and studies of narrative, and especially of those that compare scenarios to determine whether a narrative confirms or challenges dominant narratives. Relying on theme alone (whether illness narratives or Holocaust narratives) will not distinguish between the kinds of subjectivity produced by dominant narratives or the ways that counternarratives resist existing cultural categories. The theme is often the name for the larger social category. However, these categories do not exist apart from the narrative apparatus (what I am calling structure, subjectivity, alignments, and claims in the case of small-world stories) that creates a relationship between a personal narrative and the larger social category. Essentially, small-world stories make an alignment claim. When narrators see their personal coincidence stories in mythical terms (producing a small world), they claim to reproduce and reaffirm preexisting connections, at least some of which have been created retrospectively by the small-world discovery. Narratives about fellow travelers on similar life journeys or about fellow sufferers can more often produce very new connections with a new social narrative.

The danger in personal narrative is assuming that the reproduction of existing alignments affirmed or reaffirmed in narrative should be uncritically celebrated. For example, in a chapter entitled "Universalizing Your Story: Personal Mythmaking," Robert Atkinson writes, "A personal myth is the story of our life that focuses on the experiences, motifs, and emotions most common to other human beings. It is told within the framework of the sacred pattern of beginning, conflict, and resolution, of separation, initiation, and return. It connects our lives to those who have gone before us by conveying what is most important and meaningful to us, especially the ultimate concerns, events, feelings, and beliefs that have directed our growth" (1995: 83). Arguing that the pattern of narrative is sacred, Atkinson claims that the shared structure of narrative is itself profound. Atkinson leaves no room for a distinction between narrative and counternarrative and no scenario other than growth. Promoting an uncritical identity politics in which people claim that their shared experiences grant them a privileged perspective and an uncritical mode of inspiration in which other people's stories are used to inspire disaffected empathy, Atkinson's view of narrative ignores a crucial difference between stories that reproduce existing mythologies and stories that challenge them. The cost of seeing one's experiences in mythical terms can be the promotion of a dominant narrative.

The relationship between personal and larger social narratives has several structural dimensions. For small-world stories, the most obvious connection between the personal and a larger social narrative is the concept of the small world itself, represented by the coda "Small world, isn't it?" and also evidenced in the narrative structure of an unwitting protagonist who makes a discovery of an unexpected connection. The kind of characters (especially, unwitting protagonists, strangers, and benefactors) created by the narrative is essential for producing the particular kind of small world the narratives claim. Further, the connection that small-world stories describe reinforces, rather than undermines, existing social alignments. Unlike narratives that call on the similarity of fellow sufferers to create alignment, small-world stories draw on parallel lives to find points of intersection. The sense of shared experience discovered in these intersections produces surprise but does not substantially change anyone's perception or understanding of his or her experience. Narratives of fellow sufferers discovering each other often describe a moment of transformation, when the narrator discovers that he or she is not alone in these experiences. These narratives simultaneously transform both speaker and audience as they create both self-understanding and the possibility of someone else who understands. Small-world stories, depending on already existing alignments, reconfirm what one already knows and, discovering strangers to be allied after all, affirm the world to be small. No personal transformation or cultural translation is required, and without this requirement, the narratives provide no opportunity for a counter-hegemonic or liberatory discourse.

Redemption and Empathy in
        Junk-Mail Narratives

Sometimes when stories travel beyond their owners, the new tellers claim to tell the stories in the best interests of the persons who suffered the experience. Nowhere is this more true than in political support groups that use personal narratives in their efforts to persuade others to join in changing, ameliorating, or otherwise addressing the suffering. Making the claim to speak on behalf of others is always a precarious claim, open to the challenge of misinterpretation and misappropriation. At the same time, those who use this strategy argue, this use of personal narrative is a crucial and important means for creating empathy and inducing action. The use of personal narrative by political support groups raises questions that can be addressed at several levels of personal narrative research: as a linguistic category of reported speech, as a rhetorical category of persuasive argument, as cultural categories of decontextualization and relationships between public and private, as a political category of representation, and as a narrative category of allegorizing the personal. Each of these modes of analysis addresses the question of the appropriation of personal experience, and each contributes to our understanding of the concepts of subjectivity and experience.

In recent years, speaking on behalf of another has become a pivotal issue for understanding questions of authority and privilege in cultural studies.[1] The fundamental premise that grants authority to those who speak from experience is based on the idea that the person who suffered the experience is entitled to tell it. First-person experience derives its authority from its claim to be the original and thus authentic source of knowledge.[2] The use of personal stories beyond their original contexts undermines authenticity but not authority; stories can accrue authenticity as they travel. Katharine Young makes an important distinction between authority and authenticity that is useful here. She observes that authenticity is a claim to presence, first-person experience, and embodied knowledge. Authority, in contrast, gains more from detachment and distance. As stories travel, they shift from authenticity-based claims to author-ity-based claims (Young, 1997). As the story travels away from the person or persons who suffered the experience, the authority can travel also, and this is the issue of concern in appropriated stories. Narratives about personal suffer-ing are especially a contested domain in which the personal suffering is often considered local, best understood, and most accurately interpreted by those who know the experience, and appropriations are considered to be unethical and unwarranted seizures of property by a dominant group. The appropria-tion of personal stories beyond their local tellings creates several possible (and not necessarily altogether unwarranted) relationships between local and dom-inant narratives:

1. a metonymic fit between the local and the dominant, for example, when a personal experience is considered representative of a larger or universal position
2. cases in which different dominant positions compete to represent a particular local experience
3. local voices that claim exclusion from a dominant representation
4. mistaken conflation of the local with the personal
5. the general problem of the appropriation of a universal by a local and vice versa

Despite the concern in feminist studies and some other disciplines about unwarranted appropriations of the personal, the appropriation of personal stories in public life is often not only unchallenged but championed. Personal stories are found in newspaper accounts or television programs as testimonies lending credibility to an interpretation of an event, as private accounts offer-ing insight into an otherwise formal or public event, or as insiders' perspec-tives providing a measure of humanity to what might appear to be exotic, gro-tesque, or unbelievable events. Thus, stories of President Clinton loaning a bow tie to Prime Minister Yitzhak Rabin were told (by reporters as well as by Clinton himself in his eulogy), along with discussions of Rabin as a statesman and peacemaker, when Rabin was assassinated. The bow-tie story was told to demonstrate the close relationship between Clinton and Rabin, their status as friends as well as statesmen. As an example of the second category, in which a public forum appropriates a local, personal story, television coverage of the Olympic Games offers "up close and personal" portraits of the athletes. In these examples, personal and private experience is appropriated by the pub-licly told stories, but the stories retain their status as personal and even, some-times, private. Although not private, these stories operate as tokens of privacy embedded as enclaves in a public discourse. The stories retain their authenticity as personal and thereby grant authentic status to the public discourse.

Personal-experience narratives are frequently appropriated for public life. We might ask why in this particular epoch in history does the personal story play this sort of role? And what role, more precisely, does the personal narrative play in public discourse? Does the personal serve to confirm the public statements; does it keep in place the boundaries between the familiar and the exotic, or does it break these boundaries down? In many twentieth-century critiques of dominant culture, local or personal narratives have been proposed as an emancipatory alternative.[3] Often, the alternative offered to dominant culture and its dominant discourses, is multiple, competing, local discourses.[4] Feminism offers a similar model of multiple, local, personal discourses as an alternative to dominant discourses.[5] All of these conceptualizations place hope for emancipation on local discourses, often in the form of personal narratives. However, these discussions do not claim that local narratives are in themselves emancipatory; rather, their emancipatory power lies in their ongoing dialogue with and ability to undermine dominant culture. The grand narrative may have "lost its credibility" (Lyotard, 1985: 37), but the alternative is not just smaller or more local narratives but a shift in the relationship between dominant and subversive narratives. This chapter explores that shift by examining the appropriation of personal or local narratives in larger than local contexts.

The question of the role of the personal story in public life and, more particularly, the possibility that personal narratives offer a subversive and potentially emancipatory alternative to dominant narratives, raises further questions about the categories of person, experience, and public. The personal and the public are not, in Gregory Bateson's terms, "proper nots"; they are not necessary opposites. Nor do the personal and public mark discrete boundaries. Instead, the personal emerges as a category within particular public contexts. Political junk-mail stories are one of these contexts.

In a survey essay, "Public/Private Distinction," Jeff Weintraub identifies four types of public/private relationships. He begins by distinguishing between two underlying criteria for the distinction: (1) between the concealed and the accessible, and (2) between the individual and the collective. Public and private signify different territories in each of the four relationships. First, public refers to the state and private to the market economy. Second, the public realm refers to citizenship, as distinct from both the state and the market economy. Third, the public realm refers to social life, as in Erving Goffman's works *Relations in Public* and *Behavior in Public Places*. Fourth, in feminist discussions, private refers to the family or the individual, and public refers to the economic and political order.

Weintraub points out that these categories are not exhaustive, but they help us to observe how the categories blur. Personal narratives do not enter into his discussion, but they could be applied to each of the four categories he identifies. The first category is occupied with questions of jurisdiction, or what I call entitlement. "It is therefore not surprising that the use of the public/private distinction within this framework has characteristically involved a preoccupation with questions of *jurisdiction,* and especially with demarcating the sphere of the 'public' authority of the state from the sphere of formally voluntary relations between 'private' individuals" (1997: 8). The second category, focused on citizenship (using Aristotle's definition of the *citizen* as "one who is capable *both* of ruling and of being ruled," Weintraub, 1997: 12) is relevant especially to discussions of who speaks for whom in personal narratives. The third category, in which the public realm refers to social life, provides the model most familiarly found in discussions of personal narrative. In Goffman's model, and other models of interaction analysis, including those employed in discourse analysis, the concept of the person is a social concept, requiring adherence to culturally defined and socially understood boundaries of self. Goffman sees conventions of respect for the individual as parallel to conventions of respect for property: "Just as we fill our jails with those who transgress the legal order, so we partly fill our asylums with those who act unsuitably" (1963: 248). Personal narratives, in this framework, are one example of how concepts of the person are maintained and negotiated in the public sphere of social life. The fourth category, using feminist theory, focuses on the public struggle over individual rights. Personal narratives provide a particularly good example of this struggle; the struggles over a woman's right to make decisions about her body are sometimes played out through struggles over a woman's right to tell her own story.

The most problematic area of negotiation of the personal in personal narrative is the question of appropriation. Whether in face-to-face communication between equals who are members of the same community or via distant channels of communication involving dominant and dominated groups or individuals, questions of who owns a story and who can use it for what purposes emerge. These questions of rights and ownership are fundamental to cultural definitions of all of the categories of private and public, from questions of jurisdiction and citizenship to questions of social conventions and liberation from oppression.

Political junk mail often uses personal stories: the person in the story is offered as an example of the larger cause. Often, the personal-experience narrative is used as a testimony to the suffering created by a societal problem. Through these personal narrative testimonials, the person represents the world problem. The person makes the problem "real." At the same time, the problem represents the person and gives the person his or her identity as a member of a class. A familiar example of the personal-experience narrative in political junk mail (also found in magazines) is the description, sometimes accompanied by a photograph, of a child, with the plea: "You can save this child's life, or you can turn the page." Of course, whatever you might save, it is not this child's life, long lost to the past, but some child's life of which this child is the allegorical representation.

The stories I discuss here were part of political pamphlets sent by mail to elicit monetary contributions. I refer to them as "junk mail," although junk mail often refers more specifically to advertising. Political pamphlets might more often be called by more polite terms such as "promotional literature," whereas promotions and advertising would be differentiated by whether they were selling a cause or a product. Appeals for money in junk-mail letters are based on the idea that by helping the cause, you, the reader, help the person. The premise in such appropriations is a metonymic fit between the person and the cause, or an allegorical relationship between the personal and the universal: the person-writ-large and the cause-writ-locally. Although these seem to be the inverse of each other, they are quite different. The personal narrative junk-mail endeavors to conflate them. The constructedness of the relationship between the person and the cause is most evident when similar personal narratives are used in appeals for opposed causes. A controversy about the correct action, or cause, to address a particular situation calls attention to the act of appropriating the personal; an uncontested fit gives the appearance of an essential, "natural" reference, in which the cause is to the personal situation as a whole to its parts. However, the local is always a constructed political category and even, or especially, any claim of a "natural" or necessary relationship between local and global, universal, or dominant representations is an act of appropriation.

The junk-mail solicitations I collected for support of political causes range from clearly contested narratives in which opposing sides claimed the same personal stories to relatively unchallenged narratives. The best example I found of contested narratives were stories of abortion trauma, used by right-to-life groups to argue that abortion is traumatic and should be made illegal and used by pro-choice groups to argue that abortion is already traumatic and having an illegal abortion would only increase the trauma. Many groups use relatively unchallenged narratives, in part because opposing groups do not exist. Groups soliciting funds for Amnesty International (against torture of political prisoners) or for Aid to Children (against starvation and poverty) are in this category. Opposing groups sometimes use similar narratives. For example, groups both for and against gun control use stories about particular individuals who were victims of gun violence, but in addition, groups against gun control use narratives about government control more generally and about how particular gun control laws might lead to other controls.

When political junk mail uses personal narratives, a personal experience is used to represent a more-than-personal situation. The significance of the larger situation is the warrant for the appropriation of the personal. The stories are often acknowledgedly representative, as in a Jacques Cousteau Society claim, "This story, or something akin to it, has been told countless times about dolphins and porpoises." Thus, the stories make the claim that the persons described in the narratives used to solicit funds are not the only ones in their plight.

The junk-mail narratives require the reader to accept a fit between the named person and the larger situation (a metonymic fit between the person and the situation). This person is only one of many who suffers, but by introducing you, the recipient of the correspondence, to personal suffering, the political support group hopes to convince you to become involved and to contribute money toward solving the problem. I do not dispute the efficacy or appropriateness of such appeals. Rather, I want to point out that the political group has appropriated the personal story as representative of a larger, collective story (an allegorical relationship). I consider five dimensions of these appropriations:

- reported speech and the creation of a multivoiced text
- incontrovertible realities and the moral dimension of appropriated personal narratives
- the collapse of familiar and strange/the exotic other
- feminism and appropriations of the personal as political
- collective stories and the creation of empathy between fellow sufferers

Reported Speech and the Creation of a Multivoiced Text

People who are quoted are rarely present. The use of reported speech usually indicates the absence of the original speaker. That absence may be used to attribute authority, or it may be used to deprive speakers of the opportunity to offer their own interpretations of their speech, but in either case, the absence of the speaker codes some sort of relationship among all participants, present and absent, in the exchange.[6] By juxtaposing voices and thus interrupting one authoritative voice, reported speech can create the possibility of critique.[7] But this emancipatory possibility of reported speech depends on the copresence of multiple voices. The issue, in the use of personal narratives in the political support junk mail, is whether the quotation erases rather than makes present the quoted person.

The junk-mail narratives use a form of direct quotation, often indicated by quotation marks and often attributed to a particular, named speaker/author. The voices in the junk mail include the person making the appeal (evident in the signature of a particular representative, sometimes a recognized celebrity of the soliciting agency); the people whose experiences are representative of the problem the soliciting agency is trying to resolve; and you, the addressee, sometimes named, since the mail is in the form of personal correspondence. The plea for help, made by the soliciting agency, directed to you, the addressee, is made on behalf of others. The person whose story is told is no longer just a person but a representative of his or her culture or circumstance. By making the individual a representative of the larger cause, the person as individual, with a right to his or her own story, can be obliterated. I suggest that in the case of the appropriated personal narratives, the decontextualizing process of inserting the story into the fund-raising plea can create double-voicedness, but not necessarily polyphony. We recognize multiple voices, but not necessarily in conversation with each other. By erasing what might be conflicting interpretations or even slight differences between local meaning and global cause, the appropriated narratives can serve to reinforce the ideology of the cause.

In the political junk mail in which there is little contest over the interpretation of events (torture and hunger as relatively uncontested horrors), the personal narratives need only report and substantiate the evidence; the report of a single experience and the fight to restore justice in that one case seem to be symbolic representatives of any freedom fight. Where there is contest over the interpretation of the events, as in the abortion political junk mail, personal entitlement to interpretation on the basis of personal experience pits one voice against another. In the case of uncontested horrors, the local representation (the personal story) and the global cause correspond. In contested causes, each global cause offers its own interpretation of personal, local stories, and each claims to better represent and speak on behalf of the individuals whose stories are appropriated.[8]

The following narrative, from a Planned Parenthood solicitation, is told in the first person but invokes other, third-person stories as well.

> Back in October 1973, a young high school senior and her mother came into my Boston City Hospital office. I never expected that the girl who entered my office would change my life forever.
> Both daughter and mother were visibly upset.
> The 17-year-old girl was pregnant. If her father found out, she and her mother feared he would become violent. Both mother and daughter pleaded that I help, that I perform an abortion . . .

As a Resident of Boston City Hospital, I performed the abortion under supervision, following the standard medical procedures prescribed by the obstetrics/gynecology department.

But I had no idea of the nightmare that was about to begin for me.

Three months later, the district attorney's office subpoenaed the records of 88 abortions that had been performed at the hospital. The records were seized. In January 1974, a grand jury investigation began. Many doctors simply refused to testify—by invoking the Fifth Amendment. I didn't. I felt I had nothing to hide. I felt I had done nothing wrong or illegal.

A few months later I was indicted, and the following January I went on trial for manslaughter.

The parties represented in this narrative include the physician, the seventeen-year-old girl, her mother, her possibly violent father, the anonymous author of the obstetrics/gynecology department procedures, the district attorney's office, the grand jury, and the many doctors who did not speak. This combination of speaking and not-speaking participants, actual and possible acts, intentional (rule-following) and unintentional (possibly illegal) acts blends to produce a controversy that pits the past events and the speaker against the potential events and the nonspeaker. Readers of this account are encouraged to ally themselves with the actual events and the person willing to stand up for his or her actions. The speaker/narrator of this story tells two stories: the story of a girl, her possibly violent father, her request for an abortion, and the story of the doctor being indicted for manslaughter because he performed the abortion. He establishes his authority as a physician who followed prescribed procedures, and he sets himself up as an unwitting victim of a larger drama about abortion rights. His first-person testimony allows him to make the claim that he was caught in this larger drama (that "would change my life forever") and to claim, "I felt I had nothing to hide. I felt I had done nothing wrong or illegal." His personal testimony to his innocence, based on his unwitting participation in the drama, is crucial to setting up his victim status.

Although the rhetoric of the abortion rights campaign uses the concept of choice, in this case, the narrative foregrounds the role of a physician who can claim, "I had no idea of the nightmare that was about to begin for me," rather than the girl who was making a choice, and whose nightmares or freedoms involve a different set of events. She could not as convincingly claim that her victimization involved having nothing to hide or having no idea of consequences. Abortion controversies are centered around the question of who is the victim.

The following narrative from the Ohio Right to Life Society provides more evaluation than narrative events and quotes a first person named narrator to establish the authority of the speaker's evaluations of her experiences.

"Being a senior in high school and pregnant is not something I'd wish on anybody. I felt so afraid and alone," says Debby. "Realizing that there was a little
person who needed me to care for him or her made it important for me that
I do my very best to provide."

"I realized, although I could give my baby the gift of life, I could not give
it a home. It seemed clear to me then—and it still does now—that the decision for adoption gave me and my baby a real chance at life. I have never regretted it."

"Now ten years later, I feel very strongly and with all my heart that I gave
the best to everyone: my baby has a home and family that loves her, a family
has the joy of a child's laughter, and I was given a new life and freedom to go
on and enjoy it."

The participants in this exchange are an anonymous author, Debby, anybody, the baby (represented as a little person, him or her, it, my baby, and a
laughing child), and a family. These participants are represented in agreement
with the narrator's position; there is no dissenting voice. Although the narrative provides a specific, named narrator, the narrative itself is generalized; the
only specific circumstance described is that Debby was pregnant as a senior
in high school. The story is a testimony not to having experienced particular
events but to looking back ten years later and affirming her adoption decision.
The narrative provides a generalized story-scheme and the interpretation to
accompany it. First, the pregnant teen feels afraid and alone. Then, with little explanation of the connection, she decides she can do something to provide for the child and give it "a real chance at life." The last part of the story
is hypothetical ("my baby has a home and family that loves her . . .").

In both the physician's and Debby's narratives, the interpretation provided
by the teller maps onto the position described by the cause. The following
narratives, from Women Exploited by Abortion, use a combination of third-
person narrative and reported speech to provide more voices, in conflict with
each other, among the participants in the exchange:

Mary, thirty years old and pregnant, strongly wanted an abortion. She had
a chronic physical illness which her family doctor felt warranted an abortion.
After the abortion she experienced guilt and self-hatred and described it as
"the least desirable solution."

Joan, a seventeen year old, had an abortion in the first twelve weeks of her
pregnancy. She seemed to cope well. But during her second pregnancy, she
"heard" babies crying at night and all the pain came back to her.

Both narratives, told by an anonymous author, contain the before and after
voices of the protagonists and also refer to the indirect voices of other participants. Mary's narrative refers to the doctor who thought the situation warranted

an abortion as well as to Mary's direct reported evaluative remark, "the least desirable solution," and Joan's narrative refers to the indirect voices of "babies crying." The double-voiced narratives create regret, rather than critique. The later awareness makes the earlier understanding untenable and encourages the reader to similarly choose the position of awareness. In the before and after of innocence and outrage, the physician's narrative also creates double-voiced discourse, but the physician maintains his innocence as part of his outrage; the voice of outrage does not disavow the stance of innocence. Regret and outrage work differently in their double-voicedness and make different obligations on the listener/reader. The physician's narrative enacts the scene of the seventeen-year-old pregnant girl and daughter's request for an abortion. The mother and daughter "pleaded that I help, that I perform an abortion." The equation of the abortion as a plea for help creates the possibility of understanding the physician's response (the abortion) as an act of help. The physician is then out-raged that his act of help would be characterized as he having done something wrong. The narrative sets up a choice characterized as a plea for help and pro-vides evidence of the logic of the plea and his response to support his position of outrage.

The narrative of regret does not depend on evidence in the same way. Mary experiences "guilt and self-hatred" and Joan "'heard' babies crying at night and all the pain came back to her." In both narratives, regret is the self-evident log-ical response to these emotional states. Of course, both narratives could pro-vide more evidence for the change of heart, but the point of the promotional material is not to substantiate the circumstances of post-abortion regret but simply to call attention to it in the most generalized sense as an outcome of abortion. The narratives, understandably, set up syntagmatic series in which the only choice is whether or not to have the abortion. Once that choice is made, the rest of the syntagmatic chain necessarily follows.[9] Having an abor-tion leads to regret. In Mary's narrative, her chronic physical pain and the doc-tor's warrant were deceptive in providing rationale for an abortion. In Joan's narrative, "she seemed to cope well," but that, too, was false evidence, since later, "all the pain came back to her."[10]

Of course, the crucial absent/present voice in the abortion controversy is that of the fetus/baby. The controversy plays itself out in competitions to speak as the mother, on behalf of the mother, on behalf of the fetus/baby, or on be-half of the state's interests. The focus on the trauma of abortion, rather than on the rights of the embryo, has not only enabled the pro-life groups to appropri-ate abortion narratives, perhaps more important, from a political point of view, it has enabled the pro-life group to appropriate the concerns (and voice) of women, rather than only those of embryos. This is a crucial step in the abortion politics debate where anti-abortionists have tread a thin line between the competing rights to life of a mother and an embryo (Luker, 1984: 229).

Anti-abortionists sometimes run into difficulty in attempting to speak for both mothers and embryos, whose interests do not always coincide. In a Massachusetts case of a pregnant woman comatose from a car accident, both pro-choice and pro-life proponents claimed the mother's interests. The pro-choice people argued that an abortion was necessary to protect the woman's life; the pro-life people argued that if the woman awoke to find she had had an abortion, she would be traumatized and would wish she had died. Both sides claimed to speak for the woman, but in that debate, questions of pro-life versus pro-choice gave way to questions of the rights to speak for an incapacitated person, and the husband, who happened to be pro-choice, rather than a pro-life stranger, was determined to be entitled to speak for his wife.

The claims to speak for the comatose woman made by the pro-life groups have something in common with other claims typically made in the political support literature to speak on behalf of the incapacitated. The incapacitated state of those spoken for is a necessary part of the philanthropic position, and the critique of appropriated discourses, including reported speech, begins with the critique of the divide between those in a privileged position of speaking and those in a disadvantaged position that prevents their speaking.

Feminist discussions have provided a critique of representations of the woman who has no place from which to speak.[11] In an explanation for what she finds troubling about the question, "Who speaks for the jaguar," Donna Haraway argues that groups understood not to be able to speak for themselves are "permanently speechless, forever requiring the services of a ventriloquist" (1992: 312). Haraway describes the process of speaking-on-behalf, representing those who cannot represent themselves (such as the fetus and the jaguar), as removing the represented group from its context, or surround, and relocating it in a "representational practice that *forever* authorizes the ventriloquist. . . . In the liberal logic of representation, the fetus and the jaguar must be protected from those closest to them, from their 'surround'" (1992: 313). Thus, the pro-life activists argued, the comatose woman had to be protected from her husband and others who did not have her, and the fetus's, best interests at heart.

The goal of the political support junk mail is to convince readers that the interests of the philanthropic/political organization and the interests of the represented group coincide. Reported speech and appropriated personal narratives contribute to that effect by eliminating, insofar as it is possible, the distant paternalistic voice or the liberal philanthropic voice and replacing it with the personal testimony.

Reported speech in political junk mail operates in a tension between two forces of appropriation: one draws on the force of the original, authentic, and thus usually authoritative, voice, and the other locates, retrieves, and represents a stolen or silent voice, articulating the voice of groups that cannot speak for themselves. Borrowing in itself is not necessarily problematic; voices are always borrowed. Further, voices and persons are not equivalent; individuals have more than one voice. Any claim to map groups and members is a form of appropriation. The problem begins with hierarchical claims for particular voices or with any claim that one voice counts more than another. Of course, this is always the case. Reported speech offers one way for a narrator to evade responsibility for knowledge by attributing it to the quoted voice (Hill and Irvine, 1992: 17). In the political-support junk mail, reported speech is used to make the addressees of the junk mail the addressees, or witnesses, to the suffering. The person as representative, as an example, decontextualizes by removing the person being represented from the cultural context in which an event occurred and recontextualizing the personal situation within a larger social drama. In Bakhtin's understanding, the use of a person as representative can be a useful strategy. Such stories produce what Bakhtin calls "an unrealized surplus of humanness" (1981: 37). Bakhtin uses the term to refer to the ways in which a lack of fit between persons and their fates is addressed in the novel, but it is also useful for other lacks of fit between monolithic views of supposedly homogeneous local cultures and the experiences that resist the fit. In the case of the junk-mail narratives, the lack of fit is precisely what grants the solicitation its persuasive power. The excess of the person, the person who seeps beyond the boundaries of individuality and comes to represent the plight of a group, is a boundary breaker. The group soliciting funds uses these stories to break down barriers and make some other person's misfortunes just familiar enough for just long enough to persuade readers to want to help, to want to resist the dominant culture, the status quo that is depicted as creating the problem. You, the personal reader, are asked to recognize the individuality of the suffering person whose story is told and to send money (to a group, rather than an individual, but hopefully that fact will not lessen the impact of the personal story) as an act of resistance.

Incontrovertible Realities and the Moral Dimension of Appropriated Personal Narratives

What is at stake in the appropriation of stories of individual suffering for political causes, and how do these narratives claim, sustain, transform, or remove the trace of the local story? The promotional mailings claim a moral stance, and they claim to be speaking on behalf of the persons who experience suffering. Although they are vulnerable to charges of privileged misappropriation and of silencing the very voices they present, they defend that charge by claiming to speak in the interests of the people they represent. I am not interested in either defending their claims or condemning their appropriations. Rather, I find these uses of personal narrative in the name of political causes useful to expand our understanding of how claims for incontrovertible realities are located in the "real experiences" of "real people" in "real places."

Personal-experience narratives utilize the most local of categories, the person, and claim to be the most local of genres, a genre of everyday life. The narratives used in junk mail purport to be collected from the tellers whose experiences are recounted. They are appropriations of local narratives, and they raise questions about who has the right to appropriate another's personal story. They are told in first, second, or third person, each changing the relationship between the story and its audience. Some claim to be stories in the words of the person who suffered the experience; others are reports of purportedly actual people; and some, especially those in the second person, are generalized accounts of the kinds of things that happened to individuals. The promotional literature that frames the story is directly addressed to you the reader; often, the writer is identified as a particular person writing to you from his or her personal experience.

The appeal of the local drives this kind of promotional junk mail. The mail is usually sent in the form of a personal letter addressed to "Dear Friend," though innovations in computer mailing have made possible letters addressed to particular individuals. Sometimes the mail is in the form of a memorandum, and sometimes the personal stories are presented as news clippings. Locality is conveyed through reference to particular names in particular places, through photographs, and through quoted testimonials. For example, from Feed the Children:

> "I'm scared . . . I don't know if we're going to have food to eat today and none tomorrow. My kids don't know, but there have been days when I haven't eaten so they could."
> Christine, single mother of four children

Later in the letter, we are told that Christine is "not her real name." Sometimes real names are used, especially in third-person accounts. Personal-experience narratives can appear to claim unmediated status; they conceal their constructedness behind the "this really happened" frame. The use of the personal narrative not only makes the fact of the injustice described in the political appeal seem irrefutable but also works to make the particular interpretation of that injustice and its remedy persuasive. In this use of personal narrative, the personal does not provide just another perspective, another point of view that might promote relativism or even challenge ethnocentrism. Rather, the personal account in this context stands for truth and is used to promote credibility.[12] Amnesty International sometimes uses full names in their efforts to give global (or Western First World) public attention to the plight of individuals whose situations would be otherwise unknown outside their local community. For example, from a letter in the form of a memorandum:

> Mexico: On the evening of 28 October, 1999, three unidentified men entered the house of Digna Ochoa y Placido and interrogated her at length about her involvement with a local human rights group. They tied her to a chair, securing her arms and legs, and locked her in a room with an open gas canister; the telephone line was cut. After they left she managed to set herself free.

> Malaysia: Lim Guan Eng publicly criticized the Malaysian Government's handling of allegations of statutory rape made against a former chief minister. He was charged with "prompting disaffection with the administration of justice" and given two concurrent 18–month sentences—all for trying to defend the rights of a 15–year-old schoolgirl.

These journalistic third-person accounts convey evaluative, interpretive comments within the otherwise factual reporting. The first report allows the reader to infer malicious conduct. The men were "unidentified." Words such as *entered* and *interrogated at length* suggest injustice, and the open gas canister provides the narrative sign of danger that makes Ochoa y Placido's escape necessary. The second account provides more direct evaluative comment, "all for trying to defend the rights of a 15–year-old schoolgirl." The narrative refers to several stories: the public criticism of the Malaysian government, the statutory rape, and the charges and imprisonment of Eng. We infer that the fifteen-year-old schoolgirl was the victim of the statutory rape. By requiring the reader to make this inference, and by including the first mention of the girl in the final evaluative comment, the narrative makes the necessary connection between two injustices, the rape and the charges against Eng. With the connection between the two injustices, not quite sharing an enemy but linked by the failure of governmental justice, the narrative transforms individual complaints into a collective problem. This is the goal of the political fund-raising appeals that use personal narratives, and it is accomplished both by using documentable narratives about particular people and places and by using hypothetical narratives that more obviously identify a collective problem.

Susan Sarandon, a well-known actress, uses what looks like personal stationery to make what looks like a personal appeal. She frames her account, although hypothetical, as real, in contrast to her acting roles:

Dear Friend,

  I've played a lot of roles over the years.

  But few have been as important as the one I've taken on by writing to you today. Because this time I'm not acting.

  I'm writing about real life. And I'm going to ask you to imagine for a few moments that you are a woman in Colombia, Burundi or Turkey: It's night. You just got home from a community meeting. Suddenly, armed uniformed men smash in your door.

  They grab you and, beating you, drag you out into the darkness.

  You scream with all your might. But your screams are in vain.

  Because your neighbors are afraid to get involved by calling the police.

  Even more horrifying, your frantic screams may well be the last sounds anyone ever hears you make.

Sarandon goes on to say, underlined in the original, *"But the truth is, this scene is not fiction."*

Of course, this narrative, suggesting that these events happen to you, the reader, is fiction. The claim to truth is only necessary because other tropes for coding truth, such as the use of first person and the mention of specific dates and places, are not used. Sarandon cannot speak as an eyewitness or from first-person experience, but her letter does what all of the other narratives do: it asks the reader to experience suffering from a distance and then contribute money to the organization that promises to do something about the particular problem described. Why is it so important to personalize the suffering, whether in eyewitness, first-person, or, in this case, second-person imagined accounts?

  Another Amnesty International mailing uses a first-person account told from within the experience of suffering.

  I know that I shall never see another sunset. In a sense, I am glad. The burns on my feet are all infected and the pliers used on me have left some nasty gashes. I have been the object of such sadistic display that I am kept constantly awake because of the pain. It is a strange feeling to be a hostage. You are caught, beaten, tortured, but you remain hopeful. It is your strength against theirs. It is your faith in a high cause, namely the defeat of an inhuman enemy who has forgotten all feelings for kindness, understanding and compassion. I must be mad to talk of hope in this hell.

This account refers to narrative events not described. The events, too horrendous to report, are represented by their effects. The "I" has had real experiences that are probably completely foreign to the recipient of such mail.

However, the "you" who has "faith in a high cause" is not only the narrator but also anyone who has had such experiences. In addition, you, the reader, might share that faith. The persons in personal narratives used to solicit funds are not the only ones in their plight. The problem that the political funding narratives raise is that the personal is more than personal. The political cause appropriates the "excess of personalness" for its own purposes. Instead of the overdetermined signifier discussed in symbolic studies, we have an overdetermined signified.[13]

The junk-mail appeals for money are more concerned with promoting a particular interpretation of the experiences recounted in the personal narrative than they are with substantiating the factuality of the experiences. Personal-experience narratives claim entitlement to an experience.[14] The political junk-mail narratives use personal-experience narratives as representative. They claim, "this really happened," as well as "this happened to me," and they suggest that first-hand knowledge also entitles interpretation. The personal serves to establish credibility, but the goal is to persuade readers of collective, rather than merely personal, injustices and suffering. Most of the appeals involve a precise and peculiar mixing of the representational and the meaningful, and it is this slippage, this point of a break between the signifier and the signified, that I suggest is crucial to the relation between voice and authority.

The Collapse of Familiar and Strange/the Exotic Other

The junk-mail personal narratives both impose global causes on the local situations and appropriate the local through personal narratives. What is immediately evident about the personal narratives in the political campaign literature is that they are an attempt to personalize a political concern. And while that may seem to suggest a simple inversion of the feminist claim that the personal is political (here the claim would be that the political is personal), such a simple inversion will not sufficiently account for the representational problem of relating the personal experience to the cause.

The following narrative, from the Chabad Trade School, an institution offering a combination of trade education and Orthodox Judaism, appropriates the genre of Unicef appeals, the day in the life of a particular child. The letter appeals for the support of a spiritually, rather than nutritionally, deprived child.

From the Chabad Trade School:
   Dovid laughed, but there was bitterness in his laugh. "In Iran, at least I could speak the language! I don't know what I'm doing here." And the 14-- year-old boy moved off quickly to the other end of the orchard.
   Now it was Mr. Emmet's turn to sigh. Dovid knew that his parents in Iran wanted nothing to do with him, and that hurt. The hardships and political un-

rest, had prompted them to send Dovid away. In Israel, perhaps someone *could* give him what he needed: the time, attention and love . . . maybe even hope for the future . . . that they were sadly unable to provide. . . .

From all over the world they come to Israel—and from all over Israel, they come to this special school. . . .

At Chabad Trade School, Dovid can receive a *valuable skill* before he graduates at age 18, and with the *steady support and counseling* he'll receive he can recover emotionally, too. . . .

For $35, you can give Dovid wholesome meals for one week. For $110, you can provide one year's books and equipment for his first-year auto mechanics course.

As Charlotte Linde points out, narrative both negotiates the past and orients to the future (2000). The narratives included in junk-mail requests for money to support social causes especially have this future orientation. The Chabad Trade School narrative places your donation in the narrative as a direct and logical outcome of the narrative problem. This narrative combines third-person narrative including first-person fictional dialogue (coded by the evaluative comments on the speech, such as "there was bitterness in his laugh"), larger social narratives ("hardships and political unrest"), hypothetical narrative ("perhaps someone *could* give him . . ."), generalized narrative ("From all over the world they come . . ."), and future narrative (which is where you, the reader, enter the narrative). This combination of narrative tropes betrays its construction more than the use of quoted personal narrative, and in so doing perhaps diminishes credibility in the dialogue or even the existence of the characters. Knowing readers will recognize that Mr. Emmet's name means "truth" in Hebrew, the writers of this narrative ask reader not to believe in the specifics but in the larger narrative truth in which a boy without hope can find it at the trade school and in which readers' support can make that possible for real if unnamed children. Fiction, here, may undermine the credibility of the narrative provided but does not undercut the logic of the narrative and the reader's place in it.

The following narrative from Unicef is typical of third-person narratives used to describe a more generalized social problem.

Nagush Tuklu is one of Ethiopia's cave children. She's only nine years old. But each day she goes to work inside her cave—a small hole dug in the side of a dried up river bed. Though it hurts her knuckles, she patiently scrapes the damp soil inside the cave with a tin cup, to harvest the slowly seeping water by the cupful. . . . For five hours a day in the scorching Ethiopian heat Nagush mines for water. There are no holidays or days off. Her family needs water every single day.

In these narratives, the appropriation of the local is also the appropriation of the exotic. The personal becomes exotic in the hands of a global claim. This is a strategic use of difference rather than a mirror use of another to better know oneself. The exotic other is reduced to a representative in what is described as a familiar or understandable cause. Indians, dolphins, automobile crash victims, poor teenage girls, and political prisoners may be exotic, but if the cause they represent can be claimed as universally understandable, it is as if they are known, or as if the other aspects of their identities pale in importance. Diversity diminishes, and the local becomes a homogeneous representative of the larger named cause.

The following narrative, taken not from a political funding appeal but from the Banana Republic clothing catalog, illustrates how the local is easily appropriated as exotic. The Amnesty International testimony is no less exotic.

> We went to San Remo for the art film festival and discovered a lovely, unpretentious village a stone's throw from the glitz of Monaco. It's sort of an off-Broadway version of the Riviera: a town full of stubborn artists, gregarious merchants, resplendent greenhouses, friendly hotels, and delicious cheap seafood. We didn't want to let the place fade from memory, so we made this shirt from cotton as silky and light as the air in those twisting streets, and striped like the awnings along the Ligurian Sea. We feel as relaxed as San Remo whenever we wear it.

Written in the style of the traveler's account, the Banana Republic catalog depicts buyers as expatriates and adventurers who travel between jungles and famous vacation spots. Buyers are advised that such clothing "travels to meetings as easily as it did to the tropics." Paul Smith's commentary "Visiting the Banana Republic" elaborately examines this postmodern colonialist discourse as "a strategem designed both to neutralize and to legitimize the antagonisms of the colonial past and the inequities of the present." He argues:

> Like the kinds of postmodern literary and visual texts to which it is closely germane, the Banana Republic text is not just a series of appropriative moves and gestures. It can also be read as the symptom of an anxious disavowal of its own *moral* dimension. Its concern is to establish the moral veracity of its Author(s)/Producers(s), and the rewriting or restructuring of history is merely a means to that end. (1988b: 145)

The Amnesty International narrative, in contrast, makes no attempt to disavow its moral dimension. But the question here is who does the disavowing or affirming? Does it make a difference if pro-choice and anti-abortion campaigns use abortion stories for different purposes? At the very least, the presentation of these narratives in appeals for money involves appropriations of the personal for the political. To whom does the personal "belong"? How have these groups differently constituted the personal? To what lengths is this appropriate?

While the Amnesty International testimony brings distant struggles to the attention of readers in the United States, the Banana Republic narratives bring tourists to exotic places where they learn what the natives wear and return to copy fabrics and designs. Both make claims of authenticity, the political narratives claiming that such a person really exists and therefore that such a problem really exists, and the catalog narratives claiming to have found "[t]he authentic bush jacket for adventurers with a low tolerance for the ersatz."

Feminism and Appropriations of the Personal as Political

One might want to claim that appropriations of the local by the dominant culture would not necessarily look the same as appropriations by the oppressed (Kipnis, 1986: 34). Feminist discussions begin with the relations of the personal to the political and ultimately concern the possibilities of global and local resistance to dominant cultures (Bunch, 1987). For feminists, the relationship between the local and the global addresses a crucial incompatibility between respect for local differences and a universal plea for an end to oppression of women. Charlotte Bunch offers a solution in the slogan, "Think globally, act locally." For Bunch, global means for women to "come together across male divisions . . . to organize outside of male control and value systems"(1987: 334). She writes:

> Global feminism exists. Feminist activity and thought are happening all over the world. There is much diversity among us and no agreed-upon body of doctrine or central organization. Yet, there is a similarity in our approaches and in our fundamental questioning of society. While the particular forms that women's oppression takes in different settings vary and often pit some women against others, there is a commonality in the dynamic of domination by which women are subordinated to the demands, definitions, and desires of men. (1987: 331)

This approach works as long as the local and the global are in harmony against some hegemonic other, actually another global. In a move described by Spivak as "a strategic use of positivist essentialism," the local is acknowledged as authentic and, by implication, uncontested (1987: 205). The political junk mail similarly constitutes an authentic uncontested local appropriated for political purposes.

A fit between the voice of a local person and that of a larger campaign helps to support the possibility of a global struggle on behalf of local problems. This is the feminist goal represented by the "think globally, act locally" slogan. However, it also shares with the concept of cultural relativism a framework in which diversity is preserved within a universal system of respect and other principles against different and intolerable ideas, such as prejudice. The model cannot account for competition between local and global, or what I would prefer to call a competition between two locals, challenging the boundaries of the supposedly authentic local and making the local larger than local.[15] The "think globally, act locally" model helps to dismantle the global (patriarchy, for example) but leaves the local intact. It works to identify global claims, as when one particular local claims for itself the status of a standard (and, of course, this is the case in cultural relativism, in which culture claims status as a universal principle), but not when a local interpretation is privileged, in the case of personal narratives appropriated by political causes.[16]

In many poststructural models, most notably, Clifford Geertz's concept of local knowledge and Jean Francois Lyotard's concept of localized narrative, the local has become the site of resistance to dominant culture. While I agree with Geertz's preference for "local knowledge" over "placeless principle" (1983: 218), the local makes no greater claims to reality than do the universals he refutes (Geertz, 1984: 273). Geertz defends the "relativists, so-called" against the "anti-relativists, self-declared" by arguing that provincialism is a greater danger than neutrality. Among the accomplishments of anthropology, he touts, "We were the first to insist that we see the lives of others through lenses of our own grinding and that they look back on ours through ones of their own" (1984: 275). While I share Geertz's commitment to the study of the historically and culturally particular, even in his hands the inadequacy of the concept of the local is evident. Geertz is willing to discard "the presumption of a highly integrated system of behavior and belief. (There is none such, even on so tight a little island as Bali)" (1983: 187). But to address the lack of integration (or the excess of locality), he resorts to a basic tenet of structuralism, "in which matters out-of-category disturb the entire structure and must be either corrected or effaced" (1983: 180). He acknowledges, "We need, in the end, something rather more than local knowledge" but proposes only "a way of turning its varieties into commentaries one upon another, the one lighting what the other darkens" (1983: 233).

Lyotard's recommendations for the local stem from a similar concern with an alternative to hegemonic, acultural, rationalistic universals, but he goes further than Geertz in his rejection of all totalizing social theories. As Nancy Fraser and Linda Nicholson point out:

> As a result, he rules out the sort of critical social theory that employs general categories like gender, race, and class. From his perspective, such categories

are too reductive of the complexity of social identities to be useful. And there is apparently nothing to be gained, in his view, by situating an account of the fluidity and diversity of discursive practices in the context of a critical analysis of large-scale institutions and social structures. (1988: 89)

Fraser and Nicholson propose their own variation, a postmodern feminism that does not "abandon" large historical narratives but that is "attuned to the cultural specificity of different societies and periods and to that of different groups within societies and periods." Their study of "feminisms" uses metaphors of "a tapestry composed of threads of many different hues" and "a patchwork of overlapping alliances" (1988: 101–2), and all in all, their proposal depends on the same simple notion of the diverse locals as does that of Geertz.

Competition among voices cannot always be described as diversity. The metaphor of a patchwork quilt maintaining the visibility of diverse pieces only works when the pieces have a metonymic relationship to the larger-than-local quilt. There is not always a tapestry, an identifiable whole that represents the parts. Bakhtin's alternative is to "lay bare" conventions through parody to provide an "exposure of all that is vulgar and falsely stereotyped in human relationships" (1981: 162). As Maria Lugones points out, however, parody or other playfulness in the dominant world can be dangerous (Hoagland, 1987: 61). A more serious criticism of either the patchwork quilt of diversity or the laying bare of conventions is that both proposals involve an already-inscribed local, waiting to be discovered, revealed, or protected. Such locals are in fact protected by and constituted by dominant discourses and are not the "natural" havens of "truth" or justice they claim to be. The rupture in the subject-effect or the local-effect is where diversity does not partake in a larger whole, where no strategic use of essentialism works.

Few models of the local offer any understanding of relations between the center and its margins, the included and the excluded, the self-ascribed and the other-ascribed. We know that local cultures are not homogeneous entities, not unified structures represented by worldviews, but the concept of diverse localities, and even diversity within locality, only serves to preserve a conception of locals as bounded wholes. For the most part, conceptions of the local, as much as they argue for the recognition of diversity, focus more on consensus and the reproduction of the local than they do on dissent and appropriation. Giving weight to consensus plays into the hands of those who criticize the local diversity models as indeterminate comparisons in which differences do not matter.

In Bakhtin's system, the consensus of authoritative discourse is countered by indeterminate meaning, or meaning contingent upon context. Indeterminacy can look like relativism, in which the symbolic monolithic system makes all differences equal and therefore trivial, or indeterminacy can look like competition between voices struggling for a stronghold, in which not only is the monolithic global dismantled, but more important, the local is dismantled as well.

The larger problem here is the appropriation of dominant culture. Resistance involves not only the naming, citing, or parodying of authority, the dismantling of a monolithic global, but also dismantling the essentialist local.[17]

Collective Stories and the Creation of Empathy between Fellow Sufferers

The rights, obligations, and possible benefits of representation collide in the appropriation of personal narratives by political causes. First, the appropriations create problems of representation and open up questions about the rights of others to use personal stories. Second, these representations use personal stories as examples of larger, collective problems. Potentially balancing these problems is the claim made by the political causes that they use the stories only to benefit the people whose stories are told, but this benefit opens a third representation problem because the people who suffer the experiences do not speak for themselves but depend on intermediaries to plead their cause. Sorting out these problems of representation is difficult enough in any case of people speaking for others, but the problems are compounded in appropriations by political support groups of personal experience because the narratives are used to persuade others, often not fellow sufferers, to contribute financially and, presumably, to care about the suffering of the people represented in the narratives.

I have suggested that political junk mail uses personal narrative to represent collective stories. One part of producing the collective story is creating the public story. Narratives do not occupy a private space to be then transferred to a public space. Rather, the public use of personal narrative creates both the public and the private contexts for these narratives; the public use of personal stories creates the tension between public and private. The narratives represent local situations and individual experience; their locality and individuality is solicited in order to achieve the effect of real experience. This is not to say that the events recounted in the narratives did not happen to the people and did not occur in the places but that the locality and the sense of a personal drama/tragedy/suffering is invoked as an example, a proof that the political cause has real consequences for real people. The goal of the political groups is to persuade readers to understand the personal stories as collective narratives. To do this, the groups must avoid appearing to be inappropriately making public people's personal stories. The appropriations are vulnerable in particular to two challenges: the criticism that in speaking on behalf of others the privileged group is further silencing an oppressed group; and the charge of voyeurism, that personal stories of personal suffering are used to satisfy privileged readers' desires to reassure themselves that they are better off than others. Both of these challenges can be understood as discourse problems.

Many people, whether scholars, political activists, or journalists, discuss the problem of finding a way for unheard voices to be heard. The importance of revealing concealed stories cannot be underestimated. At the same time, making personal stories into public testimonies, or making public narratives responsible to the voices of the persons who have suffered the recounted experiences, often compromises the categories of local and global, personal and collective. As I have suggested, there are several possibilities of fit and conflict between these categories. The Amnesty International narratives and some others as well use personal narrative in a metonymic relationship with the larger cause; each story is representative of the larger collective story.[18]

I suggest that a key issue in disputes about the appropriation of personal stories in public contexts is how individuals and their narratives are understood to participate in larger constituencies. For example, whether or not individual stories of torture can be considered part of a collective story is a matter of dispute. Lawrence Weschler reports on this dispute in connection to controversy over the Research Center for Torture Victims in Copenhagen's efforts to provide counseling and therapy for torture victims.

> A more trenchant and substantive critique, however, has to do with the medical model underlying the work of these centers—the notion of torture victims as a group being analogous, in a way, to cancer or hypertension (or even incest) victims; the notion that they suffer from a certain definable "syndrome," so that a treatment could be developed that would be equally efficacious for victims from Sri Lanka, South Africa, or Santiago, and indeed that one element of such treatment should consist of group therapy sessions in which victims from all over the world share their common experiences. (1990: 240)

Critics argue that torture is not a "medical problem." "It is in its very essence political, social—and rehabilitation from torture can occur only in a political and social context" (a Uraguayan therapist quoted in Weschler, 1990: 240). In other words, it is quite different to constitute fellowship and the collectivity of shared narratives on the basis of shared suffering than on the basis of shared political goals. People who suffer similar experiences do not necessarily constitute a group, and the narratives told by and about that suffering (which help to constitute a sense of group and shared suffering) cannot be categorized by differentiations between the medical and the political. As Thomas Couser points out in his book *Recovering Bodies,* narratives about breast cancer are quite different than those about HIV/AIDS or those about physical disabilities or deafness (1997). Stories about HIV/AIDS can be both medical and political, for example. The distinction between the medically (therapeutically) and politically constituted collectives relies in part on a distinction between a universalizing move to understand the shared experience of fellow sufferers and a localizing move to maintain the particular political context for the oppression. The universalizing move creates new constituencies of people who, though they do not share geographic space, share suffering. As Weschler's comment acknowledges, groups sharing "cancer or hypertension (or even incest)" (1990: 240) could be understood to be constituencies of fellow sufferers. Even the creation of these groups as constituencies is a debatable proposition with some arguing against the "saturation of rhetorical space with therapeutic themes" (Cloud, 1998: 14) and others contending that the recognition of shared experience offers opportunities for personal growth, political action, and social critique. The story of the creation of narrative constituencies goes something like this: a particular situation is unmentionable and neither storyable nor tellable; some brave individuals tell their stories publicly and "break the silence"; others recognize their own stories in the public stories and begin to tell their stories as well. Newspapers, talk shows, published autobiographies, biographies, testimonials, and life stories are some of the sources for these public narratives telling collective stories. Each genre configures a relationship between the individual and the collective story, including the individual as a representative of other fellow sufferers or the individual as a counterexample. However, according to this story, the constituency is created out of a sense of mutual recognition in which people recognize others in their same plight. These constituencies are not created by the outsiders, either those who created the suffering or those who fail to understand, to listen, or to permit the stories to be told (although personal stories of suffering are sometimes created in response to those failures; that is, it is those failures that create the category of the unmentionable experience).

To participate in a larger constituency is to be recognized and to recognize others. Recognition produces affiliation. But these affiliations exist against a backdrop of distances produced by trauma and suffering. Narrative may be one means to create affiliations by bringing together people who recognize shared experience, but narrative also reproduces distances and gaps. As Cathy Caruth points out, the narrative event is always a belated event. "The story of trauma, then, far from telling of an escape from reality—the escape from a death, or from its referential force—rather attests to its endless impact on a life" (1996: 7). There are two traumas, both the encounter with death (disease, etc.) and the "ongoing experience of having survived it" (Caruth, 1996: 7). This double telling is compounded by another doubleness in trauma narratives, according to Caruth: "We can also read the address of the voice here, not as the story of the individual in relation to the events of his own past, but as the story of the way in which one's own trauma is tied up with the trauma of another, the way in which the trauma may lead, therefore, to the encounter with another, through the very possibility and surprise of listening to another's wound" (1996: 8).

The political support group personal narratives attempt to satisfy the conditions in which collective stories provide a new relationship between tellers and their audience. One way that the promotional junk mail claims to offer these conditions is by telling stories that might not otherwise be told. The junk mail invites the reader to become an empathetic listener and to participate in social change to the shared benefit of both teller and hearer. I cannot say whether or not the conditions are actually satisfied and whether the junk mail creates harm or good or both. I can only point to the areas in which the junk mail is vulnerable to failure. The first of these is that the organization promoting the political cause constitutes the collective story of the group it represents. Thus, both pro-life and pro-choice abortion groups constitute women who have had or might have abortions as a group in need of protection. Both groups appropriate personal narratives as examples of (in this case very different) traumas. The second area of vulnerability is that although the junk mail gives a voice to people who might not otherwise be heard (especially by the audiences receiving the junk mail), the exchange not only does not necessarily result in any mutual recognition in which people might recognize that "one's own trauma is tied up with the trauma of another," but it also could result in confirmation of the distance between participants, between those who suffer and those who are privileged to contribute to the well-being of people they will never know and experiences they will never have. Empathy can produce alienation. The third area is that the personal narratives in the junk mail rarely convey a double telling of encountering and surviving death. Instead, in order to promote the urgency of a situation requiring redress in the form of money, the narratives are situated as ongoing and unresolved. Nagush Tuklu's Unicef narrative uses the present tense to situate her struggle as ongoing: "Each day she goes to work inside her cave."

As vulnerable as these narratives are to claims, justifiable, that they fail to satisfy the conditions of telling trauma narrative, these conditions are part of an idealized view of narrative in which people own their own stories, in which telling one's own story gives one the power to change circumstances, or in which the exchange of stories is part of a larger system of rights and equity in the exchange of power. The junk mail also insists on a relationship between the personal experience recounted and the reader:

> I have good reason to believe it is a vision you agree with—and that's why I'm writing to ask you to join us.
> The need for you and other fair-minded people to rally to our side has never been greater.
> We count on people like you to help make the work we do possible.
> I want you to be a witness to the case of a client.
> Thanks to members like you who support our efforts . . .
> But don't just take my word for it. Please read the letter I've enclosed.
> Because I am hoping you will do two things today to help people like me.
> With your help I am confident that we will find the cure.
> It is my sincere hope that after reading both my letter and the enclosed correspondence . . . you will agree that it is profoundly important . . .
> If something this terrible should ever happen, I will know that I have done what I could to fight back against the evils . . . I hope you'll agree to do the same.

In constructing agreement and support between the author and the reader, each of these appeals works to establish the relationship of obligations or responsibility necessary for charitable giving. The appeals attempt to establish a shared struggle (based on shared values or a shared belief system) in the absence of shared experience. To accomplish the sense of shared struggle, the reader is inscribed as part of a group (of "you and other fair-minded people," or "members like you" who join with "people like me" who "will agree"). The constituency of supporters is, in almost all of the junk mail, constituted of people who are privileged never to have the experiences recounted in the narratives. Philanthropy depends on a nonreciprocal, asymmetrical relationship, so this is no surprise, but the asymmetry and nonreciprocity work against the conditions for and promises of sharing personal narratives. As described by Caruth and others, trauma victims require witnesses, rather than empathy. The junk-mail narratives are designed to create empathy and to move the emotions of the reader rather than satisfy the teller whose experiences are told. Empathy preserves a distance between those who understand and those who experience trauma; witnessing troubles that distance, and while it does not necessarily close the distance, it transforms the distance enough for the witness to be part of the constituency of sufferers.

Empathic social relationships are usually described in discussions of moral obligations, but they are also manifested in discourse patterns. I will describe just two patterns of discourse that contribute to the empathic relationship: the use of evaluation and the claim to the truth of the experience. Evaluation is crucial for demonstrating the significance of the problem and the degree of suffering; often the two are linked. Using metanarrative evaluation, some of the appeals demonstrate the narrator's commitment to his or her decision:

> I felt I had nothing to hide. (Planned Parenthood)
> It seemed clear to me then—and it still does now. (Ohio Right to Life)

Evaluation also suggests the moral/ethical reaction of the teller:

> It is your strength against theirs. It is your faith in a high cause, namely the defeat of an inhuman enemy who has forgotten all feelings for kindness, understanding and compassion. (Amnesty International)

Each of these evaluative strategies suggests that readers ally themselves with the position of the teller. The Banana Republic catalog makes use of the same strategy: "We feel as relaxed as San Remo whenever we wear it." The Chabad Trade School appeal is not metanarrative in the voice of the narrator and does not speak directly to the reader: "Dovid laughed, but there was bitterness in his laugh."

In a variation of this strategy, Susan Sarandon's narrative similarly embeds evaluation within the response to the events described; although she speaks to you, the reader, the evaluation is attached to the experience of the events rather than a retrospective response to hearing about them: "Even more horrifying, your frantic screams may well be the last sounds anyone ever hears you make."

In personal narrative, evaluation carries the burden of persuasion and more particularly works to justify actions and convey their moral and ethical position.[19] In these narratives, however, used as part of an effort to persuade readers to participate in a cause larger than the individual, the subject of the narrative can be (and usually is) eclipsed by the larger cause. It is in this sense that the personal narratives could be said to be appropriated (although as I have suggested, as long as the personal story is seen to be allied with the larger cause, the appropriation may be accepted, not challenged). The subject in these appropriated personal narratives is subjectified, both made into an object and understood as an agent at the same time.[20] Nagush Tuklu is described by her actions, but she, unlike the doctor who performed abortions, does not speak and does not offer her own judgments of her situation.[21] In many of the junk-mail narratives, situations "speak for themselves" as if the judgment of injustice or oppression is obvious to you, the reader. You, the reader, are asked to agree with the judgment offered or to make your own judgment based on the presentation of firsthand evidence (the narrative). Although the narratives may be called "personal," they locate the person differently, and each of these locations establishes a particular relationship with the reader.

The pro-life and pro-choice narratives locate the person in an interior struggle with a moral decision. The persons in these narratives speak to themselves. They use cues for interior monologue such as "I realized," "I felt," and "I have never regretted." Importantly, these are retrospective accounts, relying upon memory to establish the inner self who appears in the form of self-knowledge in these narratives.[22]

The question is, if the stories represented in these narratives are represented to publicize otherwise forgotten, concealed, unspoken, unspeakable, or unknown experience, do these representations count? Do they give voice to the otherwise voiceless? To the extent that they deny, obliterate, and obscure the voices of the persons who suffer the experiences, the answer would be no. The failure, here, could be attributed to something more fundamental than the appropriation of personal experience; it could be attributed to what Judith Butler calls "linguistic vulnerability," "the gap that separates the speech act from its future effects" (1997: 15). Appropriation is, essentially, a separation. Charges of appropriating personal narrative are directed at one kind of separation, the separation of the narrative from its "original" context. In the junk-mail narratives, in some cases at least, the "original" context is invented in order to provide firsthand evidence to support the significance and urgency of the cause. The personal narrative is separated from the context in which persons tell about experiences they have suffered to others, who then, ideally, become witnesses to that suffering. In the junk-mail narratives, the readers are far removed from the suffered experiences. The problem with this model is that it assumes that persons and their voices, and equally important, voices and their effects, are originally, naturally connected, absent the interference of appropriation, and that this connection is the ideal situation.[23]

Other separations, less the focus of appropriation, further complicate the appropriation of personal narrative. Narratives separate past and present, the world represented in the narrative and the worlds of the storytelling occasions, the narrator from the characters and from the readers, and the individual from the collective story. The most frequently appearing characters in the junk-mail narratives used by political support groups are the persons who have suffered the experiences. Absent, often, are the perpetrators of oppression or suffering. The junk mail rearranges relationships, separating some aspects and connecting others. Empathic relationships involve both detachment and affiliation. The separation is evident through critique when we ask who speaks on behalf of whom or we observe the distance between the privileged reader (and narrator) and the oppressed person whose story is told. The connection in empathic relationships is what makes the junk mail effective, measured by whether or not you, the reader, recognize your obligation to contribute to the cause.

Empathy depends on separation and is defined as a relationship that offers distance as a means of gaining perspectives on lives other than our own.[24] The junk-mail narratives create a connection between an individual traumatic story and a larger political cause. In asking the reader to imagine the life of the other, they maintain the hypothetical as a distance between the privileged reader and the oppressed subject of the story and in so doing clarify the role of the reader as philanthropist and as an agent capable of changing the world. In a subtle act of transfer in which you the reader are never the subject of the experience, you, the reader become (if persuaded) the agent who can act. This phenomenologically based premise that we can understand experience without having the experience ourselves (see Schutz 1962, 1972) can lead to uncritical promotion of the appropriation of others' narratives for the good of the privileged appropriator and without regard for the cost to those whose narratives are used. At the same time, this untethering of original experience and ownership of narrative does offer the possibility of refusing to be the subjects, to be subjected by, either our own, or others' traumas. Narrative fails its therapeutic promise but fulfills a social one.

6   *Speaking from Experience*

The great promise that narrative makes is to transcend personal experience, both by allowing us to see our own, seemingly unexplainable, experiences in other people's stories and by helping us to understand the otherwise unfathomable experiences of others. In this concluding chapter, I consider the promise and the danger of these narrative claims. In particular, I focus on the roles of entitlement and empathy in personal narratives. Entitlement and empathy are in one sense contradictory, the first claiming ownership of one's own stories and the second claiming understanding of other people's stories; in another sense, they are two dimensions of the same problem; together they negotiate the relationship between the personal and the more than personal, or allegorical, meaning of stories about experience. My goal has been to understand questions about who speaks for whom in the context of the redemptive promise of narrative. Here, I examine the intersection between personal narrative and ethnography and their shared reliance on ordinary experience.

The past decades of debate on ethnography have occurred in the context of debates about the rights to represent others' experiences. Often questions turn to the rights and interests of privileged ethnographers studying less privileged subjects, and very recently, these discussions have included not only rights but obligations. Historical events often place the privileged in the role of witness to the suffering of the subjugated. Representation is always a matter of opportunity, but sometimes it is also a matter of obligation. Ethnographers, once guided by and constrained by goals of objectivity and distance, have recognized the limits of those goals, and while not forsaking science and the possibility of accuracy, have begun to measure accuracy not only by distance but also by a culture's own measures of what looks like truth. Ethnographers who attempt to describe suffering have as their greatest task the critique of empathy: the story they tell must be accurate, and in representing a trauma, it must avoid the sensationalism that makes trauma into scandal. Examples of works facing this challenge include Barbara Myerhoff's written work and films, Charles Briggs and Clara Mantini-Briggs's study of cholera in Venezuela, Elaine Lawless's research on domestic violence, and Patti Lather and Chris Smithies's ethnography of women with HIV/AIDS, *Troubling the Angels*. These are works in the shadow of particular deaths (the very old people Myerhoff studied; Myerhoff herself; the experience of a fatal disease; the women fearing for their lives in the face of domestic violence; and the women who demand to tell their own stories in Lather and Smithies). In the context of imminent death, each story, action, and gesture, especially the most ordinary, takes on heightened representational significance. Each walk down the street represents a lifetime of walking down streets. The ordinary becomes precious, and as we know well, the precious is the most dangerous of representations; it is always precariously close to the trivial, just as its counterpart, the extraordinary, is precariously close to scandal. The ethnography of suffering requires a critique of empathy, an understanding of representation that represents emotion as neither trivial nor scandalous.

The idea that narrative can be a bridge to understanding others has occupied a central role not only in ethnography but also in its not-so-distant cousin, oral history studies. For example, James G. Blight, a scholar of international relations who has written on the Cuban Missile Crisis and Vietnam, describes empathy as "the key, the methodological Rosetta Stone of critical oral history" (2002). "Critical oral history" is a methodology created by Blight for examining recent historical events to provide reflection and retrospective insight into points of misunderstanding that led to conflict. He explains:

> By empathy, I mean nothing more exotic than seeing the events in question more or less the way they are seen by a former adversary, or even a former colleague, with whom one may disagree in some fundamental way (such as, for example, whether the risk of nuclear war in the missile crisis was great or small). I am not talking about agreement, or sympathy, or anything of the sort. I am just talking about getting inside the shoes of the other, long enough and profoundly enough to see his or her reality (2002).

The goal of mutual understanding is narrative's greatest promise. However, the metaphor of wearing another's shoes not only makes it seem easier than it is but also obscures the complex ethical issues involved. Narrative promises mutual understanding (empathy) and entitlement, and these are competing promises, the first determined by questions of translatability and border crossing, and the second by questions of custody and containment.

Discussions of the limits of narrative have focused far more on questions of representation in the sense of accuracy and objectivity than they have on the problems of empathy and entitlement. The latter, however, are also issues of representation. Scholarly discussions of narrative representation as objectivity and accuracy, on the one hand, and entitlement and empathy, on the other, parallel the tension between narrative as memory (retrieving a lost past) and narrative as a cautionary tale (used to guide present and future actions).[1]

The usual assessments of the limits of personal narrative (especially other people's stories, and as I have suggested, personal stories are inevitably other people's stories) focus on issues of representation, entitlement, interpretation, essentialism, and tellability. At one end of a continuum, narrative scholars focus on the usefulness of narrative for recording the past or competing versions of events. At the other end, they observe how narrative can be used to give voice to disenfranchised groups or provide therapeutic healing for disrupted lives (White, 1995). However, these are never separable. Questions of nostalgia and sentimentality inevitably cast a shadow on the enterprise of recovering the past. And the cautionary tales or therapeutic narratives designed to provide coherent, authentic selves out of the chaos of ordinary life are plagued by the ongoing challenges of counternarratives, the fragmentation of experience, and the blurring of personal and more than personal. Identifying the roles of empathy and entitlement in narrative helps to bring conversations about personal and allegorical representations of experience into a sustained dialogue that resists celebratory claims and interrogates narrative at its limits.

In this chapter, using the example of narratives told about disability, I trace the concept of experience (and more specifically, the privileging of the authenticity of personal experience) from the phenomenological interest in exploring given realities of everyday experience,[2] through Walter Benjamin's proposed dialectic between lived experience (*Erfahrung*) and shock experience (*Erlebnis*), to contemporary feminist understandings of experience in narrative. Narratives about disability provide an obvious site for observing empathy and entitlement, as well as nostalgia and sentimentality. They also raise important questions about the failed promise of narrative, be it the promise to provide an untold story or a counternarrative to medical discourse, the promise of greater understanding, or the question of who is served by that understanding.

I begin with Temple Grandin's story about her experiences with autism. The idea of a person with autism writing an account of her own experience provides a challenge to all of the premises of personal narrative. As Grandin herself observes, autism is defined in part by the absence of personal narrative,[3] and her narrative, written in part to reclaim and challenge the construction of autism by medical "experts," is a self-conscious performance of an unfamiliar genre. Challenging the tenet that everyone narrates—as well as its correlate, which assumes that those who do not narrate do not have a self, Grandin both claims the authority of personal experience at the same time that her stance refuses to engage in claims for entitlement or the possibility of empathy.

Oliver Sacks claims that Grandin's 1986 book on her experiences as autistic provides a voice "from a place which had never had a voice, never been granted real existence before—and she spoke not only for herself, but for thousands of other, often highly gifted, autistic adults in our midst. She provided a glimpse, and indeed a revelation, that there might be people, no less human than ourselves, who constructed their worlds, lived their lives, in almost unimaginably different ways" (O. Sacks, 1995: 10). Sacks could have been describing an anthropological study that similarly would provide a description of another culture, another way of constructing the world. Indeed, Grandin describes herself as "an anthropologist on Mars." Or Sacks's declaration of the importance of hearing a voice that had not before been heard could be the kind of declaration made about any ignored, unrepresented, or misrepresented experience (women's experiences for example) when a representative, or someone claiming to be a representative, speaks out and is heard. But revealing a heretofore unknown world is, as current anthropologists know, never neutral. Translation is domestication; what we get in the end is a combination of revelations about ourselves, or what James Clifford refers to as "partial truths" (1986a: 7), and representations, still valuable if not the window into the other that we might have understood to be the promise. We have good reason, in other words, to be suspicious of the promise to provide a voice for the voiceless or to tell the untellable. Clifford expresses this suspicion for anthropology.

> Anthropology no longer speaks with automatic authority for others defined as unable to speak for themselves . . . other groups can less easily be distanced in special, almost always past or passing times—represented as if they were not involved in the present world systems that implicate ethnographers along with the peoples they study (1986a: 10).

Kamela Visweswaran describes the postmodern penchant for coauthored texts, dispersing the previously claimed authority of the ethnographer, as "anthropology's last grasp of the 'other'" (1994: 32). Notwithstanding Grandin's description of herself as "an anthropologist on Mars," her work raises problems that are interestingly different than those confronted by ethnographers seeking to represent unfamiliar experiences. Grandin's work claims entitlement only in her interest in providing a counternarrative to existing accounts of autism (S. Smith, 1996: 239). She does not claim to speak for all people with autism, nor does she find questions of authority compelling. She presents her narrative as personal, and she makes few if any allegorical claims.

Even more insistently, Grandin resists empathy. On the one hand, the nature of her professional work, designing cattle transports, places her in what might be seen as the empathy business. She claims, for instance, that her expertise is based on understanding how cattle experience their environments. On the other hand, Grandin neither expects to understand how other people experience the world nor to have others understand her experience. As an "anthropologist on Mars," she is a visitor, a scientific observer, and she has no expectation of going native.

Grandin's autobiography is useful for exploring the representation of an individual claiming to reveal that which until now was unknown and claiming to be a voice for others who (in the case of some other people with autism literally) cannot speak for themselves. She endeavors to decipher her social world as a translator for others who cannot understand or appreciate it without a guide. As a historian of her own past, or as a narrator tacking between her past and her present, she holds these realities in juxtaposition to each other. Her narrative makes us aware of the gulf between the realities of living with autism while at times also giving the appearance of traversing them. My interest in this chapter is how narrative accomplishes the appearance of mutual understanding, or empathy, especially by setting up an alignment between subjectivities and experiences.

Discussions of personal-experience narratives sometimes promote a *natural,* uncritical concept of experience in which owning a particular identity entitles one to claim ownership of experience. The feminist slogan "the personal is political" becomes translated into the self-evidence of personal experience either as an entitled position or platform from which to speak or as an overlooked, excluded, or marginalized voice that deserves to be heard. As an entitled position, personal-experience narratives are relatively uncontested, and knowledge claimed "from personal experience" is sometimes regarded as more authentic. Alternatively, personal-experience narratives are collected and published in an effort to "grant a voice" to a group whose ideas, perspectives, or experiences have not been heard.

One way in which personal-experience narratives achieve the status of the authentic is by conflating two kinds of representation. The first is the problem of mimesis, or the relationship between the representation and the object it represents. In personal-experience narratives, the teller strives to persuade the listener that the representation corresponds to the experience represented. The second is the problem of representing the other, or the right one has to represent another. In personal-experience narratives, one claims to represent oneself.

The personal-experience narrative plays a prominent role in all of these conceptions of experience. For the phenomenologists, the question was, "What is presupposed and involved in the common-sense individual's interpretation of his own situation with respect to history?" (Natanson, 1962). Benjamin inherited this interest in what might be called everyday local history and further explored the dialectic between universal and particular histories.

Aesthetics and accountability are two sides of the same representation problem. The first is concerned with how representations transform experience; the second is concerned with how that transformation might distort or misrepresent experiences. I am less interested in collapsing the aesthetic dimension of narrative as craft and the accountability dimension of narrative as history than I am in holding both aesthetics and accountability under scrutiny as part of the question of representation and rights. Following Hayden White, I am concerned with how social rules about appropriate representations and interpretations (White refers to them as felicitous or infelicitous) constrain narratives and how narratives constrain or influence change in those rules and conventions. For White, this is a link between narrativization and moralization (1980: 18).

Ethnographies often use the present tense to avoid the suggestion of fiction.[4] They announce, "This is an account of a present and ongoing experience," and they attempt to suppress aesthetics in favor of accountability. Aesthetics and accountability play a role in all of the narratives I have discussed. Each relies on personal experience to reproduce an ideological system (Scott, 1992: 52; deLauretis, 1984: 159). The small-world story presents life as a script, as truth stranger than fiction. Small-world stories not only insist that strange things really happened, but they also insist that what happened is larger than an account of facts *because* it was so strange. Unlike ethnographies, purporting to represent in general terms a strange experience that has validity independently of the ethnographer's observations, small-world stories purport to represent a particular experience that has validity despite its unlikeliness. Ethnographers hope to be able to say, "Things happen this way, and they aren't altered by my perspective," and small-world story narrators say, "I was able to have one of those larger-than-life human experiences that makes you wonder about being part of something bigger than yourself." Similarly, the hungry-child, junk-mail advertisements make the claim, "This is still happening, right now, as you read; you can do something or turn the page." I place these seemingly different kinds of representation in juxtaposition to demonstrate that both are locked into the same problems. The reality of ordinary particular experiences stands in contrast to their allegorical renderings in ethnographies; the *petit recit* is in tension with the grand narrative (in Lyotard's terms). Grand narratives often imply and sometimes make explicit a vision of progress, an ineluctable path toward an imagined future that might or might not be reached. Personal-experience narratives do not, of necessity, have such a progression. Instead, the personal is associated with the private, the domestic, the fragmentary, the ordinary everyday lived experience.

Stephen Tyler writes, "[A] post-modern ethnography is fragmentary because it cannot be otherwise. Life in the field is itself fragmentary, not at all organized around familiar ethnological categories such as kinship, economy, and religion" (1986: 131). But the opposite of the allegorical, totalizing, narrative may not be the personal narrative. As I have suggested, the personal narrative is inevitably allegorical, as soon as it travels out of the context of personal experience, as soon as it points to the larger meaning of a personal experience. A more useful opposite may be Benjamin's concept of the ruin, or nostalgia for the personal experience (Buck-Morss, 1991: 243).[5]

What gives personal experience the appearance of avoiding or resisting the totalizing narrative is the illusion that it concerns "real" experience. Narrative about experience is granted credibility in conversation and denied credibility by historians because the teller claims the experience as his or her own. However, personal-experience narratives are mediated by the teller, by the expectations of the audience, by prior understandings of the events, and by the situation in which they are told; their truth requires negotiation and can involve contested interpretations.[6] Narratives of experience present the point of view of witness or victim—the person who "had" and therefore owns the experience (H. Sacks: 1992). Although this is a rule of conversational narrative—the narrative belongs to the person who had the experience—the configuration assumes subjectivity and identity. It assumes that one can represent oneself as a kind of person who has a particular kind of experience, which is to say that all narratives overflow their particularity, becoming allegorical. Personal narratives have the particular predicament of creating more-than-personal persons.[7]

Narratives about everyday life experiences depend not only on the validation of experience as something that truly happened but also on the validation of the identity claims necessary to support the idea that the teller is entitled to claim that experience as his or her own. It is not as simple as it sounds to say that a personal experience can be validated as true because the person who tells it claims that it happened to him or her, that is, that it belongs to the narrator. Harvey Sacks said that our experiences are just about the only thing that we can say truly belong to us, and at the same time, he pointed out, ownership of experience is often a contested territory.

Several scholars, most notably Joan Scott, have taken apart experience as a natural category. Scott has demonstrated that "experience is at once always already an interpretation and is in need of interpretation. What counts as experience is neither self-evident nor straightforward; it is always contested, always therefore political" (1992: 37). She asks, "How can we historicize 'experience'? How can we write about identity without essentializing it? Answers to the second question ought to point toward answers to the first, since identity is tied to notions of experience, and since both identity and experience are categories usually taken for granted in ways that I am suggesting they ought not to be" (1992: 33). My discussion follows from Scott's suggestion and is an attempt to interrogate the relationship between the deconstruction of experience and the deconstruction of subjectivity in order to explore the problem of how natural subjectivities are aligned with a natural category of experience. I'm in search of the murkiest examples of this alignment. This is particularly interesting when we look at claims to represent a generic experience. That is, one is claiming more than one's own experiences. Grandin's book does this in several ways. First, she speaks for others who have no voice, that is people with autism, many of whom due to their neurological differences, do not engage in the kind of description or narration that we would recognize as representing their experiences. Second, Grandin speaks about her own personal experiences but also speaks for other people with autism. Third, she speaks as an anthropologist, translating between the nonautistic perception of the artistic world and her own experience, as a person with autism. Fourth, she is not at all like any of the people with autism who do not write books about themselves; that is, she is not representative. In ethnographies, an outsider anthropologist claims to represent a general experience of others, one that he or she has also experienced as an observer. In a sense, the ethnographer has had an experience, and like other travelers, the purpose of the endeavor has been to describe it, to represent it in general terms for those back home. And Grandin is in this sense an anthropologist on Mars. She is someone who is able to report about the inner life of a person with autism to an audience who has no other access to understanding that life. As with all such anthropological journeys, the gaze is turned back on us. What we learn is how an autistic person views the world of the nonautistic, how strange she finds the rest of us. Grandin is a peculiar spokesperson in more than one sense. We probably do not question her identity as an autistic person; she is a good example of someone who constantly cautions her readers against taking her experiences as representative of all autistic persons, and she certainly is a person who can claim to understand autistic experiences, her own and others'. Just as clearly, we do question the anthropologist's identity as a person who knows enough or is entitled to write about or who constructs a discourse that conceals its apparatus for representing others' experiences.

In his essay "The Storyteller," Walter Benjamin suggests that storytelling in everyday life has fallen in value because experience has fallen in value (1968: 84). Experience in Benjamin's discussion is not information; it is not "what happened," but rather, experience is what is passed on in storytelling from the teller to those listening (1968: 159). Creating memories is one and the same with creating a subjectivity (Benjamin, 1968: 160). The distinction between two kinds of experience is crucial to Benjamin's understanding of storytelling. *Erfahrung* is the accumulated knowledge based on repeated practice, and *Erlebnis* is the lived experience, which he describes as a shock experience. Here Benjamin is contrasting our two understandings of the word *experience,* first, as accumulated knowledge—Benjamin's example is the artisan who learns to perfect a task over time (1968: 176)—and, second, as participation in or apprehension of an event or sensation. The first category is experience as knowledge; to be experienced is to know something. The second is experience as suffering; to experience an event is to suffer it. Both kinds of experience involve possession but in different ways, and I would suggest it is in conflating these two kinds of experience that subjectivity becomes aligned with experience as an essential or natural category.

Experience is what gives the artisan his or her identity. At the same time, being aligned with one's work, not separating oneself from one's knowledge, is the problem that constrains subjects to the limits of their knowledge. This is the classic problem of the housewife, a nonsubject in the world of work, or the factory worker, a nonsubject in the life of the machine. Here, where experience counts as knowledge, one person's narrative can represent a collective experience. Experience is essentially remembrance. Benjamin suggests that this sort of experience is no longer possible; remembrance of this sort, as the wisdom passed down through the ages, has been supplanted by a filtering or censoring process that leaves us with fragmented rather than integrated experiences. (I note that Benjamin invents an integrated world in order to describe its disintegration.) Benjamin's point is that shock experience is sui generis and counts for nothing; there is no possibility of the accumulation of knowledge or experience (Wolin, 1994: 233–34). In the modern age, accumulated experience is disrupted and is replaced with shock experience. Modern life, Benjamin suggested, is characterized by shock experiences, and the experience of shock is tied to the emergence of the crowd in urban life. The second use of the word *experience,* to suffer an event, is, not surprisingly, a modern invention (R. Williams, 1976: 100). The second kind of experience, in which one suffers an event, is always a shock. If in the first kind of experience, the subject is aligned with the experience—one is one's narrative—in the second kind of experience, in which one suffers events, the problem is the opposite; the experience is larger than the subject or threatens to overcome the subject, and the process of narration is a painful effort to emerge as a subject. As Dori Laub writes:

> The victim's narrative—the very process of bearing witness to massive trauma—does indeed begin with someone who testifies to an absence, to an event that has not yet come into existence, in spite of the overwhelming and compelling nature of the reality of its occurrence. While historical evidence to the event which constitutes the trauma—as a known event and not simply as an overwhelming shock—has not been truly witnessed yet, not been taken cognizance of. The emergence of the narrative which is being listened to— and heard—is, therefore, the process and the place wherein the cognizance, the "knowing" of the event is given birth to. The listener, therefore, is a party to the creation of knowledge *de novo*. (1992: 57)

Shock experience, then, creates a new kind of problematic relationship between the subject and memory; in my terms, it is a particular alignment between subjectivity and experience. The disappearance of an overwhelmed subject can take various forms. In Baudelaire's work, for example, Benjamin points out, those who are shocked are not a collective but an amorphous crowd (1968: 165). In Laub's discussion of witness accounts of the Holocaust, the subject is overwhelmed by the trauma. In both cases there is no narrative at the outset. The narrative and the subject emerge together. This same rubric is used to describe the emergence of Grandin's narrative. As Oliver Sacks would have it, we do not know that persons with autism have selves until we see this sort of narrative in which a person with autism produces her subjectivity.

But, and this is where my suspicion sets in again, I am not sure that that is what occurs in Grandin's narrative. In fact, it may be quite the contrary. She seems to be telling us that she understands the discourse of autobiography well enough to construct the kind of narrative we expect, but that aside from this production she cannot promise to be the sort of self ordinarily produced in such autobiographies. Both in her book and in the interview Oliver Sacks wrote about in the *New Yorker,* Grandin says, "If I could snap my fingers and be nonautistic, I would not. Autism is part of what I am. Donna Williams says, 'Autism is not me. Autism is just an information processing problem that controls who I am.' Who is right? I think we both are, because we are on different parts of the autism spectrum. I would not want to lose my ability to think visually. I have found my place along the great continuum" (quoted in Grandin, 1995: 60–61). Grandin describes her life in terms of her mostly successful effort to control sensory input. Too much sensory input is at the least disturbing, and usually painful. Donna Williams is on a different part of the great autistic spectrum in part because Williams has so much difficulty experiencing more than one kind of sensory input at a time. For example, Williams prefers to talk on the telephone rather than face to face, since that way she can experience only auditory, rather than also visual, input. In other words (in my own words rather than any Grandin might use), the autism makes direct sensory experience a problem; autism prevents experiencing an integrated world in which experience provides knowledge out of which one recognizes oneself. The experience of autism, then, is not unlike the fragmentary nature of modern experience as described by Benjamin except that the person with autism does not know, does not contain memories of, an integrated premodern sense of self. In the end, after reading Grandin's book, I felt that Oliver Sacks had violated her narrative by translating it into some sort of redemption for the rest of us in his claim that we finally have a glimpse into the autistic self. I was surprised that he confused the familiarity of the narrative form with the creation of the subject, especially when, in page after page, Grandin tells us all of the ways in which she does not construct her subjectivity according to those conventions.

The issue isn't meaning in the sense of perspectival determinacy—did we understand the text correctly?—but in the sense of the cultural and social conditions in which meanings are made. Focus on the first kind obscures the second kind; they are "opaque signifiers" in which we can't clarify the signifier. As Roland Barthes argues, the match is no longer possible (1968: 69). I suggest that one piece of the gap, the lack of match, what I call the vulnerability, of narrative authority (and the problem of speaking for others), is the implied redemptive promise of empathy in telling other people's stories. Personal experience gets reported (as reported speech) and translated into larger-than-personal allegorical representations. The allegorical appears to be monolithic, but it is contingent and we have to look for what holds it in place—especially the idea that personal experiences are more real than other representations. In every use of allegory, we find hidden vulnerabilities.

Both Benjamin and Joan Scott have tied our understanding of experience and subjectivity to the production of narrative. We learn from them, and from others who have written about nostalgia for narratives of coherent selves and the fragmentary nature of modern narratives, about the ways in which narratives essentialize both identity and experience. To oversimplify for a moment, what we end up with then, in the modern period, is a continuum of narrative alignments from, at one end, fragmentary narratives in which the subject is erased or overwhelmed, in which, in other words, the trauma of the loss of experience is exposed and, at the other end, seemingly coherent narratives in which identities are aligned with experiences, in which the narrator seems to represent his or her own experiences. Benjamin was more concerned with the traumas of history. Scott is equally concerned with the essentialist narratives. Both scholars have reminded us that we cannot discard either end of the spectrum, nor should we want to. To discard the fragmentary would be an act of false consciousness, a hopeless act of trying to reinstate authority (or, in Benjamin's terms, *aura*). Instead, Benjamin recommends those narratives, such as in Baudelaire, that conjure past collectivities out of modern ruins (Wolin, 1994: 235). Fragmentary narratives, then, offer some redemptive possibility.

Laments about the failures of narrative are also laments about the possibilities of redemption, and indeed, it is probably the possibilities of redemption that prompt questions about narratives' failings in the first place. For example, in a discussion of the failure of narrative as a means for feminist liberation, Naomi Schor points to "the need for narratives that redeem the past" (1995: 163).

Anthropologist Marilyn Strathern describes the feminist emphasis on experience as "knowledge which cannot be appropriated by others" (quoted in Visweswaran, 1987: 20). I question whether this is possible or desirable. Scott's discussion, also, though an indictment of the uses of experience as a natural category, ends with a call for "analysis of the production of knowledge" (1992: 37). No one advocates ignoring or discarding narratives that claim to produce coherent selves, an essential alignment between identity and experience. The question is what to do with them. Leigh Gilmore's suggestion is to "put pressure on the suggestion that coming-out narratives, confessional narratives, and consciousness-raising narratives are regressive attempts to claim a representative and mimetic function for first-person writing. Instead, these narratives can be understood as a canny raid on the discourses of truth and identity. Further, they are effective as political rhetoric precisely to the extent that they claim to 'speak the truth' at a particular time and in a particular place" (1994: 226). Similarly, in his discussion of the allegorical dimension of ethnography, James Clifford suggests, "If we are condemned to tell stories we cannot control, may we not, at least, tell stories we believe to be true" (1986b: 121).

The dismantling or deconstruction of experience and coherent selves as essentialist categories, especially in narrative, is not an academic exercise. Rather, in Benjamin's terms, it is the crucial piece to understand if we are to create a new sort of redemptive narrative to replace the failed grand narratives. In Scott's and several other feminists' terms it is the key strategy for understanding the processes of the production of knowledge and power.

Feminist discussions of personal experience as political have turned Benjamin's model on its head. Whereas Benjamin laments that experiences "are at best meaningful for the individual but have forfeited the attribute of universality from which the element of wisdom, the moral of the story, traditionally derived" (Wolin, 1994: 220), for feminists, personal stories offer the very possibilities for redemption that Benjamin desired. In feminists' hands, stories about everyday life are our collective wisdom. However, as Elizabeth Bellamy and Artemis Leontis point out, "the project of documenting women's changing 'experiences' from their own perspectives proves to be a reductive one, whose single-minded purpose is to record cultural variations on the recurring theme of rights trampled, power denied, entitlements lost, voices unheard, and/or to celebrate individual cases in which women achieve some equality with men" (1993: 176). Bellamy and Leontis suggest that "the central problem with feminism's appropriation of experience . . . is that a politics of experience has, up to this point, constituted itself only on the level of the personal" (1993: 177). They recommend following Ernest Laclau and Chantal Mouffe's suggestion to recognize "'experience' as the limit of the social" (Bellamy and Leontis, 1993: 179). The personal and the ordinary cannot be grasped without understanding the ways in which they are appropriated in public narrative. Over and over again, scholars discuss the "experiential pull" (Hall, 1994: 528), but discussion turns inevitably to the public appropriation of experience and the category of the personal experience remains unproblematized.

Using the narrative of personal experience to create identity—and this is the premise of identity politics—makes personal narratives more than personal (Fuss, 1989: 99). When essential identities depend upon narrative, that is when as in Judith Butler's example of gender as performative (1990: 25), identity must be continually performed, reenacted and retold (one must come out again in every new situation), essential identities are constantly in question. When essential identities depend on narrative, our identities are always more than our narratives. In Benjamin's terms, narratives of shock experience (reperformed identities) replace the authority and aura of a story of experience in which identity is the same as the accumulated experience of repeated practice and knowledge. In narratives in which identity is reenacted with each performance, identity cannot be stable but instead betrays its constructedness, its strategic essentialism. The problem with such strategies of essentialism, Butler points out, is that "strategies always have meanings that exceed the purposes for which they are intended" (1990: 4). When identities depend on the narration of experience, both the identity and the experience exceed the boundaries of that narrative—we are more than our narratives, and our experiences are larger than we, belonging to others as well as ourselves. The excess of identity, experience, and purposes is most evident when narratives represent more than our own experiences, as in the case of Grandin's narrative representing autistic experience more generally. That excess of representation is necessary for narrative to have meaning. Grandin resists at all points representing the inner life of autism, but it is the possibility of that larger representation that makes her narrative important, and notable to someone like Oliver Sacks.

Empathy presumes the ability to understand another's life story; its opposite, the inability to empathize, is reserved for situations that the normal person cannot imagine, including, notably, unspeakable evils and insanity (Binswanger, 1958: 226). In other words, empathy describes the sphere of the normal and allows us to imagine what any normal person would do (Binswanger, 1958: 227). Empathy is the failed promise of stories that travel beyond their owners. When we read Grandin's book, we are aware of what we have learned and of what we don't understand. The promise of empathy is most useful if we understand it, in Benjamin's terms, as nostalgia, for a lost past or never known, as a ruin, representing gaps in our shared understanding, or as a wish to understand across a divide. It is as much about the gap in recognizing that other people's stories are not our own as it is about the use of those stories to make new meanings.

To address these vulnerabilities in the retelling of other people's stories, I have proposed that we begin by asking a few questions: whose story is it (the question of entitlement), what is it being used for (what is the allegory), what does it promise (empathy, redemption, meaning), and at whose expense? Together, these questions help us to address not only how other people's stories traverse boundaries but also and importantly how they fail this redemptive promise. These are the fundamental questions ethnographers ask.

Empathy is, in a sense, the uncharted territory of ethnographic representation. Ethnographers are enjoined to understand cultures as they would understand themselves, a project that might seem at first glance to place ethnographers at a distance and thus to release them from representing their own emotional responses. The ethnographer is entitled to report because he or she is in the privileged position as witness, translator, and perhaps conduit to a larger audience. The ethonographer's empathy is inescapable and is the stance that threatens to undermine the whole enterprise. Ethnographies of suffering return us to the questions that opened the debates about ethnography. Those debates were motivated by the question of whom and what purpose ethnography serves. Is the academic pursuit of knowledge a sufficient purpose? Look at how ethnography can be misused by those desiring more power over others. Ethnographies of suffering do not escape the questions of the purpose of ethnography; rather, they insist, sometimes even more explicitly than the scientific rationale, on knowledge as redemption and on the possibility that telling untold stories might make a better world.

NOTES

INTRODUCTION: SUBVERSIVE STORIES AND THE CRITIQUE OF EMPATHY

1. Claims of this sort may be found in many books on narrative. For example, "This book is an inquiry into narrative, the primary form by which human experience is made meaningful. Narrative meaning is a cognitive process that organizes human experiences into temporally meaningful episodes" (Polkinghorne, 1988: 1). Hayden White also begins one of his books with a claim for narrative: "So natural is the impulse to narrate, so inevitable is the form of narrative for any report on the way things really happened, that narrativity could appear problematical only in a culture in which it was absent—or, as in some domains of contemporary Western intellectual and artistic culture, programmatically refused. . . . Far from being a problem, then, narrative might well be considered a solution to a problem of general human concern, namely, the problem of how to translate knowing into telling, the problem of fashioning human experience into a form assimilable to structures of meaning that are generally human rather than culture-specific" (1987: 1). See Brian McHale (1992: 4–8) for a review of narrative claims and claims for narrative.

2. The concept of a failed promise builds on Walter Benjamin's understanding of the failed promises of the Enlightenment, reason, and technology to bring forth a "truly human history" (Buck-Morss, 1991: 64). In his famous "Theses on the Philosophy of History," Benjamin outlines a redemptive criticism that depends on understanding what he described as "the secret agreement between past generations and the present one" (Wolin, 1994: 235). To counter the disintegration of experience into a meaningless series of events, Benjamin proposes the recovery of the fragmentation of the past, in part as a palliative to the myth of progress. He proposes "not to redeem the past but to redeem the desire for utopia to which humanity has persistently given expression" (Buck-Morss, 1991: 245). Benjamin's efforts to secularize redemptive criticism (Wolin, 1994: 264) provide the framework I use to understand narrative in this book.

3. I draw on Benjamin's concept of allegory, an important dimension of his redemptive criticism. In Buci-Glucksmann's interpretation of Benjamin, allegory is "the language of a torn and broken world, the representation of the unrepresentable, allegory fixes dreams by laying bare reality" (1994: 70).

4. See Leo Bersani, "The value of our capacity to identify sympathetically with the pain or suffering of others has, of course, generally been taken for granted. It has been assumed that this capacity is central both to our responses to art and to our capacity for moral behavior. . . .

sympathy associated with sexual pleasure. . . . [T]here is a certain risk in all sympathetic projections: the pleasure that accompanies them promotes a secret attachment to scenes of suffering or violence. The very operation of sympathy partially undermines the moral solidarity that we like to think of as its primary effect" (quoted in Greenblatt, 1981: 150).

5. See Mikhail Bakhtin's discussion of empathy as a foundational element of aesthetic contemplation (1990: 25).

6. For example, Elspeth Probyn in her work on autobiography, claims that the "personal voice within cultural theory highlights some crucial epistemological questions now facing the human sciences" (1993: 105).

7. For example, consider Pierre Bourdieu's important work on the public and private, everyday and extraordinary: "'Private' experiences undergo nothing less than a change of state when they recognize themselves in the *public objectivity* of an already constituted discourse, the objective sign of recognition of their right to be spoken and to be spoken publicly" (1994: 166).

8. For example, see Jonathan Yardley's review of Barbara Holland's *Wasn't the Grass Greener?: A Curmudgeon's Fond Memories:* "In all major population centers you'll find a coffeehouse where poets go to read works expressing their inmost feelings, a free and effortless new form of therapy. . . . Once considered an art form that called for practice, a poem now needs only sincerity" (*International Herald Tribune,* July 13, 1999). Also see John van Manaan on the confessional genre in anthropological writing.

9. Donna Haraway cites Linda Marie Fedigan, a feminist primatologist, who had "misgivings about the wider implications of female empathy." Haraway comments, "Empathy is both part of a code in a narrative and a culturally specific way to *construct* what counts as experience. The relevance of 'empathy' as a problematic, gender-charged scientific practice was less Fedigan's point than the salience of the debate on empathy to an insistence on seeing primates—people and animals—as complex co-actors in the crafting of knowledge at particular historical moments" (1989: 316–17).

10. Girard Genette's work on focalization (1980) and the choices a narrator makes to provide more or less information than is necessary for the listener is particularly helpful here. In a discussion of point of view and the question of how narrative perspective is oriented, Genette discusses the distinction between who sees and who speaks (186), and although his focus is works of literature, it is useful for developing a theory of the relationship between speakers and listeners/witnesses in conversational narrative.

11. Young (1987) elaborates on the points of intersection between taleworld and storyrealm and, important, does not regard these as discrete ontologies.

12. Building on William Labov's (1972) work on the concept of evaluation in narrative, I compare narrative texts to observe whether or not the storyrealm and taleworld collapse in evaluative moments. I argue that evaluation in narrative often can be used to understand the relationship between taleworld and storyrealm.

13. The Personal Narratives Group discusses "'counter-narratives'—narrative elements in personal accounts which contrast self-image and experiences with dominant cultural models" (1989: 11). M. Keith Booker argues that strategies of subversion "can be grouped according to their relationship to the dual concepts of abjection and the carnivalesque" (1991: 245).

14. For a critique of the concept of experience, see Scott (1988). For a discussion of the local, see Robbins (1993: 181), Shuman (1993a), and Visvanathan (1997: 111).

15. Adorno's actual words need to be contextualized within a dialectic on culture and barbarism: "The more total society becomes, the greater the reification of the mind and the more paradoxical its effort to escape reification on its own. Even the most extreme con-

sciousness of doom threatens to degenerate into idle chatter. Cultural criticism finds itself faced with the final stage of the dialectic of culture and barbarism. To write poetry after Auschwitz is barbaric. And this corrodes even the knowledge of why it has become impossible to write poetry today" (quoted in Zuidervaart, 1991: 7). See also specific discussions of trauma narrative, especially Caruth (1995), Couser (1997), and Frank (1995).

16. Dell Hymes discusses prejudices against narrative within the context of "cultural stereotypes [that] predispose us to dichotomize forms and functions of language use" (1996: 113). He suggests that we understand the rejection of narrative as evidence in this context. "Narrative forms of evidence would be dismissed as anecdotal, even where narrative might be the only form in which the evidence, or voice, was available. But the dismissal would be an application to others of a principle the user would not consistently apply to himself or herself—a principle, indeed, that no one could consistently apply, if I am right in thinking that narrative forms of thinking are inescapably fundamental in human life" (1996: 114).

17. Buci-Glucksmann writes, "Modernity is characterized by a loss of experience and a phantasmagoria of commodities which, like their opposite—the return to lived experience (*Erlebnis*) in Dilthey or Bergson—remain caught up in the fluid continuity of time. The experience of *Erfahrung*, on the other hand, always starts out from a break in time, in the empty, homogeneous continuity of historicism" (1984: 110).

18. See Susan Buck-Morss (1991: 68) and Anthony Wilden (1968: 164).

19. See William Labov's important discussion of narrative chronology in which he defines narrative as "one method of recapitulating past experience by matching a verbal sequence of clauses to the sequence of events which (it is inferred) actually occurred" (1972: 360).

20. *Paradigm* is Roland Barthes's term for chronological frameworks in narrative; scholars interested in narrative and memory use the term *schema* (Schank, 1990). I discuss the structural analysis of narrative, especially the work of A. J. Greimas, in later chapters.

21. In the introduction to their book, the Personal Narrative Group authors write, "The act of constructing a life narrative forces the author to move from accounts of discrete experiences to an account of why and how the life took the shape it did" (1989: 4).

22. The examples I discuss in this chapter are taken from a variety of sources, including ethnographies, newspapers, and magazines, and metanarrative comments collected in my own informal conversations with people. The examples have in common the topic of narrative about suffering, but they represent a range of historical cultural situations and are offered here not as evidence to support a position nor to generalize about narrative properties but as an indication of the diversity of problems to be considered.

23. Frederic Jameson refers to "a sometimes repressed ur-narrative or master fantasy about the interaction of collective subjects" (1981: 80).

24. Hayden White explores the crisis of representation in historical narrative. In a volume titled "Pluralism and Its Discontents," White argues against creating a separate category for measuring the validity of historical (rather than fictional) narrative. Following Ricoeur, he writes, "Historical accounts cast in the form of a narrative may be as various as the *modes of emplotment* which literary critics have identified as constituting the different principles for structuring narratives in general." He adds, "This is not to say that certain events never occurred or that we have no reasons for believing in their occurrence" (1987: 487).

25. My discussion of entitlement is based on Harvey Sacks's introduction of this concept. He specifically describes entitlement in narrative in terms of a claim to have suffered an experience (1992: vol. 2, p. 568).

26. Harvey Sacks's groundbreaking discussions of entitlement specifically use the language of having suffered an experience (1992: vol. 2, pp. 229–48). Roland Barthes discusses the assertion "this happened" in historical discourse (1970: 154).

27. See Arthur Frank's model for understanding categories of narrative. He distinguishes between what he calls restitution narratives, chaos narratives, and quest narratives, each offering opportunities to constrain or liberate tellers (1995). G. Thomas Couser builds on Frank's work in a close examination of narratives about particular illnesses and disabilities (1997).

28. The Memorial to Our Lost Children, created by Columbus, Ohio, artist Stephen Canetto, includes testimonials and artifacts provided by parents whose children had been murdered. I was involved in initial meetings to design the collection project.

29. This follows Hymes's description of "The Ethnography of Speaking" (1974).

CHAPTER 1: "GET OUTA' MY FACE"

1. See, for example, Edward Said's discussion of colonialists' claims to speak for their subjects (1978: 34–35). In a typical entitlement challenge in a film review, Laurence Jarvik and Nancy Strickland ask, "Did Louis Malle have a right to make *Au Revoir Les Enfants*?" They discuss "the propriety of a French Catholic person filming what is perceived to be a Jewish subject" (1988: 72).

2. See Aaron V. Cicourel's discussion of conversation studies and shared knowledge (1974: 42–73).

3. See, for example, Pliskin, 1975, a book-length discourse on the appropriate and inappropriate uses of information about other people in orthodox Jewish society.

4. Rather than follow conventions for describing an ethnographic present, I use the past tense to indicate observations about the adolescent community during the period 1979–81, and the present tense for this discussion. See Wolfson, 1978.

5. For a discussion of storytelling situations, see Young, (1987, chap. 1).

6. All persons' names as well as the name of the school and newspaper are pseudonyms. A question mark indicates a raise in intonation; a new numbered line indicates a pause.

7. See Amy Horowitiz's discussion of ownership in the context of culture in disputed territory. She distinguishes between appropriation and heritance (2005).

8. Richard Bauman finds that verbal punchlines that use direct discourse in contrast to preceding lines using indirect discourse are effective by rekeying a situation, overturning the apparent direction of the interaction and the moral alignments and attitudes that have seemed to control it, and establishing an ironic alternative, not as a substitute but as a coexistent perspective. The effect of the punchline is to that extent subversive, a breakthrough both on the part of the one who is reported to have spoken it and on the part of the narrator into a kind of skepticism and relativism that takes pleasure in refusing to take ideal, normative moral expectations too seriously—a "comic corrective" (1986: 75).

9. Michel Butor suggests that the use of first- or third-person narration is a literary convention:

It is easy to show that, in the novel, the simplest, most basic narrative form is the third person, and that each time an author uses another, he does so in a sense figuratively—inviting us not to take it as literally but to superimpose it on the basic form which is always implied. (1965: 75)

10. For a discussion of reported and described speech, see Ryan (1981: 127–55).

11. See, for example, Jacques Derrida's discussion of face, and thus orality, as unmediated proximity, "The face does not *signify*" (1978: 100).

12. This position is taken, for example, by Benjamin R. Barber (The most sublime event, *Nation,* March 12, 1990).

CHAPTER 2: COLLECTIVE MEMORY AND PUBLIC FORGETTING

1. See Elizabeth Bellamy and Artemis Leontis's (1993) cautions about the move from the personal to the social.

2. Narratives positioned against each other in a dialogic relationship are discussed by Edward Bruner and Phyllis Gorfain (1984), Charles Briggs (1986) and M. M. Bakhtin (1981, 1990).

3. Carol Bohmer and I discuss refugee narratives more extensively in "Representing Trauma" (2004).

4. See M. M. Bakhtin's discussion of suffering (1990: 102–4).

5. In this chapter, I endeavor to unpack the connection between structural similarities and the judgment that the story is not believable. Contemporary-legend scholars have done important work to identify similar reports of extraordinary experiences. However, in contrast to the legend scholars, I am interested in those cases in which the similarity in structure points not to a proliferating legend but to the relationship between personal and collective versions of events.

6. More is at stake in the distinction between the personal and the collective story than a difference between individual performance and collective memory. Especially, in these narratives that use personal narrative to describe group oppression, what is at stake is the distribution and ownership of knowledge.

7. *Ratified tellers* is Erving Goffman's term (1971: 565).

8. I add these parentheses as a cautionary note. Many writers on narrative make a leap from the ability to produce a coherent narrative to the idea of an integrated self, and this leap not only generates the huge claims made for narrative (referred to at the beginning of this book) but also obscures the more significant ways that narrative represents the opposite; that is, narrative represents the fragmentation of self.

9. In Derrida's terms, this is the "law of genre" (1980: 212). See also Peter Seitel's discussion of genre in *The Powers of Genre* (1999).

10. Barbara Kirshenblatt-Gimblett describes this as "cohort awareness": "Autobiography is a particularly revealing document for studying what might be called cohort awareness, the point where the individual life and the historical moment converge. Such an approach foregrounds the social nature of memory as a collaborative project" (1989: 125). Sam Schrager observes, "[E]xperience narrative mediates between individual of personal narrative and group emphasis of folk history" (quoted in Kirshenblatt-Gimblett, 1989: 143).

11. From 1982 to the present, I have conducted oral history interviews with the artisans of Pietrasanta, Italy.

12. Consider, for example, ethnographies in which the discussion is more about ourselves than about the natives, or less about the particular experiences of a particular anthropologist than about the discipline of anthropology (Clifford, 1986c, 1988). I return to this issue in chapter 6.

CHAPTER 3: ALLEGORY AND PARABLE AS SUBVERSIVE STORIES

1. *Performance arena* is John Foley's term for "the locus in which some specialized form

of communication is uniquely licensed to take place" (1995: 8). Foley observes "that the more 'dedicated' a register is to a particular function . . . the more economically it can convey meaning" (1995: 16). Allegory would qualify as a dedicated register that depends on the communicative competence of the audience (Hymes, 1974), who would be able to apply the allegory to other relevant situations.

2. See, for example, Gregory Ulmer's discussion of allegory (1983).

3. See Mark Workman's discussion of unfinished narrative (1995).

4. As Andreas Huyssen observes, "[T]he simply remembered past may turn into mythic memory . . . a stumbling block to the needs of the present rather than an opening in the continuum of history" (1986: 239). Buci-Glucksmann writes, "Allegories are always allegories of oblivion, for through them is expressed the unfreedom of men and women, and no writing which sides with victors' history, or which, even from the Left postulates an evolutionary continuity, has ever been able to reveal that infinite servitude" (1984: 46–47).

5. As Gregory Ulmer notes, "[N]arrative allegory favors the material of the signifier over the meanings of the signifieds" (1983: 95).

6. See Barbara Herrnstein Smith's *Contingencies of Value* (1988).

7. I am grateful to Diane Schaffer who collected this story as part of another research project. I discuss this material in Shuman, 1993b.

8. I borrow this phrase from Patti Lather and Chris Smithies, *Troubling the Angels* (1997).

CHAPTER 4: SMALL-WORLD STORIES

1. I refer here to the fantastic in Todorov's sense of an event that cannot be explained by the familiar world. The fantastic sets up a relationship between the real and the imaginary (1975: 25).

2. See, for example, *Small Miracles* and the many *Chicken Soup for the Soul* books.

3. Commentary on this passage and the accompanying "Haftorah" portion assigned to this passage and read along with it by Jews specifically uses the terms *reconciliation, reunification, restoration,* and *redemption.*

4. Stories told by tourists who find neighbors in exotic places often focus on the improbability of the encounter. See Martha Weinman Lear, "Close Encounters of the Improbable Kind" (*New York Times,* February, 16, 2003).

5. See Richard Bauman's discussion of the punchline in *Story, Performance, and Event* (1986). Small-world stories often begin with what would be the punchline; they could be described as stories told backwards, recovering an initial situation that is only revealed at the end.

6. From *Small Miracles,* Copyright ©1997 by Yitta Halberstam Mandelbaum and Judith Frankel Leventhal. Used with permission of Adams Media. All rights reserved.

7. See also Jack Zipes's discussion of how fairy tales preserve or critique the social status quo (1979, 1983).

CHAPTER 5: REDEMPTION AND EMPATHY IN JUNK-MAIL NARRATIVES

1. Linda Martin Alcoff reports, "There is a strong, albeit contested, current within feminism which holds that speaking for others—even for other women—is arrogant, vain, unethical, and politically illegitimate" (1995: 98). As Alcoff explains, two central premises have dominated the concerns about speaking on behalf of others: first, "a speaker's location . . .

has an epistemically significant impact on that speaker's claims and can serve either to authorize or de-authorize her speech" and, second, "certain privileged locations are discursively dangerous" (1995: 98–99).

2. In a 1991 lecture, poet David Whyte comments on "the difference between first hand experience and second hand experience. First hand experience is yours, and yet it's yours at such a depth that it joins a commonality, um, which belongs to everyone."

3. Lyotard offers the term *petit recit* as "the quintessential form of imaginative invention, most particularly in science" (1984: 60).

4. Bakhtin's dialogic is, in Iris Zavala's terms, "an 'event' in which the whole is not constructed as a single consciousness absorbing other consciousnesses as objects into itself, but is an interaction of several consciousnesses, none of which becomes an object for the other" (1990: 85).

5. "[Feminist emancipatory politics] advocate[s] multiple forms and sites of struggle. They distrust totalizing claims, large scale organization and hierarchy, and strategies or directives developed and handed down from above. They put forth visions of local politics . . ." (Alway, 1995: 136).

6. See Judith Irvine's discussion of the participant roles in speech events. Reported speech is one way of constructing absent parties to an exchange; Irvine suggests a useful distinction between alignable and excluded parties (1996: 146).

7. *Heteroglossia,* Bakhtin's term for double-voicedness, is achieved through the juxtaposition and lamination of voices, the suffering individual, whose voice appears in the form of quotation, the political observers, and the addressee. The person is made into a global issue; what is at work here is the dismantling of local culture.

In the glossary to *The Dialogic Imagination,* editor Michael Holquist defines *heteroglossia:*

> The base condition governing the operation of meaning in any utterance. It is that which insures the primacy of context over text. At any given time, in any given place, there will be a set of conditions—social, historical, meteorological, physiological—that will insure that a word uttered in that place and at that time will have a meaning different than it would have under any other conditions; all utterances are heteroglot in that they are functions of a matrix of forces practically impossible to recoup, and therefore impossible to resolve. Heteroglossia is as close a conceptualization as is possible of that locus where centripetal and centrifugal forces collide; as such, it is that which a systematic linguistics must always suppress. (Bakhtin, 1981: 428)

Bakhtin's concept of heteroglossia sees decontextualization as a virtue. Heteroglossia makes possible the critique of authoritative discourse and thus has emancipatory potential. However, all forms of decontextualization are not the same for Bakhtin; he identifies the novel as a form that decentralizes the otherwise centralizing or standardizing forces of dominant languages. The novel, as many writers on narrative have observed, provides the possibility for what Bakhtin termed *polyphony,* or the possible disjuncture between points of view of authors, narratives, characters, and, some would add, readers. Parody in the novel, to use one of Bakhtin's examples, creates a double-voicedness, which "refers simultaneously to two contexts of enunciation: that of the present enunciation and that of a previous one" (Todorov, 1984: 71).

8. See Briggs (1996). Charles Briggs's edited volume *Disorderly Discourse* includes many examples of contested causes.

9. See A. J. Greimas's discussion of "figurative trajectories" in narrative (1987: 117). Narratives utilize syntagmatic sequences to configure relationships between characters and

their actions, and at particular points in a narrative, the syntagmatic sequence creates a choice. The characters' choices are often predetermined, but the road not taken is nonetheless implied.

10. The absence of any account of the pain until it "came back to her" requires the reader/listener to infer that the abortion was the origin of the pain and it was something Joan experienced at the time. Harvey Sacks describes the relevance rules operating in such narratives as "category-bound activities," in which we understand that an activity "has a special relevance for formulating an identification of its doer" (1972: 338).

11. See Rajeswari Sunder Rajan and Zakia Pathak (1989). See also Gayatri Chakravorty Spivak's discussion of "Shabano" in "Reading *The Satanic Verses*," (1989: 88–90).

12. See Susan Stewart's discussion of the testimony of the victim: "We thereby are able to conclude that the tension between the private and the public generates certain rhetorical moves regardless of the specific content or focus of the discourse" (1988: 183–84). Further, "In the Meese Commission's Report, the tension between representation and contagion exerts an unbearable pressure, a pressure permitting the invention of a sexuality so powerful and pervasive that the state must analogously be invented in order to suppress and control it" (Stewart, 1988: 180). In abortion discussions, the issue is what has been or needs to be invented to exert what kinds of control.

13. See Laclau and Mouffe: "In a revolutionary situation, it is impossible to fix the literal sense of each isolated struggle, because each struggle overflows its own literality and comes to represent in the consciousness of the masses, a simple moment of a more global struggle against the system. . . . This is however, nothing other than the defining characteristic of the symbol: the overflowing of the signifier by the signified" (1985: 10–11).

See also the critique by John Rosenthal: "'The unity of the class' is not, then, a 'symbolic unity,' but rather precisely the theoretical unity attributed to the complexity of an 'overflowing' and overdetermining signified which is brought into relation with any fragmentary instance of struggle as its metonymic condensation. In short, 'the unity of the class' is *the signified*. (Which is not to deny that here as elsewhere 'the signified' is itself already a signifier, and that thus in a metonym we are dealing with, as Lacan puts it, 'a word-to-word connexion' and not a connection between 'word and concept' or 'word and thing')" (1988: 35).

14. Andrew Ross writes: "To ask whose interests are served by 'universal abandon' is not to hark back to a more straightforward kind of oppositional politics—our interests or their interests?—in which the left clearly 'owned' or appropriated what the right had lost. On the contrary, it is to problematize the very questions of interests in an age when interests can no longer be universalized, and for a politics in which identities are not already *there*, to be reflected as unitary in already constituted forms of struggle" (1988: xvii).

15. I have discussed this point more elaborately in earlier work (Shuman, 1986: 195).

16. I discuss the relationship between local and global in cultural studies in more detail in Shuman (1993a).

17. Or see, for example, the appropriation of the "thinking globally, executing locally" idea in the use of suitable Coca-Cola examples for different cultures, discussed in O'Barr and Moreira (1989).

18. I discuss this point in "Dismantling Local Culture" (Shuman, 1993a).

19. Charlotte Linde writes, "Narrative is thus an extremely powerful tool for creating, negotiating, and displaying the moral standing of the self. This is centrally established by the evaluation component of narrative and by the social negotiation of evaluation" (1993: 123).

20. See Slavoj Zizek's discussion of the paradox of subjectivization (1989: 171–74).

21. James Phelan's model for distinguishing between three components of character is useful here. The characters in the junk-mail narratives have elements of all three compo-

nents: "the mimetic (character as person), the thematic (character as idea), and the synthetic (character as artificial construct)" (1996: 29). Each of these character components presents different possibilities for the reader's understanding and judgment of the character's actions and words. The junk-mail narratives blur these categories so that the character represents a named person, the idea of the suffering, and the hypothetical (even you) oppressed person.

22. See Charles Taylor's discussion of "in interiore homine": "Augustine's proof of God is a proof from the first-person experience of knowing and reasoning. I am aware of my own sensing and thinking; and in reflecting on this, I am made aware of its dependence on something beyond it, something common. But this turns out on further examination to include not just objects to be known but also the very standards which reason gives allegiance to . . . By going inward, I am drawn upward" (1989: 134).

23. Judith Butler writes: "Untethering the speech act from the sovereign subject founds an alternative notion of agency and, ultimately, of responsibility, one that more fully acknowledges the way in which the subject is constituted in language, how what it creates is also what it derives from elsewhere. Whereas some critics mistake the critique of sovereignty for the demolition of agency, I propose that agency begins where sovereignty wanes" (1997: 15–16).

24. Ruthellen Josselson cites Heinz Kohut who writes, "Only through an empathic stance toward people's narration of their life experiences can we uncover the dialogic nature of the self—the dialogue within the self and the dialogue with the world that is the center of process in development and in living" (quoted in Josselson, 1995: 42). Josselson writes, "Empathy becomes an attitude of attention to the real world based in an effort to connect ourselves to it rather than to distance ourselves from it" (1995: 31).

CHAPTER 6: SPEAKING FROM EXPERIENCE

1. Citing the work of Richard Werbner, Marilin Strathern describes two kinds of narrative: "one cast in terms of an irreversible break between past and present, when the narrator looks back to good times where conditions of life were qualitatively different, while the other is a catalogue of cautionary recollections about how the significance of people's acts carry forward in time, when the circumstantial details about disputes and inheritances are forewarnings for the present relationships" (1995: 111).

2. I draw on Alfred Schutz's phenomenological work as well as on sociolinguistic studies of the everyday, such as Douglas (1970).

3. "In effect the neuro-physiological model consigns the autistic to an unautobiographical life. Multiple gaps in message transmissions force a limit to everyday autobiography, frustrating efforts to get a narrative based on memory fragments together at all, or to manipulate the story and its meanings in coherent and recitable narratives" (S. Smith, 1996: 231).

4. See Alan Singer's discussion of how fiction presupposes a worldview (1993: 7).

5. Referring to Benjamin, James Clifford writes, "the material analogue of allegory is thus the 'ruin,' an always disappearing structure that invites imaginative reconstruction" (1986b: 119).

6. "A first general point about conflict narrative is that it is difficult to sustain the premise that there can be narratives independent of the situations in which they are told" (Brenneis, 1996: 42).

7. As both Joan Scott and Teresa de Lauretis have pointed out, by reproducing or reinforcing identities/subjectivites, narratives reproduce ideological systems (Scott, 1992: 25; de Lauretis, 1984: 159).

BIBLIOGRAPHY

Abrahams, Roger. 1970. A performance-centered approach to gossip. *Man* 5:290–301.

Alcoff, Linda. 1991. The problem of speaking for others. *Cultural Critique* 20:5–32.

———. 1995. The problem of speaking for others. In *Who can speak: Authority and critical identity*, ed. Judith Roof and Robyn Wiegman, 97–119. Urbana: University of Illinois Press.

Alway, Joan. 1995. *Critical theory and political possibilities: Conceptions of emancipatory politics in the works of Horkheimer, Adorno, Marcuse, and Habermas.* Westport, Conn.: Greenwood Press.

Arendt, Hannah. 1968. *The origins of totalitarianism.* San Diego: Harcourt Brace Jovanovich.

Atkinson, Robert. 1995. *The gift of stories: Practical and spiritual applications of autobiography, life stories, and personal mythmaking.* Westport, Conn.: Bergin and Garvey.

Bakhtin, M. M. 1981. *The dialogic imagination: Four essays.* Ed. Michael Holquist. Trans. Caryl Emerson and Michael Holquist. Austin: University of Texas Press.

———. 1990. *Art and answerability: Early philosophical essays.* Eds. Michael Holquist and Vadim Liapunov. Trans. Vadim Liapunov. Austin: University of Texas Press.

Bal, Mieke. 1985. *Narratology: Introduction to the theory of narrative.* Toronto: University of Toronto Press.

Bamberg, Michael. 1997. *Narrative development: Six approaches.* Mahwah, N.J.: Erlbaum.

Barber, Benjamin R. 1990. The most sublime event. *Nation,* March 12.

Barsky, Robert F. 1991. The construction of the other and the destruction of the self: The case of the convention hearings. In *Encountering the other(s): Studies in literature, history, and culture,* ed. Gisela Brinker-Gabler, 79–100. Albany: State University of New York Press.

———. 1994. *Constructing a productive other: Discourse theory and the Convention Refugee Hearing.* Philadelphia: John Benjamins.

———. 2000. *Arguing and justifying: Assessing the convention refugees' choice of moment, motive, and host country* Burlington, Vt.: Ashgate Publishing.

Barthes, Roland. [1953] 1968. *Writing degree zero.* Trans. Annette Lavers and Colin Smith. New York: Hill and Wang.

———. 1970. Historical discourse. In *Introduction to structuralism,* ed. Michael Lane, 145–55. New York: Basic Books.

———. 1996. Introduction to the structural analysis of narrative. In *Narratology: an introduction,* ed. Susana Onega and Jose Angel Garcia, 45–60. New York: Longman.

Bateson, Gregory. 1979. *Mind and nature: A necessary unity.* New York: E. P. Dutton.

Battaglia, Debbora. 1995. On practical nostalgia: Self-prospecting among urban trobrian-
    ders. In *Rhetorics of self-making*, ed. Debbora Battaglia, 77–96. Berkeley: University
    of California Press.
Bauman, Richard. 1977. *Verbal art as performance*. Prospect Heights, Ill.: Waveland Press.
————. 1986. *Story, performance, and event: Contextual studies of oral narrative*. Cam-
    bridge, U.K.: Cambridge University Press.
Bellamy, Elizabeth J., and Artemis Leontis. 1993. A genealogy of experience: From epis-
    temology to politics. *Yale Journal of Criticism* 6(1): 163–84.
Ben-Amos, Dan, and Liliane Weissberg, eds. 1999. *Cultural memory and the construction
    of identity*. Detroit: Wayne State University Press.
Benjamin, Walter. [1955] 1968. *Illuminations*. Ed. and with an introd. by Hannah Arendt.
    Trans. Harry Zohn. New York: Harcourt, Brace, and World.
————. [1963] 1977. *The origin of German tragic drama*. Trans. John Osborne. London:
    NLB.
Bergson, Henri. 1929. *Matter and memory*. Trans. Nancy Margaret Paul and W. Scott
    Palmer. New York: Macmillan.
Berkhofer, Robert F., Jr. 1995. *Beyond the great story: History as text and discourse*. Cam-
    bridge, Mass.: Belknap Press of Harvard University Press.
Blight, James G. 2002. Critical oral history as a scholarly tool. *Chronicle of Higher Educa-
    tion Colloquy Live* <http://chronicle.com/colloquylive/2002/10/blight>.
Booker, M. Keith. 1991. *Techniques of subversion in modern literature: Transgression, ab-
    jection, and the carnivalesque*. Gainesville: University of Florida Press.
Bourdieu, Pierre. 1994. Structures, habitus, power: Basis for a theory of symbolic power. In
    Culture/power/history: A reader in contemporary social theory, ed. Nicholas B. Dirks,
    Geoff Eley, and Sherry B. Ortner, 155–99. Princeton, N.J.: Princeton University Press.
Brenneis Donald. 1996. Telling troubles: Narrative, conflict, and experience. In *Disorderly
    discourse: Narrative, conflict, and inequality*, ed. Charles Briggs, 41–52. Oxford, U.K.:
    Oxford University Press.
Brenneis, Donald, and Ronald K. S. Macaulay. 1996. *The matrix of language: Contempo-
    rary linguistic anthropology*. Boulder, Colo.: Westview Press.
Brenneis, Donald, and Fred R. Myers. 1984. *Dangerous words: Language and politics in
    the Pacific*. New York: New York University Press.
Briggs, Charles L., ed. 1996. *Disorderly discourse: Narrative, conflict, and inequality*. Ox-
    ford, U.K.: Oxford University Press.
Briggs, Charles L., and Richard Bauman. 1992. Genre, intertextuality, and social power.
    Journal of Linguistic Anthropology 2:131–72.
Briggs, Charles, and Clara Mantini-Briggs. 2003. *Stories in time of cholera: Racial profiling
    during a medical nightmare*. Berkeley: University of California Press.
Bruner, Edward, ed. 1984. *Text, play, and story: The construction and reconstruction of
    self and society*. Washington, D.C.: American Ethnological Society.
Bruner, Edward M., and Phyllis Gorfain. 1984. Dialogic narration and the paradoxes of
    masada. In *Text, play, and story: The construction and reconstruction of self and soci-
    ety*, ed. Edward M. Bruner, 56–79. Washington, D.C.: American Ethnological Society.
Bryson, Norman. 1990. *Looking at the overlooked: Four essays on still life painting*. Cam-
    bridge, Mass.: Harvard University Press.
Buci-Glucksmann, Christine. 1994. *Baroque reason: The aesthetics of modernity*. Trans.
    Patrick Camiller. London: Sage.
Buck-Morss, Susan. 1991. *The dialectics of seeing: Walter Benjamin and the Arcades Pro-
    ject*. Cambridge, Mass.: Massachusetts Institute of Technology Press.

Bunch, Charlotte. 1987. *Passionate politics*. New York: St. Martins.

Burke, Kenneth. 1950. *A rhetoric of motives*. New York: Prentice-Hall.

Butler, Judith. 1990. *Gender trouble: Feminism and the subversion of identity*. New York: Routledge.

———. 1997. *Excitable speech: A politics of the performative*. New York: Routledge.

———. 2003. Afterword: After loss, what then? In *Loss: The politics of mourning*, ed. David L. Eng and David Kazanjian, 467–73. Berkeley: University of California Press.

Butor, Michel. 1965. The Second Case. *New Left Review* 34:60–8.

Campbell, Joseph. 1956. *Hero with a thousand faces*. New York: Pantheon.

Caruth, Cathy. 1995. *Trauma: Explorations in memory*. Baltimore: Johns Hopkins University Press.

———. 1996. *Unclaimed experience: Trauma, narrative, and history*. Baltimore: Johns Hopkins University Press.

Cicourel, Aaron V. 1974. *Cognitive Sociology: Language and meaning in social interaction*. New York: Free Press.

Clifford, James. 1986a. Introduction: Partial truths. In *Writing culture: The poetics and politics of ethnography*, ed. James Clifford (with George E. Marcus), 1–26. Berkeley: University of California Press.

———. 1986b. On ethnographic allegory. In *Writing culture: The poetics and politics of ethnography*, ed. James Clifford (with George E. Marcus), 98–121. Berkeley: University of California Press.

———, ed. 1986c. *Writing culture: The poetics and politics of ethnography*. With George E. Marcus. Berkeley: University of California Press.

———. 1988. *The predicament of culture: Twentieth-century ethnography, literature, and art*. Cambridge, Mass.: Harvard University Press.

Cloud, Dana L. 1998. *Control and consolation in American culture and politics: Rhetoric of therapy*. Thousand Oaks, Calif.: Sage Publications.

Cohen, Anne B. 1973. *Poor Pearl, poor girl! The murdered girl stereotype in ballad and newspaper*. Austin: University of Texas Press.

Coles, Robert. 1989. *The call of stories: Teaching and the moral imagination*. Boston: Houghton Mifflin.

Coste, Didier. 1989. *Narrative as communication*. Minneapolis: University of Minnesota Press.

Couser, G. Thomas. 1997. *Recovering bodies: Illness, disability, and life writing*. Madison: University of Wisconsin Press.

Das, Veena, Arthur Kleinman, Margaret Lock, Mamphela Ramphele, and Pamela Reynolds, eds. 2001. *Remaking a world: Violence, social suffering, and recovery*. Berkeley: University of California Press.

de Lauretis, Teresa. 1984. *Alice doesn't: Feminism, semiotics, cinema*. Bloomington: Indiana University Press.

Deleuze, Giles, and Felix Guattari. 1983. *On the line*. Trans. John Johnston. New York: Semiotext(e).

Derrida, Jacques. 1973. *Speech phenomena, and other essays* and *Husserl's theory of signs*. Trans. David B. Allison. Evanston, Ill.: Northwestern University Press.

———. 1974. *Of grammatology*. Trans. Gayatri Chakravorty Spivak. Baltimore: Johns Hopkins University Press.

———. 1978. *Writing and difference*. Trans. Gayatri Chakravorty Spivak. Baltimore: Johns Hopkins University Press.

———. 1980. The law of genre. *Critical Inquiry* 7(1):55–82.

Dickens, Charles. [1850] 1981. *David Copperfield.* New York: Bantam Books.

Douglas, Jack D., ed. 1970. *Understanding everyday life.* Chicago: Aldine.

Dundes, Alan. 1968. Introd. to *Morphology of the folktale,* by Vladimir Propp, trans. Laurence Scott, xi–xvii. Austin: University of Texas Press.

———. 1987. *Cracking jokes: Studies of sick humor cycles and stereotypes.* Berkeley, Calif.: Ten Speed Press.

Eng, David L., and David Kazanjian. 2003. *Loss.* Berkeley: University of California Press.

Erikson, Kai. 1976. *Everything in its path: Destruction of community in the Buffalo Creek flood.* New York: Simon and Schuster.

———. 1995. Notes on trauma and community. In *Trauma: Explorations in memory,* ed. Cathy Caruth, 183–99. Baltimore: Johns Hopkins University Press.

Fairclough, Norman. 1995. *Critical discourse analysis: The critical study of language.* London: Longman.

Felman, Shoshana, and Dori Laub. 1992. *Testimony: Crises of witnessing in literature, psychoanalysis, and history.* New York: Routledge.

Finnegan, Ruth. 1998. *Tales of the city: A study of narrative and urban life.* Cambridge, U.K.: Cambridge University Press.

Fletcher, Angus. 1964. *Allegory: The theory of a symbolic mode.* Ithaca, N.Y.: Cornell University Press.

Foley, John Miles. 1995. *The singer of tales in performance.* Bloomington: Indiana University Press.

Foster, Hal, ed. 1983. *The anti-aesthetic: Essays on postmodern culture.* Seattle: Bay Press.

Foucault, Michel. 1980. *Power/knowledge.* New York: Pantheon.

Frank, Arthur W. 1995. *The wounded storyteller: Body, illness, and ethics.* Chicago: University of Chicago Press.

Frank, Gelya. 2000. *Venus on wheels: Two decades of dialogue on disability, biography, and being female in America.* Berkeley: University of California Press.

Fraser, Nancy, and Linda Nicholson. 1988. Social criticism without philosophy: An encounter between feminism and postmodernism. In *Universal abandon: The politics of postmodernism,* ed. A. Ross, 83–104. Minneapolis: University of Minnesota Press.

Frisch, Michael H. 1990. *A shared authority: Essays on the craft and meaning of oral and public history.* Albany: State University of New York Press.

Frye, Northrop. 1957. *Anatomy of criticism: Four essays.* Princeton, N.J.: Princeton University Press.

Fuss, Diana. 1989. *Essentially speaking: Feminism, nature, and difference.* New York: Routledge.

Gadamer, Hans-Georg. 1975. *Truth and method.* Ed. Garrett Barden and John Cumming. New York: Seabury Press.

Geertz, Clifford. 1983. *Local knowledge: Further essays in interpretive anthropology.* New York: Basic Books.

———. 1984. Distinguished lecture: Anti anti-relativism. *American Anthropologist* 86:263–78.

Genette, Gerard. *Narrative discourse: An essay in method.* Trans. Jane E. Lewin. Ithaca, N.Y.: Cornell University Press.

Gilbert, Margaret. 1983. Notes on the concept of social convention. *New Literary History* 14: 225–51.

Gilmore, Leigh. 1994. *Autobiographics: A feminist theory of women's self-representation.* Ithaca, N.Y.: Cornell University Press.

Ginsburg, Faye, D. 1989. *Contested lives: The abortion debate in an American community.* Berkeley: University of California Press.

Ginsburg, Ruth. 1992. In pursuit of self: Theme, narration, and focalization in Christa Wolf's patterns of childhood. *Style* 26(3):437–47.

Glassie, Henry, 1982. *Passing the time in Ballymenone: Culture and history of an Ulster community.* Philadelphia: University of Pennsylvania Press.

Gluck, Shana Berger, and Daphne Patai. 1991. *Women's words: The feminist practice of oral history.* New York: Routledge.

Goffman, Erving. 1959. *The presentation of self in everyday life.* Garden City, N.Y.: Doubleday Anchor.

———. 1963. *Asylums: Essays on the social situation of mental patients and other inmates.* Chicago: Aldine.

———. 1971. *Relations in public: Microstudies of the public order.* New York: Basic Books.

———. 1974. *Frame analysis: An essay on the organization of experience.* New York: Harper and Row.

Goodwin, Marjorie Harness. 1982. Instigating: Storytelling as a social process. *American Ethnologist* 9:799–819.

———. 1990. *He-said-she-said: Talk as social organization among black children.* Bloomington: Indiana University Press.

Grandin, Temple. 1995. *Thinking in pictures and other reports from my life with autism.* New York: Doubleday.

Greenblatt, Stephen J., ed. 1981. *Allegory and representation.* Baltimore: Johns Hopkins University Press.

Greimas, Algirdas Julien. 1987. *On meaning: Selected writings in semiotic theory.* Trans. Paul J. Perron and Frank H. Collins. Minneapolis: University of Minnesota Press.

———. 1990. *Narrative semiotics and cognitive discourses.* Trans. Paul Perron and Frank H. Collins. London: Pinter.

Gubar, Susan. 2002. Empathic identification in Anne Michael's *Fugitive Pieces:* Masculinity and poetry after Auschwitz. *Signs* 28(1):249–76.

Halberstam, Yitta, and Judith Leventhal. 1997. *Small miracles: Extraordinary coincidences from everyday life.* Holbrook, Mass.: Adams Media Corporation.

Halbwachs, Maurice. 1992. *On collective memory.* Trans. and ed. Lewis A. Coser. Chicago: University of Chicago Press.

Hall, Stuart. 1994. Cultural studies: Two paradigms. In *Culture/power/history: A reader in contemporary social theory,* ed. Nicholas B. Dirks, Geoff Eley, and Sherry B. Ortner, 520–38. Princeton, N.J.: Princeton University Press.

Haraway, Donna. 1989. *Primate visions: Gender, race, and nature in the world of modern science.* New York: Routledge.

———. 1992. Promises of monsters. In *Cultural Studies,* ed. Lawrence Grossberg, Cary Nelson, and Paula Treichler, 295–337. New York: Routledge.

Haring, Lee. 1992. *Verbal arts in Madagascar: Performance in historical perspective.* Philadelphia: University of Pennsylvania Press.

Hasan-Rokem, Galit. 2000. *Web of life: Folklore and midrash in rabbinic literature.* Trans. Batya Stein. Stanford, Calif.: Stanford University Press.

Haviland, John B. 1977. *Gossip, reputation, and knowledge in Zinacantan.* Chicago: University of Chicago Press.

Heller, Tzipporah. n.d. *Our Bodies, Our Souls.* Parts 1 and 2. Audiocassettes #HT 630A and 630B. Passaic, N.J.: Aishaudio, Aish HaTorah.

Herman, David, ed. 1999. *Narratologies: New perspectives on narrative analysis.* Columbus: Ohio State University Press.

Hewitt, John P., and Randall Stokes. 1975. Disclaimers. *American Sociological Review* 40:1–11.

Hill, Jane, and Judith T. Irvine, eds. 1992. *Responsibility and evidence in oral discourse.* Cambridge, U.K.: Cambridge University Press.

Hinchman, Sandra K., ed. 1997. *Memory, identity, community: The idea of narrative in the human sciences.* Albany: State University of New York Press.

Hirsh, E. D., Jr. 1983. Beyond convention? *New Literary History* 14:389–98.

Hoagland, Sarah Lucia. 1987. Moral agency under oppression: Playing among boundaries. *Trivia* 11:49–65.

Holquist, Michael. 1981. Introd. to *The dialogic imagination: Four essays,* by M. M. Bakhtin, ed. Michael Holquist, trans. Caryl Emerson and Michael Holquist, xv–xxxiv. Austin: University of Texas Press.

Horowitz, Amy. 1975. Re-routing routes: Zehava Ben's journey between Shuk and Suk. In *The art of being Jewish in modern times,* ed. Barbara Kirshenblatt-Gimblett and Jonathan Karp, xx–yy. Philadelphia: University of Pennsylvania Press.

Huyssen, Andreas. 1986. *After the great divide: Modernism, mass culture, postmodernism.* Bloomington: Indiana University Press.

Hymes, Dell. 1974. *Foundations in sociolinguistics: An ethnographic approach.* Philadelphia: University of Pennsylvania Press.

———. 1981. *In vain I tried to tell you.* Philadelphia: University of Pennsylvania Press.

———. 1996. *Ethnography, linguistics, narrative inequality: Toward an understanding of voice.* London: Taylor and Francis.

Irvine, Judith. 1996. Shadow conversations: The indeterminacy of participant roles. In *Natural histories of discourse,* ed. Michael Silverstein and Greg Urban, 131–59. Chicago: University of Chicago Press.

Jakobson, Roman. 1990. *On language.* Eds. Linda R. Waugh and Monique Monville-Burston. Cambridge, Mass.: Harvard University Press.

Jameson, Frederic. 1979. Foreword. In *The Postmodern Condition: A Report on Knowledge.* By Jean-Francois Lyotard. Minneapolis: University of Minnesota Press.

———. 1981. *The political unconscious.* Ithaca, N.Y.: Cornell University Press.

———. 1986. Third world literature in the era of multinational capitalism. *Social Text* 15:65–88.

Jarvik, Laurence, and Nancy Strickland. 1988. Anti-Semite and Jew? *Tikkun* 3(4):72–74.

Jason, Heda. 1975. *Studies in Jewish Ethnopoetry: Narrating Art, Content, Message, Genre.* Taipei: Chinese Association for Folklore.

Johnson, Nan. 1988. Reader-response and the *Pathos* Principle. *Rhetoric Review* 6(2): 152–66.

Jones, Ann. 1995. Crimes against women: Media part of problem for masking violence in the language of love. *Utne Reader* (May–June) 69:36; reprinted from *USA Today,* March 10, 1994.

Josselson, Ruthellen. 1995. Imagining the real: Empathy, narrative, and the dialogic self. In *Interpreting experience,* ed. Ruthellen Josselson and Amia Lieblich, 27–44. Thousand Oaks, Calif.: Sage Publications.

Josselson, Ruthellen, and Amia Lieblich, eds. 1995. *Interpreting experience.* Thousand Oaks, Calif.: Sage Publications.

———. 1997. *The narrative study of lives.* Thousand Oaks, Calif.: Sage Publications.

———, eds. 1999. *Making meaning of narratives.* Thousand Oaks, Calif.: Sage Publications.

Kipnis, Laura. 1986. "Refunctioning" reconsidered: Towards a Left popular culture. In *High theory/low culture: Analysing popular television and film*, ed. Colin MacCabe, 11–36. Manchester, U.K.: Manchester University Press.

Kirshenblatt-Gimblett, Barbara. 1975. A parable in context: A social interactional analysis of storytelling performance. In *Folklore, performance, and communication*, ed. Dan Ben-Amos and Kenneth Goldstein, 105–30. The Hague: Mouton.

———. 1978. Culture shock and narrative creativity. In *Folklore in the modern world*, ed. Richard M. Dorson, 39–47. The Hague: Mouton.

———. 1989. Authoring lives. *Journal of Folklore Research* 26(2):123–49.

Kleinman, Arthur, Veena Das, and Margaret Lock, eds. 1997. *Social suffering*. Berkeley: University of California Press.

Labov, William. 1972. *Language in the inner city: Studies in the Black English Vernacular.* Philadelphia: University of Pennsylvania Press.

Labov, William, and Joshua Waletsky. 1966. Narrative analysis: Oral version of personal experience. In *Essays on the verbal and visual arts: Proceedings of the 1996 annual spring meeting of the American Ethnological Society*, ed. June Helm, 12–44. Seattle: University of Washington Press.

LaCapra, Dominick. 1985. *History and criticism*. Ithaca, N.Y.: Cornell University Press.

Laclau, Ernest, and Chantal Mouffe, 1985. *Hegemony and social strategy: Toward a radical democratic politics*. London: Verso.

Langness, Lou, and Gelya Frank. 1981. *Lives: An anthropological approach to biography*. Novato, Calif.: Chandler and Sharp Publishers.

Lather, Patti, and Chris Smithies. 1997. *Troubling the angels: Women living with HIV/AIDS*. Boulder, Colo: Westview Press.

Laub, Dori. 1992. Bearing witness, or the vicissitudes of listening. In *Testimony: Crises of witnessing in literature, psychoanalysis, and history*, ed. Shoshana Felman and Dori Laub, 57–74. New York: Routledge.

Lebow, Richard Ned. 2001. The Holocaust and social science: A personal odyssey. In *Light from the ashes: Social science careers of young Holocaust refugees and survivors*, ed. Peter Suedfeld, 248–71. Ann Arbor: University of Michigan Press.

Lee, Benjamin. 1997. *Talking heads: Language, metalanguage, and the semiotics of subjectivity*. Durham, N.C.: Duke University Press.

Lee, Valerie. 1996. *Granny midwives and black women writers*. New York: Routledge.

Linde, Charlotte. 1993. *Life stories: The creation of coherence*. New York: Oxford University Press.

———. 2000. The acquisition of a speaker by a story: How history becomes memory and identity. In History and subjectivity, ed. Geoffrey White, special issue, *Ethos* 28(4): 608–32.

Luker, Kristin. 1984. *Abortion and the politics of motherhood*. Berkeley: University of California Press.

Lyotard, Jean Francois. 1984. *The postmodern condition: A report on knowledge*. Trans. Brian Massumi. Minneapolis: University of Minnesota Press.

Malkki, Liisa H. 1995. *Purity and exile: Violence, memory, and national cosmology among Hutu refugees in Tanzania*. Chicago: University of Chicago Press.

McCole, John. 1993. *Walter Benjamin and the antinomies of tradition*. Ithaca, N.Y.: Cornell University Press.

McHale, Brian. 1992. *Constructing postmodernism*. London: Routledge.

Messer-Davidow, Ellen. 1995. Acting otherwise. In *Provoking agents: Gender and agency in theory and practice*, ed. Judith Kegan Gardiner, 23–51. Urbana: University of Illinois Press.

Mills, Margaret. 1991. *Rhetorics and politics in Afghan traditional storytelling.* Philadelphia: University of Pennsylvania Press.

Moerman, Michael. 1988. *Talking culture: Ethnography and conversation analysis.* Philadelphia: University of Pennsylvania Press.

Moi, Toril. 1988. Feminism, postmodernism, and style: Recent feminist criticism in the United States. *Cultural Critique* 9:3–22.

Mullen, Patrick B. 1988. *I heard the old fishermen say: Folklore of the Texas Gulf Coast.* Logan: Utah State University Press.

Myerhoff, Barbara. 1978. *Number our days.* New York: E. P. Dutton.

———. 1992. *Remembered lives: The work of ritual, storytelling, and growing older.* With Deena Metzger, Jay Ruby, and Virginia Tufte. Ed. Marc Kaminsky. Ann Arbor: University of Michigan Press.

Natanson, Maurice. 1962. *Literature, philosophy, and the social sciences: Essays in existentialism and phenomenology.* The Hague: M. Nijhoff.

Nelson, Hilde Lindemann, ed. 1997. *Stories and their limits: Narrative approaches to bioethics.* New York: Routledge.

Nora, Pierre. 1996. *Realms of memory: Rethinking the French past.* 3 vols. Trans. Arthur Goldhammer. Vol. 1, *Conflicts and divisions.* New York: Columbia University Press.

O'Barr, William, and Marco M. Moreira. 1989. The airbrushing of culture: An insider looks at global advertising. *Public Culture* 2:2.

Ochs, Elinor. 1996. Narrating the Self. *Annual Review of Anthropology* 25:19–43.

O'Connor, Patricia. 2002. *Speaking of crime: Narratives of prisoners.* Lincoln: University of Nebraska Press.

Onega, Susana, and José Angel García Landa, eds. 1996. *Narratology: An introduction.* London: Longman.

Personal Narratives Group, eds. 1989. *Interpreting women's lives: Feminist theory and personal narratives.* Bloomington: Indiana University Press.

Phelan, James. 1996. *Narrative as rhetoric: Technique, audiences, ethics, ideology.* Columbus: Ohio State University Press.

Phelan, James, and Peter J. Rabinowitz, eds. 1994. *Understanding narrative.* Columbus: Ohio State University Press.

Philips, Susan U. 1993. Evidentiary standards for American trials: Just the facts. In *Responsibility and evidence in oral discourse,* ed. Jane H. Hill and Judith T. Irvine, 248–59. Cambridge, U.K.: Cambridge University Press.

Pliskin, Z. 1975. *Guard your tongue.* New York: Moriah Offset.

Polanyi, Livia. 1985. *Telling the American story.* Cambridge, Mass.: Massachusetts Institute of Technology Press.

———. 1989. *Telling the American story: A structural and cultural analysis of conversational storytelling.* Cambridge, Mass.: Massachusetts Institute of Technology Press.

Polkinghorne, Donald E. 1988. *Narrative knowing and the human sciences.* Albany: State University of New York Press.

Portelli, Alessandro. 1991. *The death of Luigi Trastulli, and other stories: Form and meaning in oral history.* Albany: State University of New York Press.

Prince, Gerald. 1982. Narrative analysis and narratology. *New Literary History* 13(2):179–88.

Probyn, Elspeth. 1993. True voices and real people: The problem of the autobiographical in cultural studies. In *Relocating cultural studies,* ed. Valda Blundell, John Shepherd, and Ian Taylor, 105–22. London: Routledge.

Propp, Vladimir. *Morphology of the folktale.* Trans. Laurence Scott. Austin: University of Texas Press.

Quilligan, Maureen. 1979. *The language of allegory: Defining the genre.* Ithaca, N.Y.: Cornell University Press.

Rajan, Rajeswari Sunder, and Zakia Pathak. 1989. Shahbano. *Signs* 14:558–82.

Ricouer, Paul. 1980. Narrative time. *Critical Inquiry* 7(1):169–90.

———. 1991. *From text to action: Essays in hermeneutics, II.* Trans. Kathleen Blamey and John B. Thompson. Evanston, Ill.: Northwestern University Press.

Rimmon-Kenan. 1983. *Narrative fiction: Contemporary poetics.* London: Methuen.

Robbins, Bruce, ed. 1993. *The phantom public sphere.* Minneapolis: University of Minnesota Press.

Robertson, Shari, and Michael Camerini. 1999. *Well founded fear.* PBS television documentary.

Roemer, Michael. 1995. *Telling stories: Postmodernism and the invalidation of traditional narrative.* Lanham, Md.: Rowman and Littlefield.

Romero, Mary, and Abigail Stewart, eds. 1999. *Women's untold stories: Breaking silence, talking back, voicing complexity.* New York: Routledge.

Roof, Judith, and Robyn Wiegman, eds. 1995. *Who can speak: Authority and critical identity.* Urbana: University of Illinois Press.

Rosemarin, Adena. 1985. *The power of genre.* Minneapolis: University of Minnesota Press.

Rosenthal, John. 1988. Who practices hegemony?: Class division and the subject of politics. *Cultural Critique* 9:25–52.

Ross, Andrew. 1988. *Universal abandon?: The politics of postmodernism.* Minneapolis: University of Minnesota Press.

Ryan, M.L. 1981. When "je" is "un autro": Fiction, quotation, and the performative analysis. *Poetics Today* 2:127–55.

Sacks, Harvey. 1972. On the analyzability of stories by children. *Directions in sociolinguistics: The ethnography of communication,* ed. John J. Gumperz and Dell Hymes, 325–45. New York: Holt, Rinehart, and Winston.

———. 1992. *Lectures on conversations.* Vols. 1 and 2. Ed. Gail Jefferson. Oxford: Blackwell.

Sacks, Oliver. 1994. An anthropologist on Mars. *New Yorker,* December 27.

———. 1995. Foreword. *Thinking in pictures and other reports from my life with autism.* By Temple Grandin, 11–16. New York: Doubleday.

Said, Edward. 1978. *Orientalism.* New York: Pantheon.

———. 1990. American intellectuals and Middle East politics. In *Intellectuals: Aesthetics, politics, academics,* ed. Bruce Robbins, 135–51. Minneapolis: University of Minnesota Press.

Schank, 1990. *Tell me a story: A new look at real and artificial memory.* New York: Scribner.

Schor, Naomi. 1995. *Bad objects: Essays popular and unpopular.* Durham, N.C.: Duke University Press.

Schrager, Samuel. 1983. What is social in social history? *International Journal of Oral History* 4(2):76–98.

Schutz, Alfred. 1962. *The problem of social reality.* Ed. Maurice Natanson. The Hague: M. Nijhoff.

———. 1972. *The phenomenology of the social.* Trans. George Walsh and Frederick Lehnert. London: Heinemann Educational.

Scott, Joan Wallach. 1988. *Gender and the politics of history.* New York: Columbia University Press.

———. 1992. Experience. In *Feminists theorize the political,* ed. Judith Butler and Joan W. Scott, 22–40. New York: Routledge.

Searle, John. 1976. The classification of illocutionary acts. *Language in Society* 5:1–23.

Seitel, Peter. 1980. *See so that we may see: Performances and interpretations of traditional tales from Tanzania.* Bloomington: Indiana University Press.

———. 1999. *The powers of genre: Interpreting Haya oral Literature.* Oxford, U.K.: Oxford University Press.

Shuman, Amy, 1986. *Storytelling rights: The uses of oral written texts by urban adolescents.* Cambridge, U.K.: Cambridge University Press.

———. 1993a. Dismantling local culture. In Theorizing folklore: Toward new perspectives on the politics of culture, special issue, *Western Folklore* 52(2, 3, 4):345–64.

———. 1993b. Gender and genre. In *Feminist theory and the study of folklore,* ed. Susan Tower Hollis, Linda Pershing, and M. Jane Young, 71–88. Urbana: University of Illinois Press.

Shuman, Amy, and Carol Bohmer. 2004. Representing trauma. *Journal of American Folklore* 117(466): 394–414.

Silverstein, Michael, and Greg Urban, eds. 1996. *Natural histories of discourse.* Chicago: University of Chicago Press.

Singer, Alan. 1993. *The subject as action: Transformation and totality in narrative aesthetics.* Ann Arbor: University of Michigan Press.

Smith, Barbara Herrnstein. 1980. Narrative versions, narrative theories. *Critical Inquiry* 7(1):213–36.

———. 1988. *Contingencies of value: Alternative perspectives for critical theory.* Cambridge, Mass.: Harvard University Press.

Smith, Paul. 1988a. *Discerning the subject.* Minneapolis: University of Minnesota Press.

———. 1988b. Visiting the Banana Republic. In *Universal Abandon?: The politics of postmodernism,* ed. Andrew Ross, 128–48. Minneapolis: University of Minnesota.

Smith, Sidonie. 1996. Taking it to a limit one more time: Autobiography and autism. In *Getting a life: Everyday uses of autobiography,* ed. Sidonie Smith and Julia Watson, 226–46. Minneapolis: University of Minnesota Press.

Spivak, Gayatri. 1987. *In other worlds: Essays in cultural politics.* New York: Methuen.

———. 1989. Reading *the satanic verses. Public Culture* 2:88–90.

———. 1999. *A critique of postcolonial reason: Toward a history of the vanishing present.* Boston: Harvard University Press.

Stahl, Sandra Dolby. 1989. *Literary folkloristics and the personal narrative.* Bloomington: Indiana University Press.

Sternberg, Meir. 1982. Proteus in quotation-land: Mimesis and the forms of reported discourse. *Poetics Today* 3(2):107–56.

Stewart, Susan. 1984. *On longing: Narratives of the miniature, the gigantic, the souvenir, the collection.* Baltimore: Johns Hopkins University Press.

———. 1988. The Marquis de Meese. *Critical Inquiry* 15(1): 162–92.

———. 1991. *Crimes of writing: Problems in the containment of representation.* Oxford, U.K.: Oxford University Press.

Strathern, Marilyn 1995. Nostalgia and the new genetics. In *Rhetorics of self-making,* ed. Debbora Battaglia, 97–120. Berkeley: University of California Press.

Taylor, Charles. 1989. *Sources of the self: The making of modern identity.* Cambridge, Mass.: Harvard University Press.

Todorov, Tzvetan. 1975. *The fantastic: A structural approach to a literary genre.* Trans. Richard French Howard. Ithaca, N.Y.: Cornell University Press.

———. 1984. *Michail Bakhtin: The dialogical principle.* Trans. Wlad Godzich. Minneapolis: University of Minnesota Press.

Tonkin, Elizabeth. 1992. *Narrating our pasts: The social construction of oral history.* Cambridge, U.K.: Cambridge University Press.

Turner, Victor. 1980. Social dramas and stories about them. *Critical Inquiry* 7(1):141–68.

Turner, Victor, and Edward Bruner, eds. 1986. *The anthropology of experience.* Urbana: University of Illinois Press.

Tyler, Stephen A. 1986. Post-modern ethnography. From document of the occult to occult document. In *Writing culture: The poetics and politics of ethnography,* ed. James Clifford and George E. Marcus, 122–40. Berkeley: University of California Press.

———. 1987. *The unspeakable: Discourse, dialogue, and rhetoric in the postmodern world.* Madison: University of Wisconsin Press.

Ulmer, Gregory. 1983. The object of post-criticism. In *The anti-aesthetic: Essays on postmodern culture,* ed. Hal Foster, 83–110. Seattle: Bay Press.

Van Maanen, John. 1998. *Tales of the field: On writing ethnography.* Chicago: University of Chicago Press.

Visvanathan, Shiv. 1997. *A carnival for science: Essays on science, technology, and development.* Delhi: Oxford University Press.

Visweswaran, Kamala. 1994. *Fictions of feminist ethnography.* Minneapolis: University of Minnesota Press.

Volosinov, V. N. [1929–30] 1973. *Marxism and the philosophy of language.* Trans. Ladislav Matejka and I. R. Titunik. New York: Seminar Press.

Webber, Sabra J. 1991. *Romancing the real: Folklore and ethnographic representation in North Africa.* Philadelphia: University of Pennsylvania Press.

Weintraub, Jeff. 1997. The theory and politics of the public/private distinction. In *Public and private thought and practice: Perspectives on a grand dichotomy,* ed. Jeff Weintraub and Krishan Kumar, 1–42. Chicago: University of Chicago Press.

Weissberg, Lilliane. 1999. Introduction. In *Cultural memory and the construction of identity,* ed. Dan Ben-Amos and Liliane Weissberg, 7–26. Detroit: Wayne State University Press.

Weschler, Lawrence. 1990. *A miracle, a universe: Settling accounts with torturers.* New York: Pantheon.

White, Hayden. 1980. The value of narrativity in the representation of reality. *Critical Inquiry* 7(1): 5–28.

———. 1987. *The content of the form: Narrative discourse and historical representation.* Baltimore: Johns Hopkins University Press.

White, Michael. 1995. *Re-authoring lives: Interviews and essays.* Adelaide, Australia: Dulwich Centre Publications.

Whyte, David. 1991. Images of fire: Poetry and the zen of primary experience. Lecture. October 28. St. Norbert College, DePere, Wisconsin.

Wilden, Anthony. 1968. *The language of the self: The function of language in psychoanalysis by Jacques Lacan.* Baltimore: Johns Hopkins University Press.

Williams, Donna. 1992. *Nobody nowhere: The extraordinary autobiography of an autistic.* New York: Avon.

———. 1994. *Somebody somewhere: Breaking free from the world of autism.* New York: Times Book.

Williams, Raymond. 1976. *Keywords: A vocabulary of culture and society.* London: Fontana/Croom Helm.

Wolfson, Nessa. 1978. A feature of performed narrative: The conversational historical present. *Language in Society* 7: 215–37.

Wolin, Richard. 1994. *Walter Benjamin: An aesthetics of redemption.* Berkeley: University of California Press.

Workman, Mark. 1995. Folklore and the literature of exile. In *Folklore, literature, and cultural theory: collected essays,* ed. Cathy Lynn Preston, 29–42. New York: Garland.

Young, Katharine Galloway. 1987. *Taleworlds and storyrealms.* Dordrecht: Martinus Nijhoff.

———. 1997. *Presence in the flesh: The body in medicine.* Cambridge, Mass.: Harvard University Press.

Zavala, Iris M. 1990. Bakhtin and otherness: Social heterogeneity. *Critical Studies* 2: 77–89.

Zipes, Jack. 1979. *Breaking the magic spell: Radical theories of folk and fairy tales.* London: Heinemann.

———. 1983. *Fairy tales and the art of subversion: The classical genre for children and the process of civilization.* New York: Wildman Press.

Zizek, Slavoj. 1989. *The sublime object of ideology.* London: Verson.

Zuidervaart, Lambert. 1991. *Adorno's aesthetic theory: The redemption of illusion.* Cambridge, Mass.: Massachusetts Institute of Technology Press.

INDEX

AMY SHUMAN is a professor of English and an adjunct professor of anthropology at the Ohio State University, where she directs the Center for Folklore Studies. She is the recipient of fellowships from the Guggenheim Foundation, the Wenner-Gren Foundation, and the National Foundation for the Humanities. Her book *Storytelling Rights: The Uses of Oral and Written Texts by Urban Adolescents* received the Katharine Briggs Award. She is currently completing a book, *Authentic Copies,* on the artisan stone carvers of Pietrasanta, Italy.

The University of Illinois Press
is a founding member of the
Association of American University Presses.

———————————————————————————

Composed in 10/13 New Caledonia
with New Caledonia display
by Type One, LLC
for the University of Illinois Press
Designed by Paula Newcomb
Manufactured by Thomson-Shore, Inc.

University of Illinois Press
1325 South Oak Street
Champaign, IL 61820-6903
www.press.uillinois.edu